CONTESTING ARCHIVES

CONTESTING ARCHIVES

FINDING WOMEN IN THE SOURCES

EDITED BY

Nupur Chaudhuri, Sherry J. Katz,
and Mary Elizabeth Perry

FOREWORD BY
ANTOINETTE BURTON

UNIVERSITY OF ILLINOIS PRESS
URBANA, CHICAGO, AND SPRINGFIELD

© 2010 by the Board of Trustees
of the University of Illinois
All rights reserved
Manufactured in the United States of America
1 2 3 4 5 C P 5 4 3 2
∞ This book is printed on acid-free paper.

Library of Congress Cataloging-in-Publication Data
Contesting archives : finding women in the sources /
edited by Nupur Chaudhuri, Sherry J. Katz, Mary Elizabeth Perry ;
foreword by Antoinette Burton.
p.   cm.
Includes bibliographical references and index.
ISBN 978-0-252-03542-5 (cloth : alk. paper)
ISBN 978-0-252-07736-4 (pbk. : alk. paper)
1. Women—Historiography. I. Chaudhuri, Nupur.
II. Katz, Sherry J. III. Perry, Mary Elizabeth, 1937–
HQ1121.C63815   2010
305.4072'2—dc22   2010006478

CONTENTS

Foreword: "Small Stories" and the Promise
of New Narratives   vii
   Antoinette Burton

Acknowledgments   xi

Introduction   xiii
   Nupur Chaudhuri, Sherry J. Katz, and Mary Elizabeth Perry

PART 1. LOCATING WOMEN IN OFFICIAL DOCUMENTS

1. Finding Fatima, a Slave Woman of Early Modern Spain   3
   Mary Elizabeth Perry

2. Revealing an Orphan's Tale from
   Nineteenth-Century Mexico   20
   Daniel S. Haworth

3. Locating Women as Migrants in
   Nineteenth-Century Tunis   35
   Julia Clancy-Smith

4. Exploring Crime and Violence in Early-
   Twentieth-Century Black Women's History   56
   Kali Nicole Gross

PART 2. INTEGRATING VARIED SOURCES FOUND INSIDE AND OUTSIDE OFFICIAL ARCHIVES

5. Spinning and Weaving the Threads of Native Women's Lives in Colonial Mexico   75
   Lisa Sousa

6. Excavating Radical Women in Progressive-Era California   89
   Sherry J. Katz

7. Recovering Women's Voices in Communist Poland   107
   Malgorzata Fidelis

8. Archival Thinking and the Wives of Marcus Garvey   125
   Ula Y. Taylor

9. Finding an Archive in Krishnobhabini Das's *Englande Bangamohila*   135
   Nupur Chaudhuri

10. Uncovering Women and Gender in Qajar Archives of Iran   156
    Mansoureh Ettehadieh (Nezam Mafi), Elham Malekzadeh, Maryam Ameli-Rezaei, and Janet Afary

PART 3. CREATING WOMEN'S HISTORY ARCHIVES

11. Revealing New Narratives of Women in Las Vegas   177
    Joanne L. Goodwin

12. Creating an Archive of Working Women's Oral Histories in Beira, Mozambique   192
    Kathleen Sheldon

Contributors   211

Index   215

FOREWORD

"Small Stories" and the Promise of New Narratives

Antoinette Burton

"May I be your sacrifice."
"My father did not accept the *lobolo.*"
"We should think of the present and the future."
"Giovanna Tellini did housework for me for four years."
"I'll tell you about one such day of standing in line at Lubelska street."
"I could not go home to my mother in the state I was in."
"This is my statement. It is not to be invalidated; it is to be carried out and done."

They are whispers and they are prayers. They are matter-of-fact and conspiratorial; agonized and embarrassed; determined and defiant. They tell us more about communist Poland, colonial India, postcolonial Mozambique, Qajar Iran, indigenous Mexico, and turn-of-the-century Philadelphia than we can ever get from monographs or textbooks alone. They are, in short, fragments of lives and dramas that we have only glimpses of but that serve as testimony to the fugitive work of gender and the equally fleeting presence of women as subjects across a vast landscape of the past. With the possible exception of Amy Jacques Garvey, even when they might be known in their respective historiographies, the women who figure in this collection are at best obscured by more important public figures, by large-scale events deemed more significant than those that frame their lives, and by grand narratives that may touch on contexts of significance to them but that effectively brush by them, in part because of the comparative lack of archival trace to secure them in the sightlines of history. If their eruption here *as history* marks a certain kind of arrival, it is also just the beginning of the interpretive work to be done with their stories and their lives. In that sense, *Contesting Archives: Finding Women in the Sources* addresses not just the terrains these particular women traversed, but a set of critical questions about the role of archives in shaping the conceptual frameworks of women's and gender history.

This volume began as a panel at the 2005 American Historical Association annual meeting in Seattle called "Women in the Documents" and then appeared as a 2008 special feature in the *Journal of Women's History* under the rubric "Finding Women in the Archive." In those contexts, four historians—Nupur Chaudhuri, Sherry J. Katz, Mary Elizabeth Perry, and Ula Y. Taylor—grappled with the challenges of unearthing heretofore unknown women and coming to grips with how and why the "smallness" of their work or their worlds illuminates dimensions of the past we need urgently to understand. As with all the essays in this expanded collection, the editors emphasized the project of encounter that their respective subjects set in motion, encouraging us to scrutinize the practice of "recovery" and to engage its limits and possibilities as historical method. So we began with Fatima (also known as "Ana"), who came into the historical record in only one extant document—and a highly prejudicial one at that. Mary Elizabeth Perry reads the Inquisition record both against the grain and in the context of what we know and can surmise about the cosmopolitan universe of sixteenth-century Málaga. Fatima emerges as a woman of purpose—if not in control of her own destiny, then at least probably mindful of her limited power in the several communities (religious, cultural, socioeconomic) she traversed. Her defiance of the ecclesiastical machinery means that she survived in history, even while her ultimate fate is unknowable. Sherry J. Katz immerses us in a completely different world—that of radical California women at the turn of the last century—and, in so doing, argues that these women were at the heart of some of the key transformations of Progressive reform and vision. Despite the localness of their work—and of course because of it—socialist-feminists like Frances Noel pioneered a dual political strategy that anticipated national feminist methods. As importantly, Katz documents her own dogged attempts at re-suturing the public and private lives of her subjects, plotting the frustrations and the thrill of discovery in turn. Ula Y. Taylor's piece on Jacques Garvey continues in this metanarrative mode, describing the "crisis of archival recognition" that historians of African American women face and that undergirded her book project on the life of a woman scarcely known except as Marcus Garvey's wife—scarcely known in part because of the apparent paucity of genuinely archival materials. The "textual snapshots" Taylor was able to glean from her research enable her to draw a fuller picture of what she termed in *The Veiled Garvey* "community feminism," itself a challenge to what have historically been individual-centered impulses of women's history as a practice. Taylor's commitment to materializing "the reality of multiple narratives" is neatly reflected in her own account, which underscores the many-tentacled lives of women and men, which, in turn, enable us to appreciate who Jacques Garvey was and what her legacy is, not just to African American women, but to women's history more generally as a political project and a method of representing the past. Last but not least is the history of Krishnobhabini Das, which Nupur Chaudhuri sets out in considerable detail. Like Fatima's, Das's life is evident from a single text; like Noel, Das struggled with the relationship between public and private; like Jacques Garvey, she was both linked to and uncontained by a conjugal relationship that at least in part enabled her to register as a subject in and of history. Chaudhuri suggests that in Das's travelogue we have an invaluable archive of gendered subjectivity—one that is not necessarily representative of Bengali women of the time but that contributes to our knowledge of how movement through imperial spaces helped to produce critical—and even feminist, nationalist—ethnographies of colonialism in the Victorian period.

To these stories are now added those of garment workers Rita Bacare and Aurora Soares, who spoke eloquently and nonchalantly to Kathleen Sheldon of their routes to factory work through bride-price rituals and, in the case of Soares, at least a dozen pregnancies. The Las Vegas Women Oral History Project gives Joanne L. Goodwin a more defined oral archive, illuminating the small but transformative community activism of Illinois native Florence Schilling McClure on that frontier town. Malgorzata Fidelis, for her part, reconstructs women's experiences under totalitarianism via a combination of written and oral sources, developing an ear for the "little window" her informants give her into big structures like the state bureaucracy in postwar Poland. Lisa Sousa has many fewer voices at her disposal, but she uses a variety of sources, as well as careful philological method, to conjure native women's status under colonial Mexican rule. The point here is not that archival records are scant; as she suggests, they showcase the wide range of labor women performed, from weaving cloth to grinding maize, and they often did so for tribute. The challenge is to capture the specificity of their embeddedness in the ecclesiastical imperium of the Spanish—and to concede that individuals will rarely be in evidence. Julia Clancy-Smith has a related challenge, in that she can read the court testimony of the Italian migrant woman Giovanna Tellini but that testimony is ultimately partial, if tantalizingly so, on the question of who Tellini actually was—raising crucial questions about the "implicit codes" of evidence-giving, the roadblocks of linguistic particularism, and the household dynamics of intimacy and betrayal that shaped the larger political economy of nineteenth-century Tunis. If, as Michel Foucault has argued, the juridical subject is a deeply contingent one, she is also almost always some form of conjugal one, as well. Here the case of Maria Petra Fernandez's "emancipation" into marriage, at her own request, is a dramatic example of how even one petition can animate discussion of who knew the law, how they manipulated it, and, of course, the near impossibility of knowing for certain whether Petra actually penned her own plea. Although they are certainly partly reconstructable from trial records, as Kali Nicole Gross deftly shows, the fates of Henrietta Cook and Katie Chizawska cannot be discerned from testimony alone. Other archival forms—like juror interviews and press coverage—allow us to see the larger context in which an African American and Polish domestic, respectively, were adjudged for the act of infanticide. That women arise so commonly in archival sources around questions of sexuality and reproduction can hardly be surprising, given the relationship between the gendered order and the social/political one, but the archives have yet to be fully plumbed on this subject, as the collaborative essay on eighteenth-, nineteenth-, and early-twentieth-century Iran indicates. The harem world was hardly closed, operating instead as a nexus of epistolary exchange, commercial transaction, and the production and circulation of medical knowledge—each of which had ramifications for the dominant regime.

In the end, the histories that have resulted from "researching around" these discrepant subjects remain fragmentary, allusive, and unsatisfactory in the best possible sense. It is certainly tempting to view them in a triumphalist mode—to celebrate their excavation and hold them up as exemplars of what we can know when we ignore the critics who even now persist in saying that such women can't be found and, when found, don't have the kinds of histories that can approximate a "true" biography or fill out a "real" history. In fact, Fatima, Noel, Jacques Garvey, and Das will never be household names, and the stories that can be gleaned from their archival traces are inevitably partial, albeit provocatively so. But as this collection also shows, those traces are more than mere documents, more than simply the foundations of historical narrative. In the hands of critical feminist historians, the varied archives of the kind we have before us are always already histories in the making.

ACKNOWLEDGMENTS

This volume is the product of a collegial collaboration that began with and has deepened the friendship of the three editors. We gratefully acknowledge the kind permission of Johns Hopkins University Press to publish the essays of Nupur Chaudhuri, Sherry J. Katz, Mary Elizabeth Perry, and Ula Y. Taylor, which were published in earlier versions in the *Journal of Women's History* (JWH). We deeply appreciate Antoinette Burton for first suggesting that we publish our four essays as a History Practice section on "Finding Women in the Archive" for the JWH, and we are grateful for the helpful comments of the readers and editors of that journal. For the authors of the essays in this volume we give special thanks, especially for their work and willingness to share their own research experiences, and for their dedication to the challenge and adventures of finding women in the sources. In addition, we are grateful for the helpful comments of the anonymous reviewers and the support of the board and the staff of the University of Illinois Press. In particular, we thank Joan Catapano, whose belief in the importance of women's history has played an instrumental role in so many publications.

INTRODUCTION

Nupur Chaudhuri, Sherry J. Katz,
and Mary Elizabeth Perry

The authors of the essays in this volume challenge the tired assumption that an archive is simply an immutable, neutral, and ahistorical place in which historical records are preserved. Rather than agreeing that an archive is merely a repository of information, these scholars view it as a site for the production of knowledge.[1] Continuing a recent trend in women's history that reconceptualizes both the document and the archive, they have found in their archival work that women's voices and their texts were often obscured or lost altogether. And they have developed methodologies for creating new archives, finding new meanings by reading documents "against the grain," weaving together many layers of information to reveal complexities, working collectively to reconstruct the lives of women in the past.

In many ways, these authors continue methodological discussions that began in the 1960s and 1970s when new social historians and women's historians sought to recover the hitherto marginalized voices of working people, ethnic-racial communities, and women of all social and economic backgrounds. They found few of their subjects in standard archival sources and instead brought a host of new and unconventional sources to the fore, including social movement newspapers, songs and material objects, and oral histories.[2] Our contributors describe the use of many varied materials in their search for women's experiences and gender ideologies as they work inside and outside the archives.

As historians of the 1960s and 1970s raised questions about who was left out of the historiography and began to reconstruct the underrepresented, they also questioned methods of archival collection that appeared to leave out the less powerful, and they made the case for preserving diverse voices and experiences. Women's historians, in particular, highlighted the exclusion of documents pertaining to women, who were not until quite recently considered legitimate subjects of history and therefore of archival collection. Nell Irvin Painter, for example, has argued that even many "achieving" women lacked their own archives because their papers were lost or destroyed or because no one considered them "important enough to warrant an archive."[3]

As historians discovered that many groups seemed to be underrepresented in or excluded from archives, they began to critique the very conception of the archive as an objective, neutral, and disinterested institution that housed historical documents and artifacts. The idea of archival objectivity and neutrality in the collection of primary sources had predominated since the mid-nineteenth century. However, as librarians and archivists now attest, the act of collection is a subjective matter involving a series of decisions regarding what to keep, what to discard, how to organize what is kept, and for what purpose. Just as a document reflects the assumptions and agendas of its creator, so, too, does an archive. Although "their origins are often occluded and the exclusions on which they are premised often dimly understood, all archives come into being . . . as a result of specific political, cultural, and socioeconomic pressures" and frequently feature documents of the powerful and privileged.[4]

Postmodern critiques of the archives have continued to challenge "assumptions of archival neutrality" and have raised critical questions about whose history gets archived and, hence, preserved.[5] In fact, Antoinette Burton's recent edited collection *Archive Stories* addresses "head-on the lingering presumptions about, and attachment to, the claims to objectivity with which archives have historically been synonymous." Many of the essays in *Archive Stories* question the objectivity of traditional archives as they explore the provenance, history, and power of specific archival sites to "shape the narratives which are to be 'found' there." Other essays "expand the definition of archival material" by naming as archives the "alternative historical material available to us when we wander outside conventional 'houses of history.'"[6] The essays in this volume further these discussions by interrogating official documents found in traditional archives for what they can yield about the women who appear in sources never intended to preserve their voices and experiences, or by claiming as archives materials by women that traditional repositories thought unimportant to include.

Yet while women have been traditionally underrepresented in archives, their voices are sometimes found in abundance. Some of our contributors have uncovered personal or organizational papers left by the women they study, although these are often filled with fragments and silences. Others have located traces of their subjects' experiences in numerous records meant

INTRODUCTION   xv

to record male-centered narratives. Even when women are not missing from the archives, reconstructing their lives and voices presents many methodological challenges.

The contributors to this volume illuminate a cross-section of divergent methodologies employed by historians of women and gender today. They make explicit the diverse methods of finding and analyzing a wide variety of sources and demonstrate much creativity in approaching hard-to-research subjects. Many of us are in one way or another "researching around" subjects who left few material traces of their own and appear in "highly fragmentary historical record[s]."[7] Others are reading "against the grain" a single official document (or a few such documents) "for subtexts and silences."[8] Still others are creating primary sources in the form of manuscript collections or oral interviews. A significant aspect of all of these methods is the importance of bringing a rich knowledge of the context and historiography into our analyses of the documents. As Ula Taylor suggests, "it is usually under the most difficult archival conditions that one must call most creatively and rigorously upon historical methods and theoretical ideas."[9] Finally, the essays here also demonstrate a methodological self-consciousness regarding historians as history makers and raise questions about the relationship between our selves and our subjects.[10]

The essays in this volume are divided into three parts. In "Locating Women in Official Documents," four historians use government or church records (and primarily single documents) to illuminate the lives of women who left no other traces in the historical record. Each of them argues that even a single document, if read with vast contextual knowledge, can be used to examine marginalized women and uncover their agency and their (however limited) power. They also point out that while these records are problematic because the female voices contained in the documents were produced by male-dominated institutions "inimical to women's interests or agency," they can reveal much about women's lives if read "against the grain."[11]

Mary Elizabeth Perry's essay analyzes an Inquisition record from 1584 that sheds light on the experience of Fatima, a Muslim slave woman in early modern Spain. Perry deploys a three-part strategy for interrogating the single extant document containing traces of Fatima. She reads the source "against the grain," exploring the "subtexts and silences that can tell us more than the formulaic questions and responses that inquisitors sought and recorded in official male-centered documents." She contextualizes the document using other relevant primary sources and the historical literature. Finally, Perry utilizes insights from other disciplines—politics, anthropology, and cultural criticism. Fatima entered the historical record because she denied a cleric's claim that she had converted to Christianity while suffering from the plague in a hospital. At great risk to herself, Fatima held fast to her Muslim identity, denying that she had embraced Christianity and had taken a new name, Ana. She was tried and convicted as an apostate Morisca, a women who returned to Islam after embracing Christianity, at a time when fears of false conversions (and Morisco rebellion) ran high among Spanish and church authorities. Perry argues that Fatima's experience "opens for us the world of minority slave women," confirming their disenfranchisement but also demonstrating their resistance to—and their empowerment despite—official power. Fatima's case also reminds us, writes Perry, "that we do not have to abandon the study of women in the past simply because they do not appear in their own writings or in multiple documents."

Daniel S. Haworth's essay also unpacks a single government document. The document from mid-nineteenth-century Mexico is an unusual record of a woman's encounter with state authority in a source base in which very few women's voices appear. The 1854 case file records the efforts of nineteen-year-old Maria Petra Fernandez to secure "a legal declaration of her adulthood," in order to marry the man of her choice against the wishes of her legal guardian. In Haworth's hands, the file illuminates the agency of two groups of women, adolescent girls and widows, in early national Mexico. Haworth reads "'against the grain' of the multiple accounts that constitute the source," taking "note of hints and implied meanings" and coming to understand the "fragmentary information by drawing on relevant secondary sources." By applying his rich contextual knowledge of Mexican law, state, and society, Haworth finds two stories, "an official story of patriarchy confirmed" and an "unofficial story of patriarchy confounded." Haworth argues that Petra, with the help of her future mother-in-law (and a lawyer and priest recruited by the widow), succeeds in winning her freedom to marry by accommodating to and utilizing the patriarchal ideology and practices of the day. His awareness of "text and subtext" enables Haworth to recover female agency and subjectivity from sources that treat women largely as objects.

Julia Clancy-Smith interrogates a single document, the criminal proceedings of Giovanna Tellini, an Italian woman in residing in Tunis in the mid-nineteenth century. Clancy-Smith tells us that this is an unusual document, for it "represents one of the few extensive records on an immigrant woman of ordinary means and the social universe she inhabited." Tellini's story also represents "a history that no one wanted" because it focuses on "undesirable women," who were neither Muslim nor French (the colonial power in Tunis) in a historiography written largely from either imperial French or nationalist North African points of view. Yet Clancy-Smith is able to explore the social world of Tellini and women like her by bringing her considerable contextual knowledge to the fore: of European migration to North Africa; of the creation and movement across borders of consular and protectorate archival collections; of the network of counselor authorities in Tunis and the common patterns of criminal proceedings; of the hybrid Sicilo-Italian and Arabic writing used in Tunis at the time. She also employs a "comparative historical perspective" to examine the Tellini proceedings alongside other similar cases. Clancy-Smith finds that Tellini inhabited a pluralistic social world made up of immigrants from many different parts of Europe and North Africa who constructed a marginal and quasi-criminal economy to survive, and that they thereby challenged the power of authorities in their daily lives. Further, Tellini's story alerts us "to rips and tears in the nets of patriarchal control," spaces that women could sometimes exploit. Clancy-Smith also uses "the Giovanna that we 'found' inside and outside the archive" to suggest new ways to view European-Muslim relations and the mobility and migration of women and men in the nineteenth century.

Kali Nicole Gross examines prison and court documents related to the case of Henrietta Cook, a young, single African American domestic worker in early-twentieth-century Philadelphia who was tried and acquitted of infanticide. The account of Cook's encounter with the criminal justice system provides us with the rare voice of a working-class black woman. It reveals a window into the ways in which standards of sexual propriety and social respectability reverberated for black women of poorer backgrounds, as they did for better-studied elite African American women, in the Progressive Era. Gross's method of "making the most of prison records . . . incomplete transcripts and court papers, and prison administrators' one-sided observations" involved knowledge of the broader historiography, and especially of how race, gender, and sexuality were constructed at the time. Her method also required empathy for her subject and careful analysis of these documents as rare texts of impoverished black women's voices and experiences. Gross suggests that seventeen-year-old Cook may have engaged in sexual intercourse "in the hopes of attaining respectability through marriage." When she found herself pregnant, however, she was desperate to retain the "appearance of chastity and respectability," attributes that were especially important for black women, who suffered from "negative assumptions about their morality." While on trial, Cook sought to project virtue "both as a means to convey legal innocence and as a measure to counteract the negative attributes assigned to blackness." Gross argues that incarcerated black women, who were often impoverished domestic workers, share much with black women as a whole in the early twentieth century, as they walked a "tightrope" regarding respectability, sexuality, and reproduction.

The second part of the book, "Integrating Varied Sources Found Inside and Outside Official Archives," contains six essays that seek to reconstruct women's experiences by weaving many partial and fragmented sources together in unique ways. These contributors suggest that even when a great variety of sources can be uncovered, interpreting them remains challenging if women's voices within the sources are filtered through others, if the documents represent scattered and incomplete fragments, if there are many silences in the extant materials, or if the historiographic context remains limited.

Lisa Sousa utilizes many diverse Spanish and indigenous language sources to illuminate gender prescriptions and roles in Nahua (Aztec) communities of central Mexico from 1520 to 1750. She argues that indigenous women of early Mexico "are not missing from the historical record, nor are they silent in the sources." On the contrary, native women can be found in many types of documents located in repositories in Mexico, the United States, and Europe: criminal records, civil documents, formal texts, and pictorial manuscripts. The challenge for Souza was not in locating sources containing traces of women, their social agency, and prescribed gender norms, but rather in "making sense of the fragmented and sometimes contradictory evidence regarding their roles and status." She describes a methodology in which she reads these diverse sources against one another to "shed light on multiple views and conflicting perspectives of gender rights and obligations." Souza likens this process to Nahua women's work of spinning and weaving, in which the raw material fragments are sifted, sorted, and spun "into threads of evidence" and further woven into multicolored fabric, "narratives that tell a coherent, complex story of Nahua women's lives." This process involved painstaking research on many continents and a deep philological understanding of the Nahuatl language and its written and pictographic forms. As she describes her work with different types of documents, Souza stresses that what was often most valuable was the "incidental information" found in them that gave her a sense of social roles, attitudes, and interactions among women and men, and relations between the Nahua and the colonial state. Sousa ends her essay with a discussion of how the process of weaving the sources together sheds light on Nahua women's labor. The economic roles and labors of men and women often overlapped, as they worked with one another to maintain the household, raise children, pay tribute, and protest Jesuit colonial authority. While women did not participate in the political apparatus, they were central to community life and to an agricultural system in which they owned and inherited land and tools.

Sherry J. Katz's essay explores the process of excavating radical women's political activism in Progressive-Era California. These early-twentieth-century socialist-feminists, who have largely rested in the margins of historical scholarship, made important contributions to social reform, including women's enfranchisement, the construction of the early welfare state, and the gendered integration of partisan politics. Because these activists left few manuscript collections or oral history interviews behind, Katz developed a method she calls "researching around our subjects," in order to reconstruct and interpret their lives. This process involved "working outward in concentric circles of related sources" that held traces of their voices and activities. Katz painstakingly mined socialist movement newspapers and manuscript collections; the varied materials of the feminist, labor, and social reform campaigns in which socialist-feminists played key roles; the collections of individuals and organizations with whom they collaborated; government documents in which they appeared; and coverage in the local, state, and national press. Integrating these layers of materials allowed Katz to construct socialist-feminists' political trajectory and social impact, but a "source base heavy in newspaper reportage and scattered organizational remains" made it difficult to reconstruct "their personal lives and the relational aspects of their political careers." Even though silences abound in this fragmented source material, Katz argues that the "researching around" methodology is indispensable to the recovery of marginalized political voices.

Malgorzata Fidelis's essay explores the process of reconstructing the lives of women industrial workers in post–World War II communist Poland. Her methodology involved both utilizing traditional official archival sources and conducting nontraditional oral history interviews. Fidelis traveled from "one archive to another in search of women's voices," sifting through many types of sources "generated by party-state institutions," a mainstay of all historical research on communist-era Poland. She was one of the first researchers to examine the records of the Women's Section of the ruling Polish United Workers' Party after they became accessible in the 1990s. Her goal was to "extract" those rare documents that contained traces of women's own perceptions or experiences. Her discussion of working in these state-sponsored archives is especially nuanced and instructive. Fidelis suggests that even "collections consciously devoted to preserving documents about women do not necessarily reflect ... women's identities and perspectives." In the case of communist state archives, women were treated like workers and peasants, ideological categories rather than social groups. Thus working in these official archives "requires taking apart layers of state agenda to see women as historical actors in their own right." In the women's section of the archives, Fidelis uncovered detailed reports on hundreds of letters from ordinary working women to the popular, but state-sponsored, magazine *Girlfriend* from 1948 to 1952. These letters "provide genuine voices of working women with no interference from censorship," as do the oral history interviews that Fidelis conducted with working women in 2002. Both of these sources suggest that women in communist Poland (as in other totalitarian states) were not merely objects of political repression or material shortages, but rather, "complex and lively characters who actively shaped their identities through interaction with state institutions." Their identities as modern, heroic socialist workers were strong, and yet they challenged party policies they believed harmful or that cut against the grain of traditional social and religious beliefs.

Ula Y. Taylor illuminates two different types of archival challenges in her essay on African American women in the Garvey movement and the Universal Negro Improvement Association (UNIA) during the 1920s. In the case of Amy Jacques Garvey (a leader of the UNIA and Marcus Garvey's second wife), Taylor encountered finding "more" than she expected. Jacques Garvey's papers were voluminous, as she was the secretary of the UNIA and had attempted to "preserve . . . [its] place in history." Yet Taylor struggled with many "archival voids" found even in very rich collections, as the records did not reveal what she expected they would: evidence of a staunch black feminist, of sisterly comrades, or contemporary co-workers willing to be interviewed. Taylor was forced to "figuratively remove" herself from the documents in order to put aside her own interpretative "longings and convictions" and resuscitate the "silenced voices" of Jacques Garvey and other women in the UNIA. She developed the concept of "community feminism" to explain their activist spirit. Community feminists played "helpmate" roles in activities designed to uplift the African American community, and yet they were also important leaders who engaged in feminist activism. In examining the life of another prominent woman in the UNIA, Amy Ashwood Garvey (a talented organizer and Marcus Garvey's first wife), Taylor encountered the problem of having too little by way of documentary evidence. Researching Ashwood Garvey, who left few "material traces," forced Taylor to employ her "historical imagination, deeply rooted in other textual scholarship on Garveyism and feminist theory, in order to compensate for the lack of records." Because Ashwood Garvey was a compelling and effective speaker for the UNIA on Harlem streets, Taylor focused on this urban space and developed the concept of "street strolling" to understand her activism. She argues that "Ashwood Garvey theorized a Pan-African struggle through public oratory and walking the 'cultural superstructure' of Harlem." Thus Taylor's essay provides a complex discussion of different archival dilemmas and how to approach them with creativity and contextual knowledge.

Nupur Chaudhuri's essay on the Indian nationalist-feminist Krishnobhabini Das brings together scattered published documents written by Das and her colleagues in order to reconstruct her life, thought, and reform work. Few traces of this late-nineteenth- and early-twentieth-century Bengali activist and author could be found in traditional archives, so Chaudhuri turned to her autobiographical writings, including a popular travel narrative and her published poems and essays, and a contemporary biographical sketch. Chaudhuri names these materials as an alternative archive (a fragmented yet coherent body of material located outside of conventional primary source repositories) for understanding not only Das, but Bengali women of her time. This archive illuminates Bengali women's family lives and the social customs that limited their choices, irrespective of class background. Chaudhuri also sees that these sources provide a window into the ways in which Das, and a larger group of female activists, took their "double subjugation" as Bengali women in a colonial context and constructed a nationalist-feminist vision for change. She argues that Das "and women like her had to negotiate their lives often in an unfriendly environment" and that "their struggles paved the way for reforms." Largely self-educated, Das articulated her nationalist-feminism in an 1885 autobiographical travel narrative titled *Englande Bangamohila* (A Bengali Lady in England), which contrasted women's position in colonial India with women's place in English society in such a way as to make the case for nationalist freedom from colonialism accompanied by changes that would emancipate women. Das proposed that modern Indian women—educated, active in public life, and independent minded—would cease to be subjugated in their homes and families. Widely known in India during her own time, but forgotten in ours, her self-made archive of published work enables us to reconstruct her life and her political commitments and allows us a glimpse into the worlds of the Bengali women of her era.

In the final piece in this part, four scholars living in the United States and Iran offer a "collaborative essay" that suggests "new venues for research on women in the Qajar era (1789–1925)." In individually written sections, each historian utilized a "different historical source to provide glimpses into gender and sexual constructs of this period." Iranian women's history is a fairly new field, and all of the sources explored here had been "previously neglected." Mansoureh Ettehadieh (Nezam Mafi) examined a legal register from a prominent notary office in Tehran. She argues that the legal contracts recorded there "reveal a legal dichotomy for women between their economic and marital rights." On the one hand, marriage laws treated women as minors, but on the other hand, women were free to engage in economic and commercial transactions, taking advantage of their opportunities in this arena. Elham Malekzadeh explored records of women's charitable giving and discovered that especially after the Constitutional Revolution (1906–11), a period of modernity and nationalism, "better-educated, more political, and more socially aware women" shifted their financial contributions from mosques and religious institutions to secular health and educational charities. "Awakened" as social activists, they became especially supportive of women's schools and orphanages, suggesting an interest in empowering women and promoting social welfare. Maryam Ameli-Rezaei uncovered private letters written by elite women in the Qajar court that provide windows "into the closed harem world." These letters also help to illuminate a transformation from Persian poetry to prose and a female prose style that tended to be more personal than that of men. Janet Afary utilized the memoirs of European physicians who spent time in the mid-nineteenth-century Qajar court to shed light on sexual and marriage practices of the era. She encountered a host of practices suggesting women's resistance to marital and sexual conformity: women's opposition to arranged marriages; secret hymen repair for women who engaged in premarital sex; and the use of contraception and abortion. Taken together, these four scholars illuminate the varied types of documents and research strategies now being employed by historians of Iranian women and gender.

In the third part of the book, "Creating Women's History Archives," two historians discuss the possibilities in constructing archives of women's experiences, in large part from women's personal and organizational papers and oral history interviews. Joanne L. Goodwin describes the dearth of materials that were available to uncover the experiences of women in twentieth-century Las Vegas, Nevada. The popular images of showgirls and prostitutes provided a master narrative of life in Las Vegas that bore "little resemblance to the lives of the women who lived there." With the help of Jean Ford, a feminist activist, legislator, and later professor of women's studies at the University of Nevada, Reno, women's history archives were created at that institution and then later at the University of Nevada, Las Vegas. Goodwin details the anatomy of that process in Las Vegas, which involved the analysis of existing archival collections in order to identify their usefulness to women's and gender history, and then acquisition and archiving of material from townswomen and ranch families, professional women, and community organizations in which women were active. When wage-earning women, women of color, and women in gaming remained poorly represented in the archive, Goodwin helped to develop an oral history project that focused primarily on women who worked in the city's casinos. From the Las Vegas Women Oral

History Project, Goodwin has begun to construct a new narrative of women's lives in the city from 1945 to 1980 that highlights four themes: migration, work opportunities for women and economic mobility, combining work and family, and community engagement. Creating an archive of women's experiences "provides alternative perspectives on women's lives and gender roles" in Las Vegas and for American women more broadly. As Goodwin points out, "without these sources, midcentury perspectives of women would remain unknown and untold."

In the final essay in this volume, Kathleen Sheldon recounts her early research on African women. When she went to Beira, Mozambique, in 1982, the country was in the midst of an internal civil conflict that meant daily life was fraught with many difficulties. In addition, very little had been written by historians on women in Africa, and historical documentation of any kind was extremely limited. Even rarer was material recording the history of women in Mozambique. With almost no archival sources on women and few secondary sources to guide her research, Sheldon felt she was "working in a vacuum" in devising a research method and locating primary sources on women in Beira. She decided to collect oral histories of working women, a process that involved using her contacts in local government and a regional branch of the national women's organization to create "a program to interview women" in three sectors of the economy in which they were employed in substantial numbers: health care (nurses and midwives), cashew processing (factory workers), and garment manufacturing (machine operators). In creating oral histories of working women, she had "source material about women's lives ... not available anywhere else." Through these oral histories, Sheldon was able to chart the positive effects of the socialist government of Mozambique on women's lives after 1975, especially on their working conditions and legal status. "Women's history was all around me," she writes, "though for the most part not in the standard archival repositories. I found it by talking to women whose memories of Portuguese colonial oppression influenced their appreciation for the improvements they were experiencing under a socialist government in a newly independent Mozambique."

Each of the twelve essays in this volume explores the challenges of finding women in the sources and proposes innovative strategies for meeting these challenges. Our hope is that the many different responses of these authors will encourage others to develop new ways to contest the archives. As historians, we respect historical evidence and archival research. Yet it is through questioning the sources and the methodologies for analyzing them that we learn more about people who have been hidden so long in historical records.

NOTES

1. Marlene Manoff, "Theories of the Archive from Across the Disciplines," *Portal: Libraries and the Academy* 4, no. 1 (2004): 10, provides a helpful discussion of the changing definitions of documents and archives. For more theoretical context for these changing views, see Michel Foucault, *The Archaeology of Knowledge*, trans. A. M. Sheridan Smith (New York: Pantheon, 1972), and Jacques Derrida, *Archive Fever*, trans. Eric Prenowitz (Chicago: University of Chicago Press, 1996).

2. See discussion in Alice Kessler Harris, "Social History," in Eric Foner, ed., *The New American Social History (Revised and Expanded)* (Philadelphia: Temple University Press, 1997), 231–55, especially 237.

3. Nell Irvin Painter, "Writing Biographies of Women," *Journal of Women's History* 9, no. 2 (1997): 160.

4. Manoff, "Theories of the Archive," especially 9–10, 14–17, 19–20; Antoinette Burton, ed., *Archive Stories: Facts, Fictions, and the Writing of History* (Durham, N.C.: Duke University Press, 2005), 6.

5. See Joanne Goodwin's discussion of this topic in this volume.

6. Burton, ed., *Archive Stories*, introduction, 1–21, especially 6, 7, and 17. Other recent collections of essays that reflect critically on the archive include Francis X. Blouin Jr. and William G. Rosenberg, eds., *Archives, Documentation, and Institutions of Social Memory: Essays from the Sawyer Seminar* (Ann Arbor: University of Michigan Press, 2006); and Margaret Proctor, Michael G. Cook, and Caroline Williams, eds., *Political Pressure and the Archival Record* (Chicago: Society of American Archivists, 2005).

7. See Katz and Taylor essays in this volume.

8. See Perry essay in this volume.

9. See Taylor essay in this volume.

10. The self-conscious examination of our relationship to, and interpretation of, the sources, as historians rooted in our own time, was an important innovation of social history (and women's history). See Kessler-Harris, "Social History," 238. Postmodern historians focus more fully on our "personal encounter[s] with the archive" itself and on "the pressure of the contemporary moment on one's reading of what is to be found there." See Burton, *Archive Stories*, 8.

11. See Clancy-Smith essay in this volume.

PART 1

LOCATING WOMEN IN OFFICIAL DOCUMENTS

1. FINDING FATIMA, A SLAVE WOMAN OF EARLY MODERN SPAIN

Mary Elizabeth Perry

Fatima, a Berber slave woman from North Africa, appears in an Inquisition report of 1584 that describes her as a "berberisca," a Muslim woman who had converted to Christianity in the city of Málaga in southern Spain.[1] Despite years of archival work, I have found her in no other documents of the period. This problem is challenging but not surprising, for existing historical records often leave women in obscurity, muted at best and usually invisible. Yet Fatima was silenced in historical records not only as a woman, but also as a member of a minority group and as a slave. It is no wonder that most historians do not even notice her invisibility in historical records.[2] To leave her in obscurity, however, is to collude in her silencing and in the writing of hegemonic history—that is, studies of the past that promote and preserve the interests of those in power.

The Inquisition undoubtedly never would have bothered to include Fatima in its records except for the fact that she challenged a cleric's account of her conversion to Christianity. When she became ill with the plague, Fatima was taken to a hospital where a cleric testified "that since the said Moor [Fatima] continued to ask for baptism and since she was not frenetic but in her sound mind and it was for her remedy and salvation, he had baptized her." After she left the hospital, however, she denied to one person that she had been baptized, asserting that she was and always had been a Muslim. Another person asked her directly about her baptism, and "she had responded that when they baptized her and converted her to Christianity, she was crazy and without sanity and without judgment." These witnesses denounced her to inquisitors as an apostate Morisca—a woman who had returned to Islam after converting to Christianity.

At this time, new converts from both Judaism and Islam triggered deep concerns among Christian rulers of the Spanish kingdoms. Ecclesiastical and lay authorities suspected Moriscos in particular of falsely "converting" in order to remain in their Spanish homes after royal decrees expelled Muslims in 1502 and 1526. The Muslim tradition of *taqiyya* deepened suspicions among Christian authorities, for this longtime teaching of "precaution" counseled the faithful living under oppressive rulers to conform externally to the dominant religion while internally remaining loyal to Islam.[3]

Because we find Fatima in a single document, much of her identity remains lost to us, eclipsed by the accusation before the Inquisition. It is true that the single document tells us about her illness and hospitalization in some detail, and particularly about her baptism and her denial of the baptism after she left the hospital. However, we do not learn from the record if she was born a slave or whether she had been enslaved following her arrival in Andalucía from North Africa. Nor do we know anything of her birth family or childhood, whether she married or had children—details commonly omitted from Inquisition records of slaves.

In fact, the single document we have raises more questions than it answers. No wonder we historians of women continue to look in the archives and old rooms that hold memories of the past—the clues to a person's identity that help us to reconstruct a life and to see how this life story reveals the society in which it was lived.[4] In my judgment, Fatima offers a valuable opportunity to study how disenfranchised people develop power and play active roles in history; in addition, Fatima shows that historians can study these very marginal people even though they appear in few historical documents.

Nevertheless, I want to acknowledge that a single Inquisition record is especially problematic as a source of information about a Muslim slave woman. It is true that Inquisition documents include testimony by and about Moriscas, women who often appear in no other records except as unnamed wives, mothers, sisters, and daughters. However, Moriscas did not write Inquisition reports, nor could these women speak openly to inquisitors without fear for their lives and their loved ones. The problems of using this single source challenge us, as Antoinette Burton suggests in her recent book *Dwelling in the Archive*, to "acknowledge that *all* archives are provisional, interested, and calcified in both deliberate and unintentional ways; that *all* archives are, in the end, fundamentally unreliable."[5]

The single source we have for Fatima tells about her only indirectly and must be read as an account of inquisitors or employees of the Holy Office who worked within the context of often-used formulae and unexamined assumptions. These men wrote down what they heard as inquisitors and asked questions to elicit responses they wanted, clearly reinforcing a form of ventriloquism in which the powerful speak for the powerless.[6] Moreover, in this power context, suspects and witnesses knew that they must speak carefully to inquisitors. Fatima, however, broke this pattern of deference to official power, for she insisted to both neighbors and inquisitors that she must be the one to define herself.

Acknowledging the limitations of our evidence in the case of Fatima, it is nonetheless possible to develop a methodology for restoring the forgotten to history by working with a single document. Using the example of women historians and literary scholars, we read this document "against the grain," looking beneath surface meanings for subtexts and silences that can tell us more than the formulaic questions and responses that inquisitors sought and recorded in official male-centered documents.[7] Moreover, we contextualize the document to recover some of the missing evidence, and we use insights from scholars in politics, anthropology, and cultural criticism to analyze the information we find.

In the following pages, I consider the context for Fatima's document and then read it closely for insights into her identity as a person, her vulnerabilities, and also her power. Although these categories are very closely intertwined, we can consider them separately as a way to better unpack what a single Inquisition record can tell us about the life of this Muslim slave woman living in late-sixteenth-century Spain. Our goal is not simply to learn more about Fatima personally, but to uncover insights that this one minority slave woman provides for historians who study many other people and periods of time. Fatima shows above all that disenfranchised people have developed strategies for empowerment and resistance that challenge assumptions of hegemonic history.

DOCUMENT AND CONTEXT

Bundled with other papers of officers of the Inquisition working in the city of Málaga, the one document we have on the life of Fatima begins by naming her:

> Ana, Berberisca by nation being a Moor [Muslim], called Fatima, slave of María López, resident of Málaga, was testified about before this commissary of this Holy Office by seven witnesses, of whom two say that a certain person whom they named had said that the said Ana, being a Moor, had become ill with the plague and, being in the hospital for the plague in the said city of Málaga, she had converted to Christianity, and a cleric named Becerra who had charge of the said hospital had baptized her and they had given her the Christian name

Ana, and that after the accused was healed and had left the said hospital, one witness says that the accused had told how she had become a Christian and that after this he knew as a certainty that the said Ana called Fatima still kept the fast of Ramadan, and that she said publicly that she was a Moor and that at the time that she converted to Christianity she was crazy. The second witness says that he asked the accused if she were Christian, and she had responded that when they baptized her and converted her to Christianity, she was crazy and without sanity and without judgment . . . and that now because she wanted to have the heart of a Moor and is said to be Christian, that she wants nothing but to be a Moor.

After more testimony, the report concludes:

[I]t was voted that because the accused did not appear to have been instructed before she was baptized nor afterward, she be ordered and compelled to keep the faith that she had promised in baptism with warning that if she acted otherwise she would be punished. It was agreed that she be placed in a convent where she would be instructed in the faith, and because through the process it was clear that the accused maliciously denied having been baptized, [and] one cannot have [illegible] nor ignorance of a fact so notable as that of baptism, it was provided that she appear in an *auto de fe* and be given 200 lashes, and thus it was executed.

Now available in the Archivo Histórico Nacional in Madrid, the document carries with it assumed but unwritten contextual information. As a report of the Inquisition, it reflects the primary purpose for the Holy Office, which was to protect the Catholic faith from heresy and contamination. Established in 1478 in the Spanish kingdoms, it had been granted by the pope as a weapon to be used especially against Jewish people who had converted to Christianity.[8] Because many of these converts had accepted baptism only under duress, Catholic officials had good reason to suspect that they had converted in name only and still retained much of their Jewish faith.

At the beginning of the sixteenth century, this suspicion of "New Christians" expanded to include Muslims who had accepted baptism. Ferdinand and Isabel had promised religious freedom to Muslims when Granada, the last Muslim stronghold in Iberia, fell to Christian soldiers in 1492. Christian zeal to convert Muslims, however, led to an armed rebellion and increasing tensions that culminated in a royal decree in 1501 that all Muslims of the kingdom of Castile must convert to Christianity or leave their Iberian homes. In large fields, Christian officials rounded up thousands of Muslims, and there prelates flung holy water over them and pronounced them Christians.[9] Not surprisingly, many Christian officials regarded these converts, like the

Judeo-*conversos* before them, as false Christians who secretly continued to practice their original faith. In both cases, the Inquisition had jurisdiction over only Christians or people who had been baptized. The issue of whether Fatima had been baptized, then, became a central question in her case.

Assimilation of "New Christians" concerned both lay and ecclesiastical authorities in sixteenth-century Iberia. They considered assimilation not as a process of mutual accommodation and understanding of other peoples, but as a means of limiting and controlling difference. The marriage of Ferdinand and Isabel had brought about what some called "a union of crowns" of the various Iberian kingdoms.[10] Yet when Charles Hapsburg, grandson of Ferdinand and Isabel, came to Iberia to claim the supposedly united throne of his grandparents, dissension and distrust erupted in local rebellions in 1520. A political imperative for this monarchy struggling to become a central state was to find a common enemy to unify its many peoples. As political theorist Anne Norton has pointed out, nations determine their own identities through what they reject.[11] Jews, Muslims, and those "New Christians" who had converted to Christianity from Judaism or Islam became politically significant counteridentities, common enemies who also justified the extension and consolidation of royal power.[12] Fatima's insistence on her Muslim identity thus raises issues of politics as well as those of religion.

Yet inquisitors' efforts to protect Spanish Christians from contamination by contact with Jews, Muslims, or suspicious converts could not seal the very permeable boundaries of this growing empire. After the earlier expulsion of Jews and Muslims, for example, Jewish and Muslim traders often entered and departed Spanish ports, especially those close to North Africa, such as Málaga, where Fatima lived when inquisitors arrested her. It was not uncommon for members of a Muslim family to convert to Christianity so they could stay in Spain, while other family members moved to North Africa, where they might turn to commerce and use their Spanish contacts.[13] Known as *Moriscos*, or "Moor-like," Muslim converts seemed to share more similarities with Muslim outsiders than "Old Christians," those Spanish Christians who did not have any Jewish or Muslim ancestors.

Muslim slaves had a unique role in early modern Spain. Often they had become enslaved as prisoners during armed conflict with Christians, who were prohibited from taking other Christians as slaves. As slaves, they might convert to win freedom from a sympathetic owner, yet as Muslims they were exempt from the decree that they must convert to Christianity or leave the Spanish kingdoms. In Spain they often came into contact with Christians, for they seldom worked in this slave economy as plantation laborers held among hundreds of other Muslim slaves. Instead, slaves in early modern

Spain more often worked in day labor, domestic service, or small workshops and protofactories. They gave their wages to their owners, women and men of more modest means who might own only one or two slaves.[14] As a Muslim slave, Fatima worked in the city of Málaga, where her owner resided, and she apparently interacted with a number of different Christians, some of whom gave testimony against her to the Inquisition.

Because Muslim and Morisco slaves often lived and worked apart from their owners, they could develop their own covert communities. One complaint of the early seventeenth century declared that slaves lived together "in their own law, keeping their sect and performing its rites and ceremonies as they could in Berbery," free to do all this "because they cannot be expelled."[15] The slaves sold produce and other food at low prices, cutting into the profits of poor Old Christians, the report asserted, and they committed robberies and murders against Old Christians. These Moorish slaves should be forbidden to live together in neighborhoods or share a courtyard, the complaint concluded, and they should not be allowed to carry arms. Insistent on preserving her identity as a Muslim, Fatima seemed to align herself with a dangerous subclass that many Old Christians resented.

The date of this report provides another important clue to the context of Fatima's case. In 1584 many Moriscos had already lived through two generations as converts to Christianity. Rather than seeming more assimilated, however, they appeared to be more rigid in their refusal to change. An instruction from Madrid about Christianizing Moriscos warned that the women were the most "obstinate," especially in preserving daily ceremonies of Islam in their homes and in keeping their children from attending the compulsory Christian schools established for them.[16] In countless Inquisition cases, Morisco women were accused of observing Muslim practices in their homes and teaching them to their families. Leonor de Morales, for example, had been denounced by her husband, who told inquisitors that she had persuaded him to follow Muslim traditions. Other witnesses said that she danced and sang as a Muslim at weddings and that she ate while sitting on the ground, cooked meat in oil, ate meat on Fridays, changed into clean clothing on Fridays, and communicated with "other Moors."[17]

Yet some Moriscos sought more than obstinate covert resistance. Moriscos of Granada, for example, openly rebelled against Christian rulers in 1568. Declaring war against Philip II and his noble supporters, these Moriscos had taken their families into the Alpujarras Mountains, where they fought a guerilla war that held off Christian forces until the last months of 1570. Ottoman Turks came to the aid of the Morisco rebels with troops and arms, confirming the suspicions of many Christians that Moriscos constituted a "fifth column" of internal spies who had been working with the Ottoman Turks. Arms also came to Morisco rebels from Berbers and other Muslims living in that part of North Africa known in this time as "Berbery."[18] Fatima's background as a "Berberisca," then, deepened suspicions about her. In fact, she may have been taken as a slave in one of the many armed skirmishes between Spanish Christians and the Muslims of North Africa.

By 1584, when inquisitors reported the case of Fatima, hopes for a peaceful resolution of the tensions between Moriscos and their Christian rulers had seriously declined. Philip II had ordered the forcible relocation of Moriscos from Granada following the defeat of their insurrection, regardless of whether they had actually participated in the rebellion. Some fifty thousand Morisco men, women, and children were rounded up to be marched or shipped to towns and cities of Castile, where officials placed them under special observation and prohibited them from living together.[19] Rarely welcomed to their new homes, these defeated Moriscos became even less likely to assimilate. In 1580, in fact, Christian officials uncovered several new plots for Morisco uprisings.[20] When Fatima was called before inquisitors, she came as member of a group that was highly suspect. At best, this group had shown long-lasting resistance to assimilation; at worst, they seemed too willing to work with the Ottoman Turks, archrivals of the Spanish Empire.

IDENTITY AND PERSON

Mindful of the historical context of an imperial Spain deeply concerned with religious conformity and internal enemies, we turn to a careful reading of the inquisitor's report of Fatima's case for what it can tell us about her personally. The report begins with words to identify her: "Ana Berberisca by nation being a Moor, called Fatima, slave of María López, resident of Málaga." What we first note is that this woman is identified by two different names: a Christian name, Ana, and a Muslim name, Fatima. She was evidently called Fatima until she became ill with the plague and went to a hospital. There a cleric baptized her and gave her the Christian name, but she resumed use of her Muslim name when she left the hospital.

In fact, it was her insistence on using her own Muslim name that brought her to the attention of the Inquisition. Throughout the report, inquisitors used Ana, even though they noted that in the first audience "she said that she was called Fatima and that she did not know that she had another name and that she was not a baptized Christian and that she knew this because always she had been and was a Moor." Both Fatima and the inquisitors understood that a name is more than a name. It denotes power and status, belonging or not belonging. A name presumes the right to give or take identity, to evoke ancestors, saints, and heroes. At this time a name especially indicated religious affiliation, for when Muslims accepted baptism they also had to show their deference by replacing their Muslim names with a Christian name. However, Fatima chose to identify herself by her Muslim name.

Inquisitors insisted on using her Christian name, but they also acknowledged her Berber connections in identifying her as a "Berberisca by nation." Most of the people of "Berbery" had retained much of their pre-Islamic culture even after centuries of living as Muslims.[21] The inquisitor's words that identify Fatima thus note her difference as both cultural and religious. Moreover, her association with nearby peoples in North Africa implied an anomalous status—a woman living between two different worlds, Christian Iberia and Muslim North Africa. Belonging neither to the one or the other, Fatima represented the dangers of liminality.[22]

The inquisition report identified Fatima not only by name, but also as the baptized slave of a woman living in Málaga. Because slaves had no legal standing except as property, the report does not give other personal information about her: family, age, marital status, occupation, or whether she had children. Inquisition records in this period usually identified non-slave women as wives, daughters, sisters, or mothers of adult men. In Fatima's case, there is no adult male to take responsibility for her, a factor that increases her anomalous status and intensifies the dangers of her liminality. This disenfranchised woman, ironically, had the freedom of not having to follow the directions of a father, husband, or son. Yet the absence of a responsible male also reveals her vulnerability, for Fatima lived in a very patriarchal society in which masculine advice and presence could be an advantage, especially in formal legal or ecclesiastical transactions. In addition, her lack of a male relative concerned authorities, who depended on fathers and brothers to police the conduct of the women in their families.[23]

María López, the owner of Fatima, offers more clues to the personal situation of this slave. The fact that Fatima's owner was a woman probably relieved Fatima from sexual services that female slaves were often expected to provide for male owners. We do not know, however, if María herself required sexual relations with Fatima, nor whether María may have hired her out to others for sex. All that the report actually tells us about this slave owner is that she was a resident of Málaga, a seaport in southern Spain not far from North Africa, which many slaves sought to reach when they attempted to flee owners in Spain.[24] Noticeably lacking in the report is any indication that María López had stepped forward either to denounce her slave for heresy or to defend her from charges against her. María made a very wise choice, for inquisitors could have held her responsible in either case, both for failure to sufficiently train her slave as a Christian and for inability to control her behavior. Moreover, some believed that a slave's conversion to Christianity obligated the owner to free the slave—a situation that María López may have wanted to avoid, especially if she, like so many small slaveholders, depended on the labor or the resale of Fatima to bring in necessary income.[25]

Fatima's case before the Inquisition gives us no indication of the work she performed. Many slave owners sent their slaves to work as domestic servants in others' homes or to make items such as ceramic tiles, bricks, or soap in small workshops. Both male and female slaves also worked as peons in construction or as stevedores in the port. Fatima may have worked in wine production or in nearby fields producing grains, fruits, and vegetables. If she had specialized skills, such as silk production or silk weaving, she could have brought in considerable income to her owner and could have been resold at a greater price than María López had originally paid for her. Although we do not know Fatima's age, resale of a female slave of childbearing years also brought a higher price.[26]

Those people who lived and worked with her knew Fatima as a slave and a Muslim who carried out certain ceremonies and traditions of Islam. These traditions may have been a strategy by which she attempted to maintain her own identity, consciously or unconsciously. Moreover, she may have wished to return to them as a way to reassert her Muslim identity after she returned from the hospital. Many religious observances—such as bathing, praying, preparing food and eating it—are ways that people have learned culture and identity through their bodies. Conversion for Fatima, as for most Muslims in early modern Spain, would have required her to forget these embodied lessons, a much more difficult task than to simply agree to become a Christian.[27]

POWER AND VULNERABILITY

When Fatima had to appear before the Inquisition, she came with even more vulnerability than most people. Her trouble began, according to the Inquisition report, when she became ill and was taken to a hospital. Often in times of plague, hospitals were used simply as a place to confine infected people in order to protect those who were still healthy. Being taken to a hospital, in fact, could be a death sentence, for there the patient would be surrounded by others struck by diseases that doctors in this period had few effective ways to cure.[28]

Fatima was vulnerable in another sense, as well, for she had talked to others about her hospital experiences. Some of these people had then denounced her to inquisitors, who were especially interested to hear about false converts. If she was vulnerable, however, Fatima seemed to be audacious, as well, and her very audacity increased her vulnerability. Yet far from collapsing in the powerlessness we might attribute to a minority slave woman, she seems to have asserted her own power to declare who she was and to provide her own explanation of why she had accepted baptism. All this directs us to the political issues in this woman's life, those questions of how others imposed power on her and how she tried to develop or assert her own power.

It would be easy to see this slave woman, Fatima, as completely disempowered. Living in a world dominated by Christians, she had been caught up in the very powerful machinery of the Inquisition. In order to survive, she had to be very aware of the power context in which she lived. When she was ill in the hospital, this power context could have seemed to her to be literally a matter of life and death. Unlike modern hospitals—or perhaps more like them than we want to think—hospitals of Fatima's time were rarely used by people with enough money and status to have their own physician or healer. As depositories for unfortunates whom others feared as carriers of contagion, hospitals often seemed simply one more step on the path to dying. Moreover, hospitals usually functioned under the direction of a religious order or corporation with more concerns about the souls than the bodies of patients.

Yet Fatima did not simply accept her powerlessness. In the power context of an early modern hospital, Fatima might well have asked herself, What can I do to receive good treatment here and improve my chances of survival? Disempowered people, as anthropologist James C. Scott has noted in his study of disenfranchised peasants in Malaysia, find many ways not only to survive, but also to develop their own "weapons of the weak"—such as pretended conformity or cheerful but slow-minded deference.[29] Perhaps Fatima realized that as a Muslim slave woman in a hospital, she had little chance of anything more than a cursory glance now and then to see if she was still alive. One possibility, then, is that Fatima consciously chose to request baptism as a way to better survive the illness and the hospital. In addition, she may have hoped that her conversion to Christianity as a slave would move her owner to grant her freedom, as happened in some cases. When her owner made no move to free her, she may have simply decided that her conversion could be a temporary measure for survival in the hospital, to be discarded when she left it.

Attempting to learn whether Fatima had deliberately hoodwinked the hospital staff, inquisitors examined the cleric who had baptized her and the head nurse who had been her godmother for baptism. The nurse testified "that among other Moorish slaves who had converted to Christianity in the said hospital that the said Fatima had requested baptism two or three times." In his testimony, the cleric who baptized Fatima stated that when he had asked her "how she wanted to be named, she had responded Ana and so he had placed the name Ana on her and that she was not forced nor pressed to be baptized but she had requested it many times and had received it with rejoicing and happiness and that she had participated in the conversion of another Moor to Christianity."

The nurse confirmed the cleric's testimony and added that "before he placed the baptismal water on the accused, the said cleric had a Berber boy ask her [Fatima] in Arabic whether she would be a Christian, and she always had responded that she wanted to be a Christian called Ana and that after becoming Christian she always passed time in the infirmary with the nurse who was her godmother and that after this at the persuasion of the accused that two other Moors were converted to Christianity before they died." This testimony, of course, called into sharp question Fatima's later explanation that she had been "out of her mind with the illness of the plague" when she allowed herself to be baptized.

Yet Fatima's going to the infirmary and helping to convert some other Muslim women might also reveal her attempts to establish a small community within the hospital. Perhaps she sought out the nurse who became her godmother because she wanted a woman who could provide nursing for her and really care about her as a person? Perhaps she helped to convince the two Muslim women to convert because she wanted to justify her own survival strategy of baptism? Perhaps she even hoped they would survive their illness and become a small support group with her and the nurse? As a slave woman, she had undoubtedly already developed survival strategies that included the friendship of other Muslim slaves who shared support, complaints, and concerns.

Once released and freed from the hospital, Fatima presumably returned to another power context—that of her home and work in Málaga. As an urban slave, she probably did not live with her owner and may have worked outside her owner's home. In this familiar setting of her own community, she told someone that she had been baptized in the hospital. This may have been simple carelessness or a quick response to a direct question about a rumor. Or it may have been a conscious decision to reassert her own identity and reestablish her own place among other Muslim slaves of her city. Muslim slaves may have developed their own form of bravado in telling of their encounters with Christian authorities, feeling especially empowered by laughing at baptism as a ruse for better medical treatment. Unfortunately for Fatima, the person to whom she spoke also noted that she continued to say that she was a Muslim and observed the fast of Ramadan. Once he had denounced her to the Inquisition, she found herself in yet another power context in which her very life was at stake.

Any person, whether Muslim or Christian, slave or free, would have realized the vulnerability of her position when required to respond to accusations before the Inquisition. Accused people were not even told why they had been arrested, and they were not given the names of those who had accused them until a much later stage in proceedings against them. Inquisitors considered contrite confession the only acceptable response, and then they required more details of the "crime" and names of "accomplices," the other people who had been involved in the offense. An accused person who confessed during torture had to affirm it the next day.

Fatima began her testimony before the inquisitors with the firm declaration "that her name was Fatima and that she did not know that she had another name and that she was not a baptized Christian, which she knew because always she had been and was a Moor." At a later hearing she repeated her statement, but she softened it by explaining that she had been "ill with the plague in the hospital in Málaga and that when she had entered it she had been a Moor and was named Fatima and she denied the rest because she was in such a state that she had no sense or judgment to understand anything and that she prayed to God to inspire her heart . . . because one still had to see that she wanted to be of a good heart and not of any evil." In the next hearing she refused to capitulate, responding that "perhaps she had agreed but that she did not agree with anyone that she had been baptized nor with anything that the witnesses had said of her had happened because she was out of her mind with the illness of the plague that she fears, and that she feels herself a Moor until God enlightens her that she is a Christian. And having been admonished by her counsel to tell the truth, [she] commended herself to God and placed her heart with him so that he would enlighten her." In another hearing "she had said that she was sick of thinking and that she would be a Christian when God wanted her to be and that she was a Moor and that she did not agree that she had been baptized."

It is true that inquisitors did not condemn her to death, but clearly they had the last word in deciding her identity and what should be done with her. Because she "did not appear to have been instructed [in the Christian faith] before she was baptized nor afterward," inquisitors agreed, she should be placed in a convent where she would be "instructed in the faith." As an enclosing hegemonic institution with strict rules, the convent could control the definition of her identity and impose a dominant form of thinking on her. In addition, because "it was clear that the accused maliciously denied having been baptized," inquisitors also agreed to sentence her to 200 lashes. This whipping would not only humble her by showing the power of the Inquisition to determine her identity as a Christian and their authority over her, it also marked her physically. Moreover, it could even be lethal, for 200 lashes could result in death.

FATIMA AND HISTORY

Despite the best efforts of inquisitors to silence her, Fatima's voice sings out in the single historical record that names her. Arrest and accusation did not prevent her from telling inquisitors her own version of what happened to her in the hospital. Nor did her slave status discourage her from insisting on her own identity as a Muslim woman named Fatima. She may have had limited choices as both slave and Muslim, but she continued to define herself and tell her own story. In the vulnerable position of a Muslim slave woman ill in a Christian hospital—and in the even greater vulnerability of a Muslim slave woman caught by the fearsome Inquisition—Fatima maintained her own identity. With considerable audacity, she told inquisitors and others that if she had agreed to convert to Christianity in the hospital, she must have been crazy. Fatima's audacity, of course, got her into a great deal of trouble. We do not know if she survived the 200 lashes and confinement in the convent. The single document that names her leaves so many questions unanswered and presents her voice only indirectly; yet it cannot silence her. Far from a victim to be pitied or an object to be lumped into an impersonal category, Fatima acts to portray herself and to protect her own interests to the best of her ability.

Although Fatima's case clearly demonstrates the power of the Inquisition, it also shows her strength in maintaining her own identity. Reading this document against the grain, we have explored questions of power, unexamined assumptions, and the significance of specific words. Furthermore, we have contextualized the document by interweaving many additional sources. Historical documents on slavery, compulsory schools for Morisco children, and Morisco resistance invigorate secondary literature on the Inquisition, the Spanish monarchy, and the Ibero-African frontier. Documents from the royal archive about the Morisco rebellion and subsequent relocation of Moriscos intertwine with an eyewitness's description and a chronicle of this rebellion. In addition, we have considered political theories about the need for counteridentities or common enemies in the unification of states. It is true that Fatima is found by name in only one historical document, but her case becomes part of a tapestry of many varied sources that place her in a specific time and place and help us to recognize meaning in her life.

As do other people forgotten in history, Fatima challenges assumptions that historians must leave the disenfranchised in silent obscurity. Her case shows that we do not have to abandon the study of women in the past simply because they do not appear in their own writings or in multiple documents. With Fatima we realize that we can listen to the voices that do come through in these indirect and far-from-neutral documents, contextualizing them and looking for layers of meanings in the words that are used and the information omitted. Fatima shows us the importance of recognizing individuals in historical records—not simply for the sake of "individualism," but because a person such as Fatima gives a face or voice to the past. This Muslim slave woman personalizes and helps to bring into human scale the institutions she encountered: slavery, the hospital, the Inquisition, an infant Spanish state. She demonstrates strategies for self-empowerment that disenfranchised people develop and find ways to use. Fatima shows us the possibilities even more than the limitations of available evidence, and she opens for us the world of minority slave women. In this world disenfranchised women suffered, but they also resisted and challenged official power.

NOTES

I acknowledge the kind permission of Johns Hopkins University Press to publish this modified version of the essay that appeared earlier in the *Journal of Women's History* (vol. 20, no. 1, Spring 2008). My thanks also to Sherry Katz, members of the Occidental College Writing Network, and editors of the *Journal of Women's History* for their helpful suggestions and comments on earlier versions of this essay.

1. Archivo Histórico Nacional (hereafter AHN), Inquisición, legajo 1953, number 19 (1584). All subsequent quotations of Fatima's case will be from this document. Note that the document has no page numbers and that inquisitors use the term *Mora*, or "Moor," to mean "Muslim." I have translated the report and have attempted to modernize language and eliminate repetitions. Some of the translations may seem unclear or grammatically awkward, but I have not wanted to change the words because the testimony may reflect the automatic assumptions of the inquisitors and also the fear of witnesses or a rush of words in the witnesses' attempts to respond to questions by inquisitors.

2. Ada María Díaz discusses the invisible invisibility of minority women in "Toward an Understanding of Feminismo Hispánico in the USA," in Barbara Hilkert Andolsen, Christine E. Gudorf, and Mary D. Pellauer, eds., *Women's Consciousness, Women's Conscience*, (San Francisco: Harper and Row, 1987), 51–61. More on the challenges of studying minority women is found in Mae Gwendolyn Henderson, "Speaking in Tongues: Dialogics, Dialectics, and the Black Woman Writer's Literary Tradition," in Judith Butler and Joan W. Scott, eds., *Feminists Theorize the Political* (New York: Routledge, 1992), 144–66; bell hooks, *Yearning: Race, Gender, and Cultural Politics* (Boston: South End Press, 1990); Toril Moi, *Sexual/Textual Politics: Feminist Literary Theory* (London: Methuen, 1985);

Joan W. Scott, *Gender and the Politics of History* (New York: Columbia University Press, 1988); Paul Julian Smith, *Representing the Other: "Race," Text, and Gender in Spanish and Spanish American Narrative* (Oxford: Clarendon Press, 1992); Sidonie Smith, "Who's Talking/Who's Talking Back? The Subject of Personal Narrative," *Signs* 18, no 2 (Winter 1993): 392–407; Gayatri Chakravorty Spivak, *In Other Worlds* (London: Methuen, 1987); Trinh Minh-ha, *When the Moon Waxes Red: Representation, Gender, and Cultural Politics* (New York: Routledge, 1991); and Trinh Minh-ha, *Woman, Native, Other: Writing Postcoloniality and Feminism* (Bloomington: Indiana University Press, 1989).

3. Two helpful sources on *taqiyya* are Louis Cardaillac, "Un aspecto de las relaciones entre moriscos y cristianos: polémica y taqiyya," *Actas del coloquio internacional sobre literatura aljamiada y morisca* (Madrid: CLEAM, 1978), 3:107–22; and Henri Lammens, *Islam: Beliefs and Institutions* (London: Methuen, 1968). See also *The Holy Qur'an: Text, Translation and Commentary,* trans. and comm. Abdullah Yusef Ali, 2 vols. (Cambridge, Mass.: Hafner, 1946), sura 16:106 at 1:685. For an example of Moriscos and *taqiyya,* see "Respuesta que hizo el mufi de Oran a ciertas preguntas que le hicieron desde la Andalucía," May 3, 1563, published in Mercedes García Arenal, *Los moriscos* (Madrid: Editora Nacional, 1975), 44–45.

4. See the very important discussion of life stories and research methodologies in Nwando Achebe, "Getting to the Source: Nwando Achebe—Daughter, Wife, and Guest—A Researcher at the Crossroads," *Journal of Women's History* 14, no. 3 (Autumn 2002): 9–31, at 15–16, especially; and Mary Maples Dunn, "Dialogue," *Journal of Women's History* 14, no. 3 (Autumn 2003), which discusses the success of Laurel Thatcher Ulrich in using a single document to reveal a whole society in her *A Midwife's Tale,* at 136, especially.

5. Antoinette Burton, *Dwelling in the Archive: Women Writing House, Home, and History in Late Colonial India* (Oxford: Oxford University Press, 2003), 26, author's emphasis.

6. Ventriloquism and confession are discussed in Mike Hepworth and Bryan S. Turner, *Confession: Studies in Deviance and Religion* (London: Routledge and Kegan Paul, 1982); and Michel Foucault, *Discipline and Punish: The Birth of the Prison* (New York: Random House, 1995), 35–42, especially.

7. For reading against the grain, see Annette Kuhn, "Passionate Detachment," in *Women's Pictures: Feminism and Cinema* (Boston: Routledge and Kegan Paul, 1982) 15. Joëlle Rollo-Koster demonstrates how a papal document can be useful in writing women's history in her essay "The Women of Papal Avignon: A New Source," *Journal of Women's History* 8, no. 1 (Spring 1996): 36–59. In an interesting parallel to how we are trying to read an Inquisition record to uncover the life of Fatima, Linda Gordon provides an excellent example of finding the voices of poor immigrants in records kept by social workers in nineteenth- and twentieth-century Boston in her book *Heroes of Their Own Lives: The Politics and History of Family Violence* (Urbana: University of Illinois Press, 2002), 13–17, especially.

8. An earlier inquisition had been established in the Crown of Aragon, but it was under papal direction. A very helpful source on the Spanish Inquisition is Henry Kamen, *Inquisition and Society in Spain in the Sixteenth and Seventeenth Centuries* (Bloomington: Indiana University Press, 1985).

9. For terms of capitulation of Muslims in Granada, see Luis del Mármol Carvajal, *Historia del rebelión y castigo de los moriscos del reino de Granada* (1600), published in

Biblioteca de autores Españoles (Madrid: Atlas, 1946), 21:146–50. Antonio Domínguez Ortiz and Bernard Vincent, *Historia de los moriscos: vida y tragedia de una minoría* (Madrid: Revista de Occidente, 1978), discuss the subsequent conversion of Muslims, 15–22.

10. For example, J. H. Elliott, *Imperial Spain 1469–1716* (London: Penguin, 1990), 15–129; and Stanley Payne, *A History of Spain and Portugal* (Madison: University of Wisconsin Press, 1973), 1:170–87.

11. Anne Norton, *Reflections on Political Identity* (Baltimore: Johns Hopkins University Press, 1988); and Mary Elizabeth Perry, "The Politics of Race, Ethnicity, and Gender in the Making of the Spanish State," in Tom Lewis and Francisco J. Sánchez, eds., *Culture and the State in Spain 1550–1850* (New York: Garland, 1999), 34–54.

12. For more on counteridentities and national identity, see Peter Sahlins, *Boundaries: The Making of France and Spain in the Pyrenees* (Berkeley: University of California Press, 1989), 9, 107, and 123.

13. Andrew C. Hess, *The Forgotten Frontier: A History of the Sixteenth-Century Ibero-African Frontier* (Chicago: University of Chicago Press, 1978).

14. For more on slavery, see Biblioteca Nacional (hereafter BN) ms. 18.735, "Informe sobre los moros esclavos y libres de Sevilla" (n.d., but probably early seventeenth century); Antonio Domínguez Ortiz, "La esclavitud en Castilla durante la edad moderna," *Estudios de Historia Social de España* 2 (1952): 369–428; and Aurelia Martín Casares, *La esclavitud en la Granada del siglo XVI: género, raza y religion* (Granada: Universidad de Granada and Diputación Provincial de Granada, 2000).

15. BN, ms 18.735, no. 53, *Papel de lo dañosso que es en los reynos de que aya moros y moriscos* (n.p., n.d., but after 1619).

16. "Informe de Madrid a Valencia sobre instrucción de los moriscos," printed in García Arenal, *Los moriscos*, 116–25, 122, especially.

17. AHN, Inquisición, legajo 2075, no. 11, dated 1601.

18. For the Alpujarras rebellion and the role of the Turks, see Ginés Pérez de Hita, *Guerras civiles de Granada, 1595–1597*, ed. Paula Blanchard-Demouge, 2 vols. (Madrid: Bailly-Bailliére, 1913–15), 2:253–61, especially.

19. Mármol Carvajal, *Historia del rebelión*, 323–24, especially; Archivo General de Simancas (hereafter AGS), Cámara de Castilla, legajo 2166; AGS, Cámara de Castilla, legajo 2161, part 1; AGS, Cámara de Castilla, legajo 2196.

20. Celestino López Martínez, *Mudéjares y moriscos sevillanos* (Seville: Rodríguez, Giménez y Compañía, 1935), 57, especially.

21. Kahina and the Berbers are discussed in Michael Brett and Elizabeth Fentress, *The Berbers* (Malden, Mass.: Blackwell, 2005), 85–86. For Berber resistance to Arabization, see Brett and Fentress, *The Berbers*, 135–42, especially, and Maya Shatzmiller, *The Berbers and the Islamic State: The Marinid Experience in Pre-Protectorate Morocco* (Princeton, N.J.: Markus Wiener, 2000).

22. Liminality has especially come to our attention through the work of Victor W. Turner, such as his *The Ritual Process: Structure and Anti-Structure* (Ithaca, N.Y.: Cornell University Press, 1969).

23. More discussion of gender, shame, and honor is in the essays edited by J. G. Peristiany in *Honour and Shame: The Values of Mediterranean Society* (London: Weidenfeld and Nicolson, 1965).

24. Many cases of Muslim slaves attempting to flee to North Africa from the Spanish coast appear in Inquisition records; see, for example, the case of Juana, slave of Francisco de Piña, in AHN, Inquisición, legajo 2075, no. 14.

25. Martín Casares, *La esclavitud*, 236–59; Juan Aranda Doncel, *Los moriscos en tierras de Córdoba* (Córdoba: Monte de Piedad y Caja de Ahorros de Córdoba, 1984), 142–51.

26. Aranda Doncel, *Los moriscos*, 142–51.

27. The strength and complexities of embodied knowledge are discussed in chapter 2 of Mary Elizabeth Perry, *The Handless Maiden: Moriscos and the Politics of Religion in Early Modern Spain* (Princeton, N.J.: Princeton University Press, 2005), 38–64.

28. I discuss hospitals and disease in my book *Crime and Society in Early Modern Seville* (Hanover, N.H.: University Press of New England, 1980), 238–40, especially; for more on medicine in Spain at this time, see Luis S. Granjel, *La medicina española del siglo XVII* (Salamanca: Ediciones Universidad de Salamanca, 1978); for a broader view of hospitals and history, see Michel Foucault, *Madness and Civilization: A History of Insanity in the Age of Reason* (New York: Pantheon, 1965).

29. James C. Scott, *Weapons of the Weak: Everyday Forms of Peasant Resistance* (New Haven, Conn.: Yale University Press, 1985).

2. REVEALING AN ORPHAN'S TALE FROM NINETEENTH-CENTURY MEXICO

Daniel S. Haworth

Recently, while working in the state archives of Guanajuato, in north central Mexico, I stumbled across a woman's story embedded in government documents from the mid-nineteenth century. Government in early national Mexico was an exclusively male domain; hence, internal government communication ordinarily omitted the female perspective. An exception to that rule emerged in a case file from early 1854 describing the efforts of nineteen-year-old María Petra Fernández to secure *habilitación de edad*, a legal declaration of her adulthood.[1] The precipitating factor was that Petra, an orphan, wanted to marry Cayetano Olmedo against the wishes of her guardian, Antonio Leiva. At the time, another year would elapse before she reached the age of majority, and until then, she could marry without Leiva's consent only if the governor emancipated her. Petra's request for what she deemed an "indispensable license" initiated a flurry of discussion between the governor and officials in her home town of Celaya.[2] The resulting documentation, twenty-five pages in total, was loosely sewn into a single volume and eventually filed with otherwise unrelated records—a report notifying the governor of a prison break; a ledger accounting for travel permits issued by the municipal government; a discussion of the ongoing attempt to confiscate an unauthorized history of the recently concluded war with the United States (1846–48); and so forth—all grouped according to place and date of origin.

The value of Petra's case file lies in its illumination of the adolescent woman's experience in early national Mexico. Petra represents a historical subject marginalized by the patriarchy of her time and, in the present, by the chronological and thematic focus that characterizes the scholarship on Mexican women. It is well known that in Mexico's patriarchal social order, law and custom regarded the woman as an eternal minor, subordinate to male authority in theory if not always in practice.[3] That reality also applied to adolescents and children, especially girls, who existed in the shadow of legally empowered adults and so rarely appear in the archive. While the study of children is a developing field in Latin American history, adolescents remain largely unexamined.[4] Compounding the obscurity of the adolescent woman is the fact that, chronologically speaking, the historiography of women in nineteenth-century Mexico concentrates on the closing decades of that century, when the economic liberalism favored by the ruling elite spawned rapid growth and an array of corresponding social changes. The historical features of that of age make it fertile ground for inquiry into the origins of patterns characterizing women's experience in the twentieth century. Historians have consequently made great strides in elucidating the insertion of women into the emerging capitalist order; their mobilization and collective effort to define their rights as citizens within the family and the workplace; the ways modernization impacted conceptions of sexuality and gender; and the origins of contemporary feminism. Women in the early national period, in Mexico as elsewhere in Latin America, have received comparatively little attention.[5] The same can be said for women of Petra's age group.

By claiming the right to marry the man of her choosing, Petra declared the end of her adolescence. Then as now, adolescence constituted an ambiguously defined transition from childhood to adulthood, mediated by law and custom. According to the law in effect at that time, a person became an adult at twenty-five years of age.[6] Of course, factors other than the law determined the duration and significance of adolescence; of these, gender and cultural tradition exerted the most influence, mitigated by the social status and economic condition of the individual. Young men gradually acquired the trappings of adulthood in their twenties, and though they could remain bachelors without compromising their autonomy, they entered the fullness of adulthood upon marrying. Young women ordinarily remained under parental authority for much longer, with marriage as the only socially acceptable means to leave their parents' household.[7] The problem for Petra was that marriage in and of itself would not end her subjugation. She feared that Leiva opposed her choice because he intended for her to marry one of his sons instead. She had to marry Cayetano, not just because she loved him, but also out of an urgent desire to liberate herself from Leiva.[8]

Before the case file can be mined for historical insight, however, its specific purpose must be taken into account. The file documents the legal process by which officials determined the merits of Petra's request, and it records the governor's eventual decision. Because his decision constituted a legally binding act, the file was furthermore an indispensable compendium of findings that established the legitimacy of his ruling. The story the file purports to tell is one of a paternalist government adjudicating a dispute between a guardian and his female ward. Hence, the file presents a carefully crafted official narrative suited to the objectives of the regime that produced it. This function in turn affected the way the file documented Petra's experience. Official imperatives determined the inclusion of certain details, the omission of others, and how those details were presented.[9]

Insofar as Petra was the object of the case file and not its subject, discerning her as a historical subject and assessing the deeper significance of what would seem to be a straightforward conflict over marriage choice poses a methodological challenge. To unpack the case file, I read "against the grain" of the multiple accounts that constitute the source. In doing so, I take note of hints and implied meanings, and I expand upon fragmentary information by drawing on relevant secondary sources. From those clues I deduce an alternative story to the one presented on the surface of the documentation. This essay employs the technique of narrative history to address Petra's case file on two levels: that of the text, an official story of patriarchy confirmed; and that of the subtext, an unofficial story of patriarchy confounded.[10] The essay shows a young woman resisting her subordination by selectively accommodating patriarchal concepts and institutions, all with the help of her prospective fiancé and his widowed mother. Petra's case file is thus an archive that preserves a story of female agency encrusted with an assertion of male authority.[11]

Although she was central to the legal proceeding it describes, the case file provides only a partial image of Petra herself. What personal detail it does contain allows us to envision Petra as an individual. Our image of her grows sharper still when Petra is considered within the context of her place and time. She inhabited a world defined by her physical surroundings, social relations, and, above all, her status as a female orphan. Examining each of these elements brings us closer to her perspective.

Petra was born and raised in Celaya, a town in south central Guanajuato, 150 miles northwest of Mexico City. Celaya was the seat of a municipal district encompassing an array of hamlets, haciendas, and small farms that dotted the surrounding countryside. The town lay in the heart of the Bajío, a rich agricultural region stretching across the southern half of Guanajuato and parts of two neighboring states. The prosperity of its hinterland enhanced the town's importance as a center of administration and trade. Celaya was then as now a pleasant place. Its fourteen hundred buildings were organized into attractive, well-lit blocks with the towers of the Temple of San Francis, the town's architectural jewel, rising above them. Celaya boasted a press, a theater, a granary, and a textile factory that was an important source of local employment. Around 37,000 people lived there as of 1854, qualifying it as a city by the standards of the day.[12] Like provincial cities throughout Mexico, Celaya was an urban island in a rural sea. For that reason, if not also for the difficulty of overland travel, the population was tight-knit and insular.[13] Mexico's corporatist social tradition mediated interpersonal relations, whereby the groups to which a person belonged—family, occupation, neighborhood, and the like—defined that person's standing in the community more than individual attributes. For Petra, that made Celaya less a city than a small town, bound by the familiarity inherent to a constrained social environment in which personal affairs could be subject to public scrutiny. Indeed, the prospect of her marriage and details of her dispute with Leiva were regular subjects of local gossip.[14]

A window onto Petra's early life is opened by the copy of her baptismal certificate, which accompanied her petition. She had been baptized on February 1, 1835, in the presence of her parents, José María Fernandez and María de la Luz Lejarra, and her godmother, Marcela Escarda.[15] Petra was born into a typical family consisting of biological (her parents) and fictive (her godmother) elements that, according to longstanding Hispanic tradition, were to enmesh her in a protective web of relations. Moreover, evidence in her file indicates that her family was predominantly female in composition. She had one and perhaps two sisters, while there is no reference to any brothers.[16] Whatever comfort that might have given Petra was disrupted by the absence of her parents and godmother, who appear nowhere else in the file, and the lack of grandparents or other extended family, of whom there is no mention. Orphanhood deprived Petra not only of the security of an intact family, but also of any advantage she might have gained by having a father to serve as a sympathetic male advocate.

Instead, Petra would grow up under the care of a guardian, Antonio Leiva. That she avoided placement in an orphanage indicates that her parents had died and that she had not been abandoned. In larger towns or cities like Celaya, abandoned children without extended family to serve as the responsible next of kin commonly wound up in orphanages run by the Catholic Church, or in private homes, where they frequently performed domestic service for the adoptive family.[17] Petra instead became a ward of the state. Family law placed responsibility for children like her in the hands of the local judge, who was to appoint a guardian for them.[18] Assuming the magistrate was conscientious, it stands to reason that Leiva, who already had children of his own, could afford to maintain Petra and her sisters, as well. Yet life for Petra was hardly easy. The case file includes an account by the local priest, in which he reported that Petra "is on the verge of abject misery, and the pressure of the case obligates me to confess . . . that *I myself have helped her to buy shoes.*"[19] She was evidently a neglected appendage to the Leiva household.

On becoming Petra's guardian, Leiva assumed all the rights of her father, including the right to overrule her marriage choice. Petra was therefore triply subordinated, as an orphan, as an adolescent, and as an unmarried woman. Yet she was not altogether powerless. As we shall see, she counted on help from Cayetano and his mother, who supported her morally and perhaps financially, enabling her to pursue *habilitación de edad* and so to resist Leiva.

Petra initiated the process with a petition to the governor that merits quotation in full because of the insight that it provides into her case:

> Your Excellency [Gov. Francisco Pacheco],
>
> María Petra Fernández . . . in light of your Excellency's well-known willingness to hear this appeal . . . does formally declare: that Cayetano Olmedo, the tobacco administrator for this city, sought permission to marry me from Antonio Leiva. He being my guardian, his consent is required by law in the absence of my parents and grandparents, yet Mr. Leiva refused, and opposes the marriage without reason, in my opinion, given that Mr. Olmedo is widely known among the population as an honorable man of means, one who derives from his position the necessary resources to uphold his matrimonial responsibilities and comply with the corresponding obligations.
>
> Given these facts, with no judge willing to strike down Mr. Leiva's resistance, and having exhausted all other appropriate means, I must now respectfully resort to Your Excellency as I do, so that in view of the irrational and illogical resistance of my guardian, I request, in conformity with Title II, Book X, laws IX and XVIII, of the New Compilation, the consent I have thus far been denied, and the concession of the license that is indispensable for my marriage to Mr. Olmedo.
>
> In these terms: entering a hopefully adequate plea as sustained by all the reasons that to it pertain, I implore you to decree as I have asked, this being just.[20]

Although Petra's signature appears at the close of the petition, the words may not have been hers. Her signature, made up of carefully formed letters written in a heavy hand, is inconsistent with the flowing penmanship of the text. The phrasing limns an anonymous presence, someone familiar with the legal code, implying that she may have worked with an attorney.

Petra's case hinged on laws that prohibited the abuse of patriarchal authority. Her citation of the New Compilation (*Novísima Recopilación*) referred to a Spanish legal code, enacted in 1806 and in force in Mexico at the time of its War for Independence (1810–21). Laws IX and XVIII of Book X, Title II, concerned conflict between minors and adults over marriage choice.[21] Law IX, issued in 1776, known as the Royal Pragmatic on Marriage, required the minor to obtain parental permission in order to wed. Yet it also prohibited parents and guardians from forcing a minor to marry and so addressed Petra's fear that Leiva wanted her to marry one of his sons. The extent of her desperation is conveyed by the fact that Law XVIII, issued in 1803, allowed young women like her, who lacked surviving parents or grandparents, to marry without the consent of their guardian upon attaining the age of twenty. To reach that age Petra would have to wait nearly a year, a year too long in her estimation. But she would not have to wait, because Law XVIII also empowered her to marry without parental consent, regardless of age, if and only if the highest official in the province (i.e., the governor) granted her *habilitación de edad*.

Dictatorship vested the governor with that authority. The year before Petra filed her appeal, Gen. Antonio López de Santa Anna took the helm of a nation weary of the political turmoil exacerbated by Mexico's defeat in the U.S.-Mexican War. Santa Anna, in this latest of his many stints as president, believed he had a mandate to bind the country together under a singular authority. To that end, he abolished state legislatures and town councils, and even the states themselves, redesignating them as "departments" controlled by appointed governors. He also replaced the array of state civil codes and ruled by decree. The centralist jurists who advised him regarded the New Compilation as the model for a nationwide legal system, making it the point of reference, if not the actual foundation, of national law under the dictatorship.[22] Santa Anna set himself up a quasi-monarch, the patron of a troubled nation. The governor stood as the dictator's surrogate, the provincial apotheosis of paternalist rule.

To determine the merits of her request, Governor Pacheco directed Celaya's two justices of the peace and its parish priest to report what they knew about the case. Under the administrative scheme imposed by Santa Anna, a justice of the peace was the highest municipal official, appointed by and answerable to the governor. The priest had no formal administrative role but was important nonetheless as the arbiter of moral issues in the community. His inclusion in the proceedings bespoke the influence of Catholic tradition on what was otherwise a secular matter, and of the precedent set by Spanish colonialism, which had consigned conflicts over marriage choice to ecclesiastical jurisdiction.[23] Collectively, the president, justices of the peace, and priest expressed the working logic of the dictator's political project. Santa Anna aimed to reestablish the paternalist pact between the government and society that had once been the hallmark of colonial rule. According to that model, the president, like the king before him, embodied the interests of the subject population, ruling in its name through his designated local representatives. This was an explicitly gendered political construct built upon a patrimonial legal system. Both mirrored the patriarchal social order whose precepts would play a normative role in Petra's case.

Those precepts lay at the heart of the governor's instructions to the officials in Celaya. They were ordered "to report . . . whether you fear [that Petra's request will lead to] a disastrous outcome, or the contrary, or if the resistance manifested by the young woman's guardian is reasonable or purely capricious, and all else you deem necessary to illustrate the substance of the case."[24] The governor's instructions made clear that Petra could defy Leiva only if her examiners believed that to do so would conform to and so uphold patriarchal propriety. From the official standpoint, it was not Petra's qualities that mattered to the outcome of the case, per se, but rather those of the men responsible for her.

The suitability of Cayetano as her prospective husband was the most prominent issue in the deliberations. The assessment of his suitability focused on his capacity to support a wife and family. Cayetano's youth—he was only a few years older than Petra—made this a serious question. The trio of officials concurred with Petra's assertion that Cayetano's work as the local tobacco administrator proved his financial stability. The tobacco trade had long been a lucrative sector of the Mexican economy, so lucrative that it was subject to a state monopoly. Cayetano was a tax farmer, a private investor who held a contract with the state government entitling him to enforce the tobacco monopoly. As such, he controlled the local marketing of tobacco products, collected the excise tax levied on them, and was entitled to keep a portion of the money. His position testified to his financial resources and, of equal significance, his connections and prospects. Cayetano was poised to become an *hombre de bien,* a man of standing.[25]

Social quality also factored into the assessment of Cayetano's suitability. In the words of Justice of the Peace José María Ramírez, Cayetano was a young man of "good conduct." The judge also noted that Cayetano himself had been granted *habilitación de edad* three years earlier, in 1851, "in order to administer his assets."[26] This laconic description hinted that Cayetano had acquitted himself well after being thrust into adulthood by an undisclosed event. The priest, Antonio Casalot, declared that the Olmedo family was renowned for its "modest well-being, its exquisite dealings with others, [and] its moral reputation." The Olmedos, he continued, enjoyed "extensive relations with the leading families of [Celaya]—the Linares, the Villaseñor, the Caballero, the González, the Herrera, the Arizmendi, the Rábago, the Maldonado, the Concha, etc." By all accounts, then, Cayetano was a more-than-suitable match. The official portrait of him implied that the orphaned Petra would be marrying well—or even marrying up, gaining admission into the select circle of the town's *gente decente*. To reinforce that image, and to discredit Antonio Leiva's opposition, the priest observed that Leiva had no quarrel with the marriage of Petra's sister to a humble clerk from a family with "no name." "Which of the sisters," Casalot asked, "will be better placed?"[27]

The priest furthermore warned the governor that if Petra should be denied her request, it would be difficult for her and Cayetano to break off their engagement, so greatly did they desire each other, and that "a scandal would surely result."[28] Casalot's preoccupation revealed an enduring notion of honor inherited from the Spanish colonial era. Honor denoted the modulation of sexual propriety and social standing. It was, as Patricia Seed explains, "a complex social code that established the criteria for respect in Hispanic society."[29] Without the sanction of marriage, the ongoing relationship between Petra and Cayetano would be illicit. To forestall improper contact in instances like this, it was customary to separate the couple by cloistering the woman, to place her *en depósito*, until the situation was resolved. The priest reported that Petra's brother-in-law had pleaded for her to remove herself to a nearby hacienda, lest she succumb to temptation and elope. She preferred instead to remain alone at the house Leiva maintained in town, visited only by her sister. She would stay close to Cayetano even if that heightened the threat of scandal. Casalot urged Governor Pacheco to rule in Petra's favor and end "the ongoing distraction this case has caused [Cayetano] to the detriment of his obligations, which threatens to erode his position in the community."[30]

As for Petra, Casalot emphasized that her future hung on the outcome of her appeal. To make the point, he painted a gloomy picture of what would become of her should she be denied. He portrayed Antonio Leiva as an uncaring guardian who disregarded Petra's long-term interests. He worried that in growing older, Petra would inevitably lose her youthful attractiveness and would not easily draw the attention of another suitor of Cayetano's quality. This he asserted would be a tragedy, because she had no patrimony to preserve her. In other words, Casalot feared that Petra would fall into an insecure spinsterhood. In this, the priest played upon the archetype of the vulnerable unmarried woman, who would surely languish without a man's support. The governor should therefore grant what Petra requested both for her good and that of Cayetano.[31]

Casalot and the justices of the peace of Celaya set forth a gendered rationale for approving Petra's request. They assured the governor that her emancipation would conform to the patriarchal norm on three counts. First, Leiva had disregarded his paternal responsibility to Petra, exposing her to shame and insecurity. Second, Cayetano possessed the background, character, and financial means to support Petra as his wife. Marrying her would moreover advance him to the next step in his maturation, by establishing him as a patriarch in his own right. Third, the marriage would carry the community's imprimatur. "In my opinion and that of the sensible persons of this city with whom I have consulted on this matter," intoned Justice of the Peace Joaquín Galván, "I consider [the marriage] conducive to the happiness of both parties."[32] In accordance with the officials' recommendation, Governor Pacheco emancipated Petra so that she might transfer her dependence from Antonio Leiva, her guardian, to Cayetano Olmedo, her prospective husband.[33]

Whereas the text of the case file is one of a paternalist state reaffirming the patriarchal compact between man and woman, an altogether different story emerges from the testimony of the local priest, Antonio Casalot. His report makes it possible to map a hidden subtext of patriarchy confounded by following the track of interpersonal relations leading to Petra's appeal. He had been embroiled in the case from its beginning, owing to his position as the curate of Celaya. As such, Casalot oversaw the observance of Catholic rites and served as the pastoral counselor for his parishioners. It was in this latter role that he interacted with Petra, Leiva, and the Olmedos. Casalot was by no means a neutral observer. His aforementioned comment that he had felt moved to buy Petra shoes betrayed his disapproval of her care under Leiva. Yet Casalot took no part in the dispute between Petra and Leiva over Cayetano until the Olmedos approached him for help.[34] Motivated, it seems, by his sympathy for Petra, the priest agreed to approach Leiva on their behalf.

In his meeting with Casalot, Leiva left no doubt of his low regard for Petra and the Olmedos. He derided Cayetano as an "inexperienced youngster," with neither the aptitude for nor dedication to a job that would never provide him the financial means to support a family. He dismissed Petra as lazy, undisciplined, unversed in the management of a home, and altogether unfit to be a wife. Leiva insinuated that what passed between Cayetano and Petra was merely lust or infatuation, an ephemeral desire that would soon dissipate and cause them regret once consummated. Moreover, Leiva charged, Cayetano was motivated to marry Petra primarily by a desire to "free himself of the maternal yoke." The ire directed at the mother, Clara Olmedo, indicated her centrality in the dispute. Without her, any possibility for Petra and Cayetano to marry might have been lost.[35]

Although she was never explicitly identified as such, Clara was evidently a widow. Details from the priest's letter lend credence to this conclusion. For example, she lived with Cayetano, the two of them forming a single household so interdependent that neither mother nor son ever "thought to separate from one another should he marry, so as not to multiply the expenses of children, attending to the home, daily necessities, etc."[36] In fact, Clara held considerable wealth, which she allowed Cayetano to administer. That this responsibility fell to him, and not to his father or an elder brother, implies that the family included no other male member. Cayetano may have been Clara's only son, or her only child, who had taken on a man's role three years earlier. Justice of the Peace José María Ramírez stated that in 1851 the state government had granted Cayetano *habilitación de edad* so that he could take charge of his assets.[37] That was likely the year his father died, the assets in question being Cayetano's share of the patrimony, with the rest going to Clara.

The widow in early national Mexico, like her counterparts throughout the Hispanic world, occupied an ambiguous position. Under the Spanish legal tradition, she enjoyed more expansive property rights as a widow than she had as a married woman. The law regarded the widow as a female head of household. She inherited half of her deceased husband's property and controlled that property along with any that she brought into or acquired during her marriage. She also could act as the guardian of property her minor children inherited from their father, until the children came of age. Control of property, though, did not necessarily translate into autonomy. This was especially true if adult male family members—sons, brothers, in-laws—intervened in family affairs. Hence the conventions of a patriarchal society limited a widow's freedom of action. While these general patterns applied to all widows, individual cases often differed from the norm, depending on the particular circumstances of the widow's life. Judging by what Casalot observed about Clara, she was indeed exceptional.[38]

Clara belonged to the propertied class of Celaya. According to Casalot, she was financially secure and hardly the burden on Cayetano that Leiva made her out to be, because her personal fortune amounted to over ten thousand pesos. At a time when a small family could live comfortably for a year on a thousand pesos, Clara had all the money she needed and more.[39] She most likely came by her fortune as a matter of inheritance augmented through lending, shrewd investment, or both. Indeed, the priest's description of her financial relationship with her son leaves the impression that Cayetano depended on Clara as much, if not more, than she did on him. Her money, part of which she invested in Cayetano's activities, dramatically boosted his liquidity, giving him the luxury to capitalize his business ventures without going into debt. Even so, access to his mother's funds was conditional. Casalot asserted that "were they to be at odds with each other, [Clara] might be obliged to retract her promises to him [i.e., she might refuse to continue combining her resources with his], and he, unprotected, would have trouble obtaining another guarantor because of the scandal created by his ingratitude." For that reason, the priest concluded, Cayetano "has the greatest interest in remaining at his mother's side, for in his new condition [as a businessman and prospective husband], he needs her more than ever."[40]

Casalot's account allows us to infer what joining the Olmedo family signified for Petra. Marrying Cayetano would insert Petra into a family structure distinct from the rigid patriarchy maintained by her guardian. Clara and Cayetano appear bound by financial synergy and commitment to each other's interests. While Clara was not necessarily a matriarch, Cayetano does seem to have respected her. He was the family's public face, but not its patriarch. At the minimum, the Olmedo family was matrifocal and, with the addition of Petra, would become predominantly female in composition. To what degree that scenario might privilege the female voice in family affairs can only be guessed and would depend on the mix of personalities involved. Clearly the Olmedo family offered Petra emotional and economic security, a comfort that would have enhanced the romantic love she shared with Cayetano.

The final element in this subtext of patriarchy confounded is one of unacknowledged aid. Here we return to the petition that initiated Petra's pursuit of emancipation. Whoever drafted the petition had the specialized knowledge necessary to cite chapter and verse of the elements of family law applicable to Petra's case, suggesting that she worked with an attorney. But if, as Casalot claimed, she could not afford shoes, then surely she could not afford a lawyer. It stands to reason that the Olmedos referred her to one and supplied the funds for his fee. Petra's eventual success therefore signaled triumph for a young woman who, with a widow's help, escaped her guardian and married the man of her choice by using the legal system to selectively accommodate the patriarchal order.

In Petra Fernández and Clara Olmedo we have examples of marginal voices encountered in an archive of women's interaction with patriarchal authority in early national Mexico. They represent the diversity of female perspectives waiting to be uncovered in a documentary collection not normally recognized as a source of women's history. Petra, an adolescent and an orphan, ensured the preservation of her voice by initiating a bureaucratic process that would define her passage to the circumscribed adulthood of the married woman. Clara, a widow, is a more faint though no less vital presence in the record. Her recruitment of the priest Antonio Casalot to advocate for Petra contributed to the eventual creation of a rich source imprinted by the social and interpersonal context that culminated in Petra's application for *habilitación de edad*. Nonetheless, because the case file details the deliberations of male officials, it marginalizes the women responsible for its creation. This essay has demonstrated how awareness of text and subtext in such instances is essential to recovering the female subject from a source that treats her as an object.

NOTES

1. "Espediente formado a consecuencia del ocurso en que Da. María Petra Fernández solicita habilitación de edad para contraer matrimonio sin consentimiento de su tutor, con Cayetano Olmedo," [Celaya,] Guanajuato, 1854, Archivo Historico del Estado de Guanajuato, Fondo Secretaría de Gobierno, Sección Secretaría de Gobierno, box 277, folder 1. [Hereafter AHEG/Fernández.]

2. Petra Fernández to [Francisco Pacheco], Celaya, January 4, 1854, AHEG/Fernández, folio 2v. A comparative perspective on the way conflicts over marriage choice drew the government into the private realm of the family can be gained from Patricia Seed, *To Love, Honor, and Obey in Colonial Mexico: Conflicts over Marriage Choice, 1574–1821* (Stanford, Calif.: Stanford University Press, 1988); and Kathryn A. Sloan, *Runaway Daughters: Seduction, Elopement, and Honor in Nineteenth-Century Mexico* (Albuquerque: University of New Mexico Press, 2008).

3. A representative sample of the recent scholarship on women in nineteenth-century Mexico includes Silvia Arrom, *The Women of Mexico City, 1790–1857* (Stanford, Calif.: Stanford University Press, 1985); Heather Fowler Salmini, *Women of the Mexican Countryside, 1850–1990: Creating Spaces, Shaping Transitions* (Tucson: University of Arizona Press, 1994); Deborah E. Kanter, "Native Female Land Tenure and Its Decline in Mexico, 1750–1900," *Ethnohistory* 42, no. 4 (Autumn 1995): 607–16; Francoise Carner, "Estereotipos femeninos en el siglo XIX," in Carmen Ramos Escandón, ed., *Presencia y transparencia: la mujer en la historia de méxico* (Mexico City: El Colegio de México, Programa Interdisciplinario de Estudios de la Mujer, 2006); Margaret Chowning, *Rebellious Nuns: The Troubled History of a Mexican Convent, 1752–1863* (New York: Oxford University Press, 2006); María Teresa Fernández Aceves et al., eds., *Orden social e identidad de género: México, siglos XIX y XX* (Mexico City: CIESAS and Universidad de Guadalajara, 2006); Ana Lidia García Peña, *El fracaso del amor: género e individualismo en el siglo XIX mexicano* (Mexico City: Colegio de México; Universidad Autónoma del Estado de México, Centro de Estudios Históricos, 2006); and Julia Tuñón, comp., *Enjaular los cuerpos: normativas decimonónicas y feminidad en México* (Mexico City: El Colegio de México, 2008).

4. Regarding the historiography of Latin American children, see Asuncion Lavrin, "Mexico," in *Children in Historical and Comparative Perspective,* Joseph M. Hawes and N. Ray Hiner, eds. (New York: Greenwood Press, 1991); Ann S. Blum, "Children without Parents: Law, Charity, and Social Practice in Mexico City, 1867–1940" (PhD dissertation, Berkeley: University of California, 1998); Tobias Hecht, ed., *Minor Omissions: Children in Latin American Society* (Madison: University of Wisconsin Press, 2002); Nara Milanich, "The *Casa de Huérfanos* and Child Circulation in Late Nineteenth-Century Chile," *Journal of Social History* 38, no. 2 (2004): 311–40; Ondina E. González and Bianca Premo, eds., *Raising an Empire: Children in Early Modern Iberia and Colonial Latin America* (Albuquerque: University of New Mexico Press, 2007); and Pablo Rodriguez and Maria Emma Mannarelli, eds., *Historia de la infancia en América Latina* (Bogotá: Universidad del Externado de Colombia, 2007).

An exception to the lack of scholarly attention to adolescent females is Ramón A. Gutiérrez, *When Jesus Came the Corn Mothers Went Away: Marriage, Sexuality, and Power in New Mexico, 1500–1846* (Stanford, Calif.: Stanford University Press, 1991).

5. The early national period remains a frontier in the historiography for Latin American women in general. See Carmen Ramos Escandón, *Género e historia: la historiografía sobre*

la mujer (Mexico City: Instituto Mora; Universidad Autónoma Metropolitana, 1992), 31–32; and Edna Acosta-Belén, "Opening New Paths: Research on Women in Latin America and the Caribbean" (Washington, D.C.: Woodrow Wilson International Center for Scholars, 1993), 13–14. For exceptions to this pattern listed among the works cited in note 3, see Arrom, *Women of Mexico City;* and García Peña, *El fracaso del amor.*

6. The law in question came from an eighteenth-century Spanish edict. See note 21.

7. Gendered distinctions in the relationship between marriage and adulthood are addressed in Arrom, *The Women of Mexico City.* The study of children and childhood in nineteenth-century Latin America offers additional insight into the nature of adolescence as a life stage and legal category. See, for example, Blum, "Children without Parents"; Hecht, *Minor Omissions;* González and Premo, *Raising an Empire;* as well as the discussion of children and adolescents in Gutiérrez, *When Jesus Came.*

8. Petra's fear that Leiva intended for her to marry his son is mentioned in Casalot to [Pacheco], January 26, 1854, AHEG/Fernández, folio 17v.

9. This observation on the archive as a site of official memory is adapted from Jacques Derrida, *Archive Fever,* trans. Eric Prenowitz (Chicago: University of Chicago Press, 1996). On the epistemological challenges associated with Derrida's idea, see Sandhaya Shetty and Elizabeth Jane Bellamy, "Postcolonialism's Archive Fever," *Diacritics* 30, no. 1 (Spring 2000): 25–48; and Carolyn Steedman, "Something She Called a Fever: Michelet, Derrida, and Dust," *American Historical Review* 106, no. 4 (October 2001): 1159–80.

10. The conceptualization of patriarchy confirmed and confounded is adapted from the narrative framework of Sandra Lauderdale Graham, *Caetana Says No: Women's Stories from a Brazilian Slave Society* (New York: Cambridge University Press, 2002).

11. This observation engages what Carmen Ramos Escandón has termed the woman's historical "presence and transparency." See Ramos Escandón, ed., *Presencia y transparencia.*

The various ways in which women in nineteenth-century Mexico asserted their autonomy, both individually and collectively, are illuminated by Chowning, *Rebellious Nuns;* Fowler Salmini, *Women of the Mexican Countryside;* and García Peña, *El fracaso del amor.*

12. Datos para la memoria, que se ha de presentar a la 16 Legislatura del Estado en Enero de 1852. Noticia de las poblaciones que en el Estado de Guanajuato, cuentan de cuarto mil habitants arriba, Guanajuato, 1852, AHEG, Fondo Secretaría de Gobierno, Sección Secretaría de Gobierno, box 248, folder 1.

13. For example, to travel from Mexico City to Celaya took at least a week. See Map 3.1, "An Isochronic Map of Mexico in the Early Nineteenth Century," in Richard Salvucci, *Textiles and Capitalism in Mexico: An Economic History of the Obrajes, 1539–1840* (Princeton, N.J.: Princeton University Press, 1987).

14. Gossip is reported in Antonio Casalot to [Francisco Pacheco], Celaya, January 26, 1854, AHEG/Fernández, folios 13r, 17v.

15. [Certificate of Baptism for María Petra Fernández], Celaya, February 1, 1835 [copy], AHEG/Fernández, folio 1.

16. Petra's sister Regina is identified in Casalot to [Pacheco], January 26, 1854, AHEG/Fernández, folio 16r.

17. A distinction was drawn between children orphaned by the death of their parents, and those orphaned through abandonment (known as *hijos expósitos*). On orphans and orphanages in Mexico, see Blum, "Children without Parents." For a comparative example addressing orphans in Chile, see Milanich, *"Casa de Huérfanos."*

18. Family law regarding the disposition of orphans derived from eighteenth-century Spanish jurisprudence. See T. Esquivel Obregón, *Apuntes para la historia del derecho en México*, tomo 3, *La Nueva España, derecho privado y derecho de transición* (Mexico City: Editorial Porrúa, 1943), 57–59.

19. Leiva had at least one child, a son. See n. 17. On Petra's penury, see folio 16v. The emphasis given at the end of this paragraph is reproduced from the original document.

20. Fernández to [Pacheco], January 4, 1854, AHEG/Fernández, folio 2.

21. For the complete text of these laws, see *La Nueva Recopilación*, Libro 10, in Marcelo Martínez Alcubilla, comp., *Códigos antiguos de España*, vol. 2 (Madrid: n.p., 1886). Law IX is found on pp. 1714–15, and Law XVII on p. 1717.

22. On the workings of the Santa Anna regime, see Carmen Vázquez Mantecón, *Santa Anna y la encrucijada del estado (1853–1855)* (Mexico City: Fondo de Cultura Económica, 1986); and Will Fowler, *Santa Anna of Mexico* (Lincoln: University of Nebraska Press, 2007).

23. Patricia Seed examines ecclesiastic oversight of conflicts over marriage choice in colonial Mexico. See Seed, *To Love, Honor, and Obey*. On the role of priests in Mexican society through to the nineteenth century, see William B. Taylor, *Magistrates of the Sacred: Priests and Parishioners in Eighteenth-Century Mexico* (Stanford, Calif.: Stanford University Press, 1996).

24. Pacheco to Jueces 1° y 2° de Paz y Curra Párroca de Celya, Guanajuato, January 19, 1854 [copy], AHEG/Fernández, folio 4.

25. On the tobacco monopoly in early republican Mexico, see David W. Walker, "Business as Usual: The *Empresa del Tabaco* in Mexico, 1837–44," *Hispanic American Historical Review* 64, no. 4 (November 1984): 675–705. Regarding tax farming, see Barbara A. Tenenbaum, *The Politics of Penury: Debts and Taxes in Mexico, 1821–1856* (Albuquerque: University of New Mexico Press, 1986). The nature of the *hombre de bien* as a social category is discussed in Michael P. Costeloe, *The Central Republic in Mexico, 1835–1846: Hombres de Bien in the Age of Santa Anna* (New York:Cambridge University Press, 1993).

26. José María Ramírez to [Pacheco], Celaya, January 24, 1854, AHEG/Fernández, folio 6.

27. Casalot to [Pacheco], January 26, 1854, AHEG/Fernández, folios 16, 17r.

28. Ibid., folio 17v.

29. Seed, *To Love, Honor, and Obey*, 62. On the function of honor in Mexican culture, see also Gutiérrez, *When Jesus Came*. Ann Twinam notes that social status and gender mediated the ascription of honor; see her *Public Lives, Private Secrets: Gender, Honor, Sexuality, and Illegitimacy in Colonial Spanish America* (Stanford, Calif.: Stanford University Press, 1999).

30. Casalot to [Pacheco], January 26, 1854, AHEG/Fernández, folios 17v, 18; Lee N. Penyak, "Safe Harbors and Compulsory Custody: *Casas de Depósito* in Mexico, 1750–1865," *Hispanic American Historical Review* 79, no. 1 (February 1999): 83–99.

31. Casalot to [Pacheco], January 26, 1854, AHEG/Fernández, folio 17v.

32. Felipe Galván to [Pacheco], Celaya, January 26, 1854, AHEG/Fernández, folio 10v.

33. Feliciano Segovia to [Pacheco], Guanajuato, February 22, 1854, AHEG/Fernández, folio 20; Pacheco penned his ruling in the margin of this document.

34. Casalot to [Pacheco], January 26, 1854, AHEG/Fernández, folio 14r.

35. Ibid., folio 13v–14r.

36. Ibid., folio 17r.

37. Ramírez to [Pacheco], January 24, 1854, AHEG/Fernández, folio 6.

38. On widowhood, see Arrom, *The Women of Mexico City;* and Manuel Ramos Medina, comp., *Viudas en la historia* (Mexico City: Condumex, 2002). The discussion presented here also reflects observations by Alida Metcalf and Julie Hardwick, who examine colonial Brazil and early modern France, respectively. Like Mexico, those places based their legal systems on Roman law. See Metcalf, "Women and Means: Women and Family Property in Colonial Brazil," *Journal of Social History* 24, no. 2 (winter 1990): 277–98; and Hardwick, "Widowhood and Patriarchy in Seventeenth-Century France," *Journal of Social History.* 26, no. 1 (Autumn 1992): 133–48.

39. The value of a peso in early national Mexico was approximately equal to that of the U.S. dollar. On the cost of living in Mexico, see Costeloe, *Central Republic,* 20. The amount of Clara Olmedo's fortune is cited in Casalot to [Pacheco], January 26, 1854, AHEG/Fernández, folio.16r.

40. Casalot to Pacheco, January 26, 1854, folio 17r.

3. LOCATING WOMEN AS MIGRANTS IN NINETEENTH-CENTURY TUNIS

Julia Clancy-Smith

In 1868 the Italian consulate in Tunisia instituted criminal proceedings for grand larceny and contraband against Giovanna Tellini, a forty-year-old Italian citizen. Tellini resided in Tunis, a port city experiencing massive subsistence immigration from adjacent Mediterranean islands—Sicily, Malta, and Sardinia—as well as from southern Europe. The lengthy transcript rendered in the hybrid Sicilo-Italian and Arabic employed in Tunis at the time represents one of the few extensive records on an immigrant woman of ordinary means and the social universe that she inhabited.[1]

Giovanna's first testimony to the court convened in the Italian consular building located in a mostly "European" neighborhood of the Tunis *medina* [walled city] and took place on February 27, 1868. In response to the set questions always posed to those giving testimony, Giovanna identified herself in the following manner: "I am Giovanna Tellini, daughter of Antonio; I am forty years old, born in Cala [Pisa] and residing in Tunis for the past ten years. I am single, an Italian citizen, Catholic, and illiterate. I rent the shop [in Tunis] from the Greek, Dimitri Papadopolo, but I am partners in business with Annetta, a Spanish citizen, single, as well, as with 'Dimitri L'Inglis' ['Dimitri the Englishman'], who is imprisoned at this moment."[2] Giovanna added that she shared the house with her *sedicente marito* ("common-law husband"), a Spaniard named Niccola Sabuquillo. Her twenty-nine-year-old Spanish friend Annetta Barbera, born in Algeria but a Spanish citizen, resided in the same dwelling, apparently with her common-law husband, as well. When in February 1868 the authorities burst into their dwelling-cum-shop, where the alleged fencing operations transpired, all the inhabitants, with the exception of Giovanna, had been bedridden for weeks with typhoid fever, then raging in Tunisia.[3]

When I first came across Giovanna's story nearly a decade ago, I was in the midst of a book-length study of trans-Mediterranean migrations to North Africa, particularly to Tunisia, between 1830 and 1881, when France invaded the country and declared it a protectorate. The study investigates the entire spectrum of Tunisian/North African responses to subsistence immigration of highly varied types and guises. Thus I initiated my research in the National Archives of Tunisia, although a range of collections from other countries had to be brought into play for reasons addressed momentarily. But the handwritten manuscript of fifty-three unnumbered pages detailing the Tellini affair was discovered in an unlikely place—across the Mediterranean in Nantes—where some, but not all, of the protectorate archives were relocated after Tunisian independence in 1956, in addition to consular records for the precolonial era. Mention of the trial or of its many protagonists was never found again in the more than ten collections consulted.[4] This does not mean, however, that we should neglect sources that prove to be blind alleys. Indeed, a seemingly fruitless search points toward novel kinds of evidence for building the context around a particular case, or others like it, which, combined with a comparative historical perspective, can be deployed to know and understand more.[5]

Although I immediately realized the potential of this unusual document—rare for its length, richness of detail, and recording of "direct" (although problematic) testimony, among other things—its value became fully apparent only after years of additional research into the larger structures in which Giovanna's story was imbricated. Returning to the trial record at the end of a research journey allowed me to better mobilize the highly fragmented bits and pieces of data, as well as inquire about other sources—city space, for example—that lie for the most part outside of written records composed by those in power, who were exclusively male.[6] Taking up Giovanna at this point and locating her in wider, multiple fields of social actors, structures, and relationships brought a clearer sense of fleeting facts and ostensibly trivial details and made me conscious of the silences, excisions, and distortions in the available secondary literature on this period and place.

This essay first considers why older scholarly literature virtually ignored migrants and mobilities, despite the fact that North Africa constituted a particularly active migratory frontier throughout the nineteenth century. Subsequently, the problems posed by studying people in motion are addressed, especially for women, whose social worlds suffered tremendous flux because of myriad intersecting forces—local, regional, transnational, and global. Third, different archives are surveyed for what is there, what is not there, and why; and the pitfalls of relying on written evidence for communities characterized by high illiteracy and extreme linguistic pluralism are touched upon. Next, through a sort of exegesis, I interrogate the trial proceedings to mine nuggets of information, particularly those hidden in plain view, to evaluate their suitability for reconstructing an immigrant woman's life and to ascertain their limits, falsehoods, or half-truths. In concluding, I suggest how the Giovanna that we "found" inside and outside the archive might undermine standard historical narratives. Given the current state of the field and the difficulties inherent in the documentation, the essay offers up more queries than definitive answers, but it is the questions that we are after.

ERASURES: THE SECONDARY LITERATURE

Until the past decade, the history of precolonial and colonial Tunisia had two principal actors: "the Tunisians" and "the Europeans," the latter almost exclusively male and mainly merchants or consuls.[7] The story of population displacements to the Maghrib, especially nineteenth-century migratory streams from the Mediterranean islands, constituted the history that nobody wanted, because it undermined the two master narratives, one imperial, the other nationalist, both intimately related. Most historians of French North Africa—of whatever nationality or training—slighted the troublesome not-quite-European or non-French nationals settling in Tunisia before and during colonialism. Scholars trained principally in North African Muslim societies focused on Arabs, Berbers, or Muslims, while relegating others—including indigenous Jews—to monolithic, largely residual categories, such as "the settlers" or "the Europeans," or "colonized."[8]

For numerous reasons, women were virtually absent from these narratives, but the primary force for invisibility was that scholars of the French Empire only belatedly embraced the study of women, gender, and empire. Immigrant women who lived and worked in precolonial Tunisia suffered the most radical erasures because, in the view of both imperial and nationalist historians, their stories represented either an ideological cul-de-sac or an embarrassment. Giovanna and her associates were neither French nor Arab Muslims, neither colonizer nor colonized—nor were they even considered "European" by bourgeois northern Europeans resident in Tunisia. Giovanna's presence—along with thousands of Sicilians and Italians who vastly outnumbered French nationals in the country before and after 1881—belied the imperial claim that Tunisia was destined to be, and therefore became, "French." For nationalist historians, the Annettas and Giovannas of Tunis constituted an anomaly unworthy of a footnote because they did not fit into the (male) nationalists' boxes or categories employed to characterize the past and therefore the independent present.⁹ Nevertheless, a collaborative undertaking is now under way on both sides of the sea to rewrite the narratives of North Africa and Europe as intertwined Mediterranean—not merely national or imperial—histories.¹⁰

ORDINARY WOMEN IN A MOBILE WORLD

What rendered Giovanna and others like her largely invisible? First, as a migrant, she was not firmly attached to a stable, "legible" space. States have always attempted to control the flow of people, commodities, and ideas, but the nineteenth century witnessed a dramatic expansion in the modern state's drive for what James C. Scott terms the "legibility" of populations and resources.¹¹ Nevertheless, specific categories of social actors—children, servants, women of modest means—were relegated to footnotes or banished from the record until circumstances arose that forced open their lives to outside scrutiny. For this period and milieu, mobility and morality were intimately related in the minds of male authorities. Women in motion "without men" or kin guardians were the most suspect but, paradoxically, the most likely to be studiously ignored until some transgression—accusations of smuggling, theft, or prostitution—dredged up their stories or fragments of them. Giovanna was living in a state of concubinage with Niccola; her life represented a moral affront to the keepers of the record that may have concealed her existence until things changed for the worse. Second, she made an "honest living" by trafficking in contraband and stolen goods in what might be called the informal-sector economy. She did not work in a factory, nor was she involved in a trade union—as unions did not yet exist—that might have kept records. Thus Giovanna's work, social rank, and, above all, gender conspired in the silencing.

Women as migrants—their journeys, trajectories, motives for leaving home, and experiences as expatriates, foreigners, or diaspora members—pose challenges. Women often traveled under their husband or father's name, so ship manifests omit data on individual women arriving by sea in Tunis, as nearly all immigrants did. European women traveling alone, unaccompanied by male relatives, were theoretically subject to special limitations by the Tunisian state when they landed in port. But rudimentary record keeping, together with the consular system of naming and counting male nationals and protégés—mainly bourgeois—means that credible statistics on arrivals or departures from the port for Tunis lack, for the most part. And many subsistence immigrants arrived in small boats maneuvering the waters between Sicily, Malta, and Tunisia with "human contraband"—those without papers—and therefore left virtually no trace behind.

Giovanna did not relocate to Tunis through state-sponsored labor transfers, but rather, she participated in spontaneous emigration to secure work, land, and livelihood. Her decision to leave home raises much larger issues about women and sea travel within the framework of the gendered nature of physical displacements in the Mediterranean, which for men represented a place of adventure, discovery, escape, romance, or conquest. The question needs to be posed: What kinds of access did women enjoy to the Mediterranean in an age when sail transportation gave way to steam travel and transnational movements assumed global proportions?

In a sense, Giovanna resembled the female members of largely French Catholic missionary orders that left home in the same period to proselytize and tend to "wayward women" in North Africa and elsewhere in the Ottoman Empire. The best example is the Congregation of Saint-Joseph de l'Apparition, which arrived in Tunisia around 1840; assuming a new spiritual identity, the sisters relinquished their birth names (and families), rendering it difficult to trace them in this period.[12] Thus if states have always worked to fix "desirable" subjects or citizens in place, while keeping others out, the "disparity in the mobility of men and women within states or across borders" needs to be explicitly acknowledged.[13] However, this disparity does not mean that women were less mobile than men; rather, restrictions on women's physical displacements—imposed by families, religious authorities, states, or international entities for a wide range of motives—were the product of gender ideologies and thus differed in nature and in consequences.

The preceding section touched upon some of the challenges in locating Giovanna as a migrant and reconstructing her trajectory in space. Let's consider archival records that might help to get a better GPS reading on her. Because of the nature of the Tunisian state and of consular authority, most immigrants' stories can be only partially reconstructed, if at all, once they landed in Tunis. The record becomes meatier when immigrants faced adversity—lack of housing and work or poverty—or got into trouble over unpaid debts or criminal charges that resulted in entanglement with local authorities, either Tunisian or consular, or both. Regrettably, documentation informing us about the initial decision to strike out and leave home, wherever home may have been, for North Africa in the first place is wanting.

STATES, ARCHIVES, AND SOURCES ON WOMEN AS MIGRANTS

To study migrants, the historian needs to travel to locate data often dispersed over considerable distances. But this travel does not suffice, because the scholar must know not only the history behind the collections consulted, but also the physical displacements to which many diplomatic, state, or colonial records were subjected in the postcolonial period, often with considerable loss of documentation as archives were repatriated or moved around.[14] The "repatriation" of the French colonial archives from Algeria to Aix-en-Provence, and the partial transfer of archives from precolonial and colonial Morocco and Tunisia to Nantes, constitutes the most extreme case of dispersal.

In making sense of the recondite shards of evidence, I rely to a great extent upon the discipline of ethnography, recently reinstated as an invaluable methodological approach because historians now realize that detail and description do not merely amount to detailed description, as the story, like the devil, is the details. My methodology is to follow people around on their daily rounds—to shadow them, tail them, imagine where they might be, what they might be doing, and why—and then look into written and other kinds of records to determine if traces remain. Here, space and built environment provide critical evidence for the past, since the places through which a woman moved not only shaped the arc of her biography, but also contain clues about what, who, and why, clues frequently lacking in written documents. In short, our enterprise—locating Giovanna—and the nature of the documentation demand the skills of the muralist and miniaturist informed by the ethnographer's beady, if sympathetic, eye. Let's adopt the perspective of the muralist first when constructing the immediate world around Giovanna after she stepped off the boat in a Tunisian port.

Enter the Tunisian state and European diplomatic representatives: the political and legal grid into which Giovanna was inserted when she relocated to Tunis shaped her daily life to varying degrees and, in consequence, how much we can learn about her, or conversely, how little. In her first and lengthiest testimony, Giovanna stated that she had moved from a town near Pisa in Tuscany to Tunis, where she had been "residing for the last ten years." Thus she left Italy around 1858, a country then experiencing great political turmoil as a modern nationalist state was painfully stitched together from a collection of kingdoms in the Italian Peninsula, Sardinia, and Sicily. Political conditions in Italy meant that Italian consular records of correspondence exchanged with the Tunisian state and located in the National Archives in Tunis are discouragingly slim; indeed, until unification, five different consular authorities represented Italians resident or working in Tunisia.

When the relatively meager Italian files remaining in Tunis are compared to the vast quantity of documentation—an embarrassment of riches—generated by the French and British consuls and consulates during the nineteenth century, one is reminded that strong states produce more documentation on nationals or protégés in diaspora than weak ones. For Giovanna and her community, the Italian consular authorities would appear to represent the single most important source of documentation for reconstructing their lives as expatriates in Tunisia, but owing to political upheavals across the Mediterranean, this did not necessarily prove true.

Fortunately, European consuls did not only collect data and dirt on their own nationals or protégés, but recorded information on individuals under other jurisdictions. Because the system of justice in precolonial Tunisia was marked by extreme legal pluralism, any communal fracas or dispute invariably involved a huge cast of characters from across the Mediterranean under different regimes of legal protection. Several of the witnesses called by the prosecution to testify against Giovanna were French protégés: Nicola Milone, a Greek Orthodox, claimed France's protection, while Sa'id Zuavi, an Algerian Muslim, was a French subject.[15] These factors together explain why the sole surviving transcript of the Tellini proceedings (as far as can be ascertained) is located in France.

Complicating efforts to recuperate the local social worlds of immigrants in a nineteenth-century Mediterranean port city is the fact that Tunisia had been ruled by a semi-independent Muslim dynasty since the eighteenth century, although it was theoretically a province of the Ottoman Empire. By virtue of treaties signed with an array of European powers, this dynasty did not normally have legal jurisdiction over non-Muslim Europeans unless homicide was involved. With the creation of the first municipal council for Tunis, followed by the establishment in 1860 of an urban police force (*Zabtiya*) counting some four hundred agents, the record of arrests of prostitutes, smugglers, thieves, brawlers, and drunks becomes thicker. But here the rules of consular jurisdiction intervened to create breaches in the bureaucratic grid of surveillance and in our written data.

By treaty, the native Tunis police were circumscribed in what they could do to, and with, resident Europeans apprehended for disturbing the peace, misdemeanors, or crimes. While extremely useful, those records offer limited possibilities for capturing the lives of city inhabitants under European protection.[16] However, Giovanna and other witnesses mention the fact that several members of the thieves' band were incarcerated in a Tunisian prison. Would prison records tell us anything more? Unfortunately, those records yield little, if any, documentation, precisely because those incarcerated for alleged crimes were under European consular protection and not subject to local jurisdiction. In any case, the nineteenth-century Tunisian state, like its Italian counterpart, might be considered a weak state, one that did not generate the same quantity of documentation that France or Great Britain did. Finally, another key source of state-generated documentation is the census, one of the most powerful tools for modern political elites seeking to impose legibility upon the people, territories, and resources under their governance. But the first census for Tunisia's population came only in 1906 under the French protectorate, and it counted only French nationals and, to an extent, resident Europeans. Therefore, another potential data bank of evidence, however problematic by nature, is not available.

What about nonstate sources—the press, or civic or cultural associations? Print culture and publishing came belatedly to Tunisia only after the mid-nineteenth century, much later than in Europe, and tardy even relative to Egypt or the Ottoman heartlands. Cultural and social organizations were few in Tunis in the pre-1881 era and were the purview of the middle classes; unfortunately, most documentation generated by those associations has not survived.

However, another factor was at play. What we might call "sex and the city" shaped the written record, as well—the moral norms and worldviews shared both by elite resident Europeans—the consuls and big-time merchants and their social peers, the Tunisian Muslim ruling class. Documentation for the study of "unruly women," whether indigenous or immigrant, in nineteenth-century Tunisia is surprisingly scarce. Aside from travelers' accounts, data on sexual traffic between different religious communities is scant—with the exception of the few spectacular cases of interconfessional sex that ended in violence and often in tragedy.[17] As was universally true elsewhere, women from the "lower orders" of urban society were regarded as morally dangerous and prone to sexual misconduct. One would think that the Tunisian state, consular officials, the police, and religious morality minders would have done their utmost to superintend the behavior of women like Giovanna to ensure conformance with the law and with sociomoral conventions.

Yet in practice, European consuls and beylical authorities preferred relying upon *conversation* more than written correspondence when the delicate, and shameful, matter of female sexual behavior was addressed—whether concubinage, as in Giovanna's case, or adultery, or prostitution. Letters exchanged between European diplomatic representatives and officials in the Tunisian government often used less formal notepaper rather than official letterhead; correspondents employed coded language or circumlocutions, such as the expression "the woman in question." In these somewhat exceptional written documents, reference is made to earlier conversations regarding how to proceed with a "woman of easy virtue." The letter exchanged between Richard Wood, the British consul general to Tunis, and the Tunisian prime minister's office in 1876 is representative. It is marked "private," and in it Wood states the following:

I have had the pleasure to receive your *private* [emphasis mine] letter of the 11th of October conveying to me the request of his Excellency the Prime Minister in the name of His Majesty the bey [ruler] to embark by the first conveyance *the woman in question* [emphasis mine] with injunction never to return to this country again. I will do my utmost to carry out the wishes of His Highness, which are founded on considerations, the importance of which have not escaped my attention. In anticipation that His Highness would decide that she should be sent out of the country, I wrote yesterday to a friend at Malta to persuade some family to receive her. It is not every family that will receive a stranger in their house.[18]

This last remark—almost a throwaway—opens up an entire social universe concealed from the historian's gaze until now. It offers evidence, if only a shred, about the fate that awaited women, like Giovanna, after their trials, and also tells us that European consuls made private arrangements with families (who may have been acquaintances) to banish "wanton women" from the places and populations under their legal authority. It is significant that Wood does not mention enclosing the "woman in question" in Malta in a convent—of which there were many in the period—which might have furnished documentation. Rather, the English consul stated that he would locate a family in Malta, one not related by kinship to the female deportee, to act as moral guardians—an informal agreement leaving little or no record.

However, there was one record-keeping institution in Tunisia from the 1840s that was very concerned about the morality of its members—the Church and Catholic female missionaries—but we will deal with parish documents when evaluating what Giovanna says, or appears to say, about herself in the next section. Suffice it to say that missionary records have proven invaluable if, as is true of all sources, they are employed critically. Unfortunately, Catholic records still remaining in Tunisia are poorly organized and archived, if at all, and very difficult of access; once they are repatriated to France, they are often not made readily available to researchers.[19]

THE *PROCEDURA PENALE:* WHO WAS GIOVANNA TELLINI?

The trial proceedings contain oral testimony as well as appended documents produced by on-site investigations of Giovanna's residence; the testimonies stretched over a three-month period, from February 27 until May 20, 1868, perhaps to give some witnesses time to recover from typhoid fever. At first glance, the material contained in the transcripts seems to unlock the local social universe of the down-and-out, hustlers, risk takers, and ordinary folks going about their business, or at least a slice of that universe. But the single most critical element in that opening up was the consulate, with its own peculiar system of justice. Consulates oversaw the drawing up of affidavits, written statements made before a competent authority, and depositions, the written testimony of witnesses under oath. These legal acts were conveyed by signature and seals. When an alleged crime occurred, consular authorities followed the local legal culture for gathering, organizing, and filtering words, and thus social facts, through established procedures governing admission of evidence. In consequence, there were, or might be, fairly high levels of distortion in the record. This means that before the historian can even tackle what is in—or not in—the transcribed testimony, she or he must thoroughly understand how the consular system of justice, in this place and at this time, operated. In addition, the researcher should discover the customary ways of doing things, often unwritten and understood only to social actors in the period, which could take precedence over the formal rules of the game in consular proceedings.

Finally, when perusing the proceedings in their entirety, one is immediately struck by how crowded the record is with people who are poorly identified. The congestion in terms of individuals named during oral testimony brings to mind Laurel Thatcher Ulrich's wry observation in *A Midwife's Tale*: "Opening a diary for the first time is like walking into a room full of strangers."[20] In light of these elements, the document itself, the trial proceedings, must be interrogated from a number of different angles: as an ethnographic record providing key evidence about material conditions and daily life; as an artifact translating the cultural and linguistic pluralism of city people who occupied more or less the same social rank; as a libretto showing how the regime of legal pluralism worked in the decades before 1881; and as a genre of diplomatic inquiry that shaped oral testimony to no small degree by forcing words into a menu of predetermined questions, thus deeply marking the responses. Now let's look at what the record appears to tell us.

We begin by listening again to Giovanna's "words" from February 27, 1868, to see what meanings can be wrung from them, as terse as they are: "I am Giovanna Tellini, daughter of Antonio; I am forty years old, born in Cala [Pisa] and residing in Tunis for the past ten years. I am single, an Italian citizen, Catholic, and illiterate. I rent the shop from the Greek, Dimitri Papadopolo, but I am partners in business with Annetta, a Spanish citizen, single, as well as with Dimitri L'Inglis, who is imprisoned at this moment."[21]

Giovanna identifies herself as Antonio's daughter—is her father or family in Tunis with her? It seems not, since she does not identify him as "Antonio, the owner of the shop near a specific city landmark" in the way she locates other city residents in her testimony. Other details provided indicate that the household Annetta and Giovanna shared was composed of people not related by kinship but rather by economic and/or criminal activities (as well as, perhaps, by love and affection). Next she furnishes her birthplace near Pisa in northern Italy. While she offers no explanation for why she came to Tunis around 1858, several questions spring to mind: for example, was her relocation related to political turmoil in Italy attendant to unification? On the other hand, we know that Pisa is not far from Leghorn/Livorno, which had traditionally furnished Italian expatriate merchants and traders to Tunis since the eighteenth century, although they were usually middle-class and many of them were Jewish.

However, Tuscany furnished maids and domestic help to European residents in Tunisia during the nineteenth century, since women from northern Italy were regarded more positively than their sisters from the south, especially from Sicily, whose women were reputedly "slovenly" and of "loose morals."[22] A later testimony, furnished on March 23, 1868, by the middle-class, literate Jewish businessman Elia Fargion, enlightens us: "Giovanna Tellini did household work for me for four years, and during that time I can not complain about her loyalty. For the last two years she comes to my house from time to time when I am lacking [domestic] help, and I still cannot find fault with her and remain surprised to hear that she was arrested."[23]

Perhaps she had set out for Tunisia to find household employment or been recruited through word-of-mouth circuits; but written contracts were rare in this period for this kind of domestic work, closing off another possible source of additional information. We can speculate that Giovanna sought a more remunerative profession by going into small-scale retailing in association with Annetta, since she states that they kept a shop as a living. Her testimony, as well as that of others, indicates that the rented building served as home, a store for selling secondhand clothing, and as a café, the "Caffe della Genina," located somewhere in the lower medina, where the down-and-out clustered together. A final query must be raised about the initial reasons for expatriation from Italy and the search for work. We do not know that Giovanna left Cala directly for Tunisia. Her partner, Annetta, whose family originated in Spain, was born in Oran, Algeria, soon after the French conquest in 1830; at some time, Annetta left Algeria for Tunisia, perhaps also in search of work. Thus we know virtually nothing of Giovanna's life before she arrived in Tunis, or where she might have resided and worked after leaving northern Italy and reaching North Africa in circa 1858.

Subsequently, she states that she is single and Catholic—what does this tell us in terms of her identity and social positioning, which in turn might connect to additional sources of information? At this point, church records in Tunis, whether missionary or diocesan, demand scrutiny. The practice of concubinage, which church authorities from the period refer to obliquely as a "serious moral problem" among the immigrant Catholic population in Tunis, seems to have been widespread, although there is no scholarly study of this. Had she been married in the church in Tunis, that sacrament would have been registered in the diocese of Tunis. And if Giovanna had been born in Tunis, she might have appeared in diocesan records, but that was not the case—at least according to her testimony. By stating that she was Catholic, she may have meant that she attended mass regularly or took part in the most important annual celebration in the country—the public procession in honor of the Virgin of Trapani. All of the witnesses unfailingly state their religion, Jewish, Greek Orthodox, Muslim, or Catholic, because religious affiliation was one of the central elements determining legal status, although not the only one, because of the tangle of legal pluralism and foreign diplomatic protection. Thus Giovanna's claim to be Catholic can be interpreted in a number of ways.

Her common-law marriage deprives us of church documentation, but that arrangement does not appear to have been terribly shameful. Giovanna readily admits to the consul that she is living with Niccola; she does not attempt to dissimulate, as far as we know. Finally, the typhoid fever epidemic should alert us to the possible existence of other sources, in this case hospital or clinic records, although none of the people who mentioned the epidemic stated that members of Giovanna and Annetta's households used neighborhood health facilities. In fact, these were very few and exclusively run by French Catholic missionaries, mainly the Sisters of Saint-Joseph; most of the records from this period do not appear to have been saved.[24]

THE *PROCEDURA:* LANGUAGES OF IDENTITY AND SPACES

Let's return to Giovanna's first testimony and the menu of predetermined questions, since that dictated in large measure her responses. How much of her words can we really hear? And do we know whether the "implicit codes" governing female evidence in court differed from that of men—if, as the saying goes, women tell stories and men give testimony? No, we do not. But subsequent witnesses, male and female, interrogated after her, run through the same list of identifiers in the same order. The Maltese servant employed in Annetta's household, Gianmaria, identified himself as "nearly fifteen years old, native resident of Tunis, English citizen, single, Catholic, and illiterate," a repertoire that follows closely the litany of other respondents, male and female.[25] Note, too, that many of those questioned do not know their birth dates with any certainty.

One crucial issue never explicitly addressed in the proceedings is language, which leads us to consider problems of translation. While Giovanna spoke northern Italian and probably understood the questions posed, Gianmaria, the servant, may not have understood Italian very well—or not at all—since the majority of impoverished Maltese residing in Tunisia spoke only Maltese, although the middle class in Malta or in diaspora used Italian as their written language. The witnesses and the accused called to testify spoke at least six different languages in various forms: Arabic, Greek, Spanish, French, Maltese, and Italian. Who rendered their words into the chancellery style of Italian used in these proceedings, a style that closely resembled French and British documents of similar nature? And how were the translations done? We have few definitive answers. At one point in the proceedings transcript, the notary enters into the record that "the judicial consul . . . is being assisted by Emanuele Cesana, the interpreter," although this was one of the few instances that we are allowed to know this.[26] Yet the widespread presence of local Arabic terms for people, places, and things, especially food items, shows that the myriad languages spoken in Tunis bled into one another in daily usage. For example, Giovanna claimed to have purchased a pair of weighing scales in the *succo* for ten *piastres,* employing the Arabic *suq* or market in an Italianate linguistic form.

Two other issues arise regarding the "rules of the game" for gathering, translating, and committing evidence to writing. What is truly unique about this record is that it let slip, in an aside, a hitherto unknown fact about consular investigations. The consul searched Giovanna's person (*sulla persona*) looking for stolen goods concealed on her body, a fact that leads us to ask how social class entered into this procedure.[27] Would middle-class women have been subjected to the same treatment, to a physical search? It is highly implausible. Although no incriminating possessions were found on her person, Giovanna's shoes appeared to be stained with a substance implicated in the burglaries, so these were confiscated. The second issue relates to the all-important matter of space and its uses.

The actual spaces where proceedings were held were critical in shaping responses to questions, even those following a set menu. An imposing, august room where the accused was questioned or witnesses for the prosecution were interviewed may well have intimidated many of the people hauled in before consular authorities. Another related question is whether other witnesses were present during interrogations, for, as we all know from watching *Law and Order,* this practice greatly influences testimony. As Gianmaria Hiberras, the Maltese servant, testified, something that he said "provoked a commotion in the room," a fact that was dutifully entered into the transcript of his testimony—the only time that such a notation was made, but it deepens our understanding about how things were done. Moreover, the consular authorities running the show hailed from the upper reaches of European expatriate society, something immediately made known by their dress, language, and style of speech. And the fact that consular authorities were able to round up so many people who often had "no known address" in Tunis and force them to participate in the inquiry is telling. It suggests that the consuls had networks of spies and informants who trolled city streets keeping track of people—for a price.[28] Thus space and social positioning in combination could play a major role in what people said, how they were interpreted or understood, and how words were committed to writing.

These observations lead to another. Through her own on-site investigations, the historian must be intimately acquainted with the places and built environments in which the historical actors under study lived out their days. Thanks to an intimate knowledge of the present-day Tunis medina, I ascertained that the spaces evoked by witnesses in the trial "made sense." For example, in testimony given on February 28, 1868, Mordachai Tapia stated: "I am twenty-six years old, born in and residing in Tunis, a subject of the *bey* [ruler of Tunisia], Jewish, a musician, and can write in Arabic." Mordachai added: "I do not know Tellini and Annetta. I play music in a *caffee dei mori* [Arab coffeehouse] during Ramadan, but I have two or three times seen two women, one of whom is called 'La Spagnola' ["The Spanish woman"]. I did not know that they had a shop near the market known as 'Suk l'Uzar.'"[29] The market quarter named by Mordachai still remains in today's Tunis, and other witnesses name that market in testimonies. Moreover, his testimony seems credible because the cultural practices mentioned in passing—Jewish musicians playing in coffeehouses during the long Ramadan nights—have been documented by historical and anthropological studies.

Therefore, the places and spatial practices evoked largely in asides from a trial held more than a century and a half ago can be aligned more or less with the actual layout of today's medina. Yet this part of Tunis is currently threatened by renovation projects that risk destroying what remains of nineteenth-century Mediterranean quarters, known as "Malta Saghira" (Little Malta), or "Little Sicily."[30] And so the historian also needs to be aware of future plans for urban neighborhoods representing incommensurable social and historical documents, since these could well disappear before long or even from one day to the next.

THE BETRAYAL

The most detailed testimony was given by someone from within the household itself. Gianmaria Hiberras, the Maltese servant who had worked and resided at Annetta's shop-residence for years, was intimately, perhaps too much so, aware of what transpired in the dead of night. At first Gianmaria denied everything, claiming to have been asleep when the burglars returned to the house with their stolen booty. However, in a burst of solidarity with her own servant, Giovanna betrayed Gianmaria by claiming that he had placed the stolen items in her room to frame her. Gianmaria returned the favor by changing his testimony in the middle of the interrogation and ratting on his mistress.[31]

From the servant we learn intimate details of burglary and fencing in the medina. Here is how it worked, at least according to Gianmaria. Giovanna's role was to store, conceal, and fence what her male acquaintances—two Greeks named Dimitri and Atanasio; an Italian, Veglione; and Niccola, the Spaniard—stole from houses, shops, or other neighborhood establishments, such as the inn. The adjacent shop of "the Djerbi *bakkal*" (a grocer from the island of Djerba) was hit twice by the robbers, who hauled off rice, soap, sugar, coffee, nuts, and a large scale. When the band returned with the purloined goods, the burglars hid them in Annetta's house and waited for a few days before dividing up the loot; the sugar found in Giovanna's room was a gift for serving as an accomplice and was used in her coffee shop. Stolen items not retained for personal consumption were then sold or bartered in markets in Tunis, in the port of La Goulette, and even as far away as Algeria.[32]

But how can we evaluate Gianmaria's testimony, and according to which standards? Once again, the historian must have mastered not only the "big picture"—for example, the fact that a flourishing contraband trade existed between French Algeria and precolonial Tunisia during the nineteenth century—but also the intermediate "layers" sandwiched in between the wide-angle frame and the microlevel details of daily life. The fact that the shopkeeper who suffered repeated burglaries hailed from the island of Djerba rings absolutely true, since the grocery trade was monopolized by Djerbans until very recently.[33] Therefore, each "fact" in the testimony has to be weighed, "held up to the light," and juxtaposed with "facts" from other historical cases that have been authenticated, or at least firmly established.

PARDON TALES

In her first sworn testimony, given on February 27, 1868, Giovanna denied everything. Asked if she knew where the stolen goods, including skeleton keys, found in her room and house came from, she stated, "*Non ne so niente*" ("No, I don't know"). When confronted with Gianmaria's testimony as well as with the huge stockpile of stolen items seized from her dwelling during her second testimony on March 2, 1868, Giovanna broke and appealed to gender norms to clear herself of the charges: "I want to correct what I said the other time. I was fearful ["*compresa della paura*"] that if I failed to narrate the events the way they want me to, they would carry out threats against me. I am a weak woman ["*una donna debola*"] who gave in, but now that I have heard that the great part of them [the thieves] are under arrest at the Driba [Tunisian prison], I want to tell the truth."[34] Here we encounter classic pardon-tales discourse first studied by Natalie Zemon Davis. In many of these accounts, the accused admits to guilt, fear, and weakness, assumes responsibility for immoral actions, begs forgiveness, and reenters social collective life. Hopefully a pardon, inspired by prevailing male views of female nature as intrinsically weak, would be forthcoming. However, the goal of reintegration into the local community in which Giovanna lived was not assured.[35] But before considering Giovanna's possible fate, another matter demands our attention.

Do we know with any degree of certainty that she was truly guilty? The longest testimony was provided by Gianmaria, whose detailed narrative of what was stolen and how corroborated with the mountain of physical evidence shown to witnesses, including Giovanna. Could he have been bought off by the prosecution? It seems unlikely because many of the tiny, seemingly unimportant details that he recounts are duplicated in similar cases from the period. Let's listen to what he says: "Yesterday evening, I [Gianmaria] was lying in bed when I saw Giovanna get up and open the door. I did not hear any sound like whistling, because you know how when they [the thieves] steal, they whistle."[36] Here the power of comparative historical analysis emerges, since by juxtaposing similar cases the historian can evaluate the significance and credibility of whistles in the night, which appears to have been a common mode of communication for nocturnal operations of a dubious sort in the Tunis medina.

Nevertheless, the paramount question whose answer we may never know is: Who ratted on the operation in the first place? And why did the neighborhood yield up its secrets to the authorities, who tended to differ in social class, power, religious affiliation, and nationality, secrets as often guarded as revealed?[37] These queries may never be fully answered for this story, but they guide the historian when trying to make sense of cases like it. And digging into similar dramas can subsequently open up previously murky areas of Giovanna Tellini's trial.

THE END OF THE STORY: WHAT WAS GIOVANNA'S FATE?

As is true of most of these accounts, the next chapter remains, alas, a mystery (not in the least because many documents in this series in the protectorate collection in Nantes have disappeared from the archives). So we speculate by reflecting upon how different societies control and punish women and men deemed deviant, although in different ways. Traditionally, women judged unruly or criminal were confined to asylums, convents, state-run brothels, prisons, or guarded houses, or expelled to bleak, largely uninhabited islands, such as the Kerkeneh islets, which served as an open-air prison for Tunisian Muslim prostitutes. Imperial states with distant colonies forcibly exiled women regarded as socially dangerous—the dumping of working-class English women branded as morally undesirable in colonies like Australia comes to mind.[38]

Yet as an Italian national and as a female, Giovanna would not normally be locked up in a Tunisian prison or asylum, and the consulate lacked its own long-term prison facilities. Men under European protection were at times incarcerated for short periods in Tunisian prisons; those convicted of murder were often packed off on vessels for repatriation or simply exiled by force on any passing ship that would take them onboard. When and why were the imprisoned thieves sprung from the Tunisian prison—and what happened next? Were they then deported back to Sicily, Spain, or Greece? Did Giovanna remain in Tunis after 1868, return "home," or move on, perhaps to Algeria along with Annetta? Could Giovanna have ended up in a convent run by the Sisters of Saint-Joseph in Tunisia? Or did the Italian consul make private arrangements to have her repatriated and placed under home arrest, as the British consul Richard Wood had done in 1876? And if the Tellini drama was representative of the historical realities and relationships of a particular time and place, can it serve to change the narrative?[39]

CONCLUSIONS: TRANSFORMING THE NARRATIVE

As we have established, female voices are rarely heard in the documents, and when they are, the circumstances surrounding their production were frequently inimical to women's interests or agency. On the other hand, the blank spaces in the consular documents on Giovanna's life story alert us to rips and tears in the nets of patriarchal control, openings that women, such as Giovanna and Annetta, exploited to their advantage—for a while at least. As a history that no one wanted because it centered upon undesirable women, accounts such as this one were largely excised from both the colonial and nationalist narratives. How might Giovanna's story, however incomplete, serve to refashion conventional historical writing?

By reassembling in brick-and-mortar fashion pieces from her life trajectory, a more complex tableau of a Mediterranean port city comes into focus. We appreciate how female immigrants found work in a precolonial, preindustrial state and how they tapped into the dense social networks that converged in Tunis and included a surprisingly diverse range of folks—Jewish musicians, Maltese servants, Muslim day laborers, and so forth. At another level, the story shows how ordinary people thwarted the state, the police, and consular authorities—momentarily—and also at times victimized their own neighbors by robbing them of their few cherished possessions. The critical issue of the nature and tenor of daily relationships between "Europeans" and North Africans in this majority Muslim Arab society before colonialism also emerges from the proceedings. As a tale whose plot, cast of characters, and denouement (frequently unknown) reoccur in other Mediterranean ports, Giovanna's trial can inspire historians to rewrite the narrative of those port cities irrespective of what side of the sea they occupied and in turn undermine the Orientalist paradigm, unfortunately still with us.[40]

The story of Giovanna and of her social universe dispels two pernicious, if enduring, historical myths. The first is that of the "lawless Barbary states." As we have seen, precolonial Tunisia was governed by a Muslim dynasty that observed international treaties and laws and also "made room" for subsistence immigrants from across the Mediterranean, irrespective of religion. The second myth is that of an age-old, impenetrable Christian-Muslim Mediterranean frontier shaped by implacable hatreds and impervious to all, or most, exchanges—with the exception of warfare and violence. Therefore, this fragment from an ordinary woman's life story can, if interpreted closely, serve as a much-needed antidote to polemical writings, which for decades have discredited Mediterranean Muslim societies by portraying them as innately hostile to, and intolerant of, Europe and all things European.[41] Finally, this history of women and men on the move in a very small place challenges traditional histories that have overlooked semiconcealed migrations and mobilities across the globe during the long nineteenth century.

NOTES

1. Agenzia e Consolato Generale di S. M. Il Re d'Italia a Tunisi, anno 1868, no. 31, Procedura Penale Contro Giovanna Tellini e Biagio Veglione, in sous-série, Tunisie, premier versement, carton 381, "correspondence entre le consulat français et les consuls étrangers à Tunis," in Centre des Archives Diplomatiques de Nantes, hereafter "Procedura." The first

testimony of Giovanna Tellini, February 27, 1868. Many thanks to Dr. Deborah Kaye, the University of Arizona, for invaluable assistance in translating this challenging text.

2. The seemingly insignificant phrase "Dimitri L'Inglis" contains potentially critical information about language and communication in this polyglot society marked by high rates of illiteracy. "L'Inglis," an infelicitous rendering of the Italian *L'Inglese*, or "the English man," is closer to the Arabic *l'inglizi*. It suggests that the secretary recording the interrogation either wrote down the term as used in spoken, "street" Italian or employed the form of written Italian known derisively by northern Europeans as the "bad Italian" of Barbary owing to its mongrel nature, especially the heavy influence of Arabic.

3. "Procedura," February 27, 1868, first testimony of Giovanna Tellini.

4. Archives Nationales de Tunisie; Centre des Archives d'Outre-Mer, Aix-en-Provence; Maison Méditerranéenne des Sciences de l'Homme, Aix-en-Provence; Chambre de Commerce et d'Industrie Marseille; Centre d'Archives Diplomatiques de Nantes; Public Record Office, Foreign Office; Bodleian Library; Rhodes House Library; St Antony's College, Private Papers Collection.

5. Edmund Burke III, "The Mediterranean before Colonialism: Fragments from the Life of 'Ali bin 'Uthman al-Hammi in the Late Eighteenth and Nineteenth Centuries," in Julia Clancy-Smith, ed., *North Africa, Islam and the Mediterranean World: From the Almoravids to the Algerian War*, (London: Frank Cass, 2001), 129–42.

6. Julia Clancy-Smith, *Mediterraneans: North Africa, Europe, and the Ottoman Empire in an Age of Migrations, c. 1800–1900* (Berkeley: University of California Press, forthcoming).

7. Anne-Marie Planel, "De la nation à la colonie: la communauté française de Tunisie au XIXème siècle d'après les archives civiles et notariées du consulat général de France à Tunis," 3 vols. (Paris: Doctorat d'état, École des Hautes Études en Sciences Sociales, 2000).

8. Julia Clancy-Smith, "Changing Perspectives on the Historiography of Imperialism: Women, Gender, Empire," in Israel Gershoni, Amy Singer, and Y. Hakan Erdem, eds., *Middle East Historiographies: Narrating the Twentieth Century* (Seattle: University of Washington Press, 2006), 70–100. Silvia Finzi, ed., *Mestieri e professioni degli Italiani di Tunisia/Métiers et professions des Italiens de Tunisie* (Tunis: Éditions Finzi, 2003); the Finzi family, Jews from Tuscany, were among the many immigrants who settled in Tunisia in the nineteenth century.

9. Julia Clancy-Smith, "Women, Gender and Migration along a Mediterranean Frontier: Pre-Colonial Tunisia, c. 1815–c. 1870," *Gender and History* 17, no. 1 (April 2005): 62–92; and Nadia N. Mamelouk, "Leïla, 1936–1941: bien plus qu'une revue feminine," in *Leïla, revue illustrée de la femme, 1936–1941* (Tunis: Éditions Hafedh Boujmil, 2007).

10. Tunisian historians are currently making the most concerted effort to integrate minorities, women, immigrants, and other marginalized groups into historical narratives: Habib Kazdaghli, Dalenda Larguèche, and Abdelhamid Larguèche, eds., *Les communautés méditerranéennes de Tunisie: actes en hommage au Doyen Mohamed Hédi Chérif* (Tunis: Centre de Publication Universitaire, 2006); and Dalenda Larguèche, ed., *Histoire des femmes au Maghreb: culture matérielle et vie quotidienne* (Tunis: Centre de Publication Universitaire, 2000).

11. James C. Scott, *Seeing Like a State: How Certain Schemes to Improve the Human Condition Have Failed* (New Haven, Conn.: Yale University Press, 1998), 1–8; and Willem

van Schendel and Itty Abraham, eds., *Illicit Flows and Criminal Things: States, Borders, and the Other Side of Globalization* (Bloomington: Indiana University Press, 2005).

12. Sarah A. Curtis, "Emilie de Vialar and the Religious Reconquest of Algeria," *French Historical Studies* 29, no. 2 (2006): 261–92.

13. Hamilton Sipho Simelane, "The State, Chiefs and the Control of Female Migration in Colonial Swaziland, 1930s–1950s," *Journal of African History* 45, no. 1 (2004): 103–24; quote page 103. Donna R. Gabaccia, *Italy's Many Diasporas* (Seattle: University of Washington Press, 2000); and Donna R. Gabaccia and Franca Iacovetta, eds., *Women, Gender, and Transnational Lives: Italian Workers of the World* (Toronto: University of Toronto Press, 2002).

14. Antoinette Burton, ed., *Archive Stories: Facts, Fictions, and the Writing of History* (Durham, N.C.: Duke University Press, 2005); and Antoinette Burton, *Dwelling in the Archive: Women Writing House, Home, and History in Late Colonial India* (New York: Oxford University Press, 2003).

15. "Procedura," April 27, 1868, testimony of Nicola Milone; February 27, 1868, testimony of Sa'id Zuavi.

16. Julia Clancy-Smith, "Making a Living: The Sea, Contraband, and Other Illicit Activities in the 19th-Century Mediterranean World," in *A Colonial Sea: The Mediterranean, 1798–1956*, eds. Manuel Borutta and Athanasios Gekas (2010); and Dalenda Larguèche, *Territoires sans frontières: la contrebande et ses réseaux dans la régence de Tunis au XIXe siècle* (Tunis: Centre de Publication Universitaire, 2001).

17. Dalenda Larguèche and Abdelhamid Larguèche, *Marginales en terre d'Islam* (Tunis: Cérès Productions, 1992); Abdelhamid Larguèche, *Les ombres de la ville: pauvres, marginaux et minoritaires à Tunis (XVIIIème et XIXème siècles)* (Tunis: Centre de Publication Universitaire, 1999); Mohamed Kerrou and Moncef M'Halla, "La prostitution dans la Medina de Tunis aux XIXe et XXe siècles," in Fanny Colonna and Zakya Daoud, eds., *Être marginal au Maghreb* (Paris: CNRS Éditions, 1993); and Christelle Taraud, *La prostitution coloniale: Algérie, Tunisie, Maroc* (Paris: Payot, 2003).

18. Richard Wood, October 12, 1876, série historique, carton 288, dossier 413, ANT.

19. Julia Clancy-Smith, "Women, Gender, and Missionary Education: North Africa," in *Economics, Education, Mobility and Space*, vol. 4, *Encyclopedia of Women and Islamic Cultures*, ed. Suad Joseph (Leiden: E. J. Brill, 2006), 283–85.

20. Laurel Thatcher Ulrich, *A Midwife's Tale: The Life of Martha Ballard, Based on Her Diary, 1785–1812* (New York: Vintage, 1990), 35.

21. "Procedura," February 27, 1868, first testimony of Giovanna Tellini.

22. Julia Clancy-Smith, "Marginality and Migration: Europe's Social Outcasts in Pre-Colonial Tunisia, 1830–81," in Eugene Rogan, ed., *Outside In: On the Margins of the Modern Middle East* (London: Routledge, 2002), 149–82.

23. "Procedura," March 23, 1868, testimony of Elia Fargion.

24. Planel, "De la nation."

25. "Procedura," February 27, 1868, testimony of Gianmaria Hiberras.

26. "Procedura," February 28, 1868, testimony of Biagio Veglione.

27. "Procedura," Trasferta d'Ufficio, February 27, 1868.

28. The transcript of the proceedings lists at least seventeen witnesses either native to or residing in Tunis, from very different social backgrounds.

29. "Procedura," February 28, 1868, testimony of Mordachai Tapia.

30. Daniela Melfa, "Regards italiens sur les Petites Siciles de Tunisie," *Revue de l'Institut des Belles-Lettres Arabes* 70, 199 (2007): 3–28; and Daniela Melfa, *Migrando a sud: coloni italiani di Tunisia (1881–1939)* (Rome: Aracne, 2008).

31. "Procedura," February 27, 1868, testimony of Gianmaria Hiberras.

32. Ibid.

33. Julia Clancy-Smith, *Rebel and Saint: Muslim Notables, Populist Protest, Colonial Encounters (Algeria and Tunisia, 1800–1904)* (Berkeley: University of California Press, 1994).

34. "Procedura," March 12, 1868, second testimony of Giovanna Tellini.

35. Natalie Zemon Davis, *Fiction in the Archives: Pardon Tales and Their Tellers in Sixteenth-Century France* (Stanford, Calif.: Stanford University Press, 1987).

36. "Procedura," February 27, 1868, testimony of Gianmaria Hiberras.

37. Leslie Peirce, *Morality Tales: Law and Gender in the Ottoman Court of Aintab* (Berkeley: University of California Press, 2003); and Joanne Ferraro, *Nefarious Crimes, Contested Justice: Illicit Sex and Infanticide in the Republic of Venice, 1557–1789* (Baltimore: Johns Hopkins University Press, 2008).

38. Philippa Levine, *Prostitution, Race and Politics: Policing Venereal Disease in the British Empire* (London: Routledge, 2003).

39. Countless archival records document the contraband trade and demonstrate similarities with the Tellini case, although few provide such great detail. Julia Clancy-Smith, "The Maghrib and the Mediterranean World in the Nineteenth Century," in *The Maghrib in Question: Essays in History and Historiography*, ed. Michel Le Gall and Kenneth J. Perkins (Austin: University of Texas Press, 1997), 222–49.

40. This particular case study in immigration complicates today's hysteria about labor migrations; "Europeans" settling in North Africa to scratch out a living is counterintuitive, since it is assumed that people in search of work and a secure life always come from the global south.

41. Bernard Lewis, *What Went Wrong? Western Impact and Middle Eastern Response* (New York: Oxford University Press, 2002), to name but a few of his works.

4. EXPLORING CRIME AND VIOLENCE IN EARLY-TWENTIETH-CENTURY BLACK WOMEN'S HISTORY

Kali Nicole Gross

On October 20, 1906, authorities in Philadelphia, Pennsylvania, charged Henrietta Cook, a black seventeen-year-old, with murder. The alleged crime took place at the house where she roomed.[1] Cook, at that time using the name Cooper and with a man posing as her husband, rented the second-story front room of Rachel Martin's home at 1526 South Capitol Street. Martin, an African American widow, most likely rented the house herself and took in boarders to help make ends meet. The practice was fairly common, and city property records list an Edward Omasta as the sole owner.[2] Capitol Street—roughly one mile south of the city's largest black neighborhood—was a narrow, racially diverse block comprising two-story row homes.[3] But while blacks and whites lived in close proximity, they maintained, perhaps not surprisingly, very separate lives. Kate Welsh, a white resident in 1528 South Capitol, would later testify that she did not know Martin's name until the day of the murder.[4] Yet it is likely that the two never forgot each other after that bleak day. The corpse of a newborn discovered in the common outhouse behind their homes would have served as a grim reminder.

Although her actions likely left a lasting impression on the residents of Capitol Street, as well as on many other Philadelphians, histories of black women like Henrietta Cook are rare. Whereas African American women's history has flourished in the last few decades, witnessing a growing body of research on enslaved women, reformers, educators, and artists, there are few historical studies of black female crime and violence.[5] Yet prison and court records help to document these otherwise invisible women—typically impoverished domestics accused of nonviolent crimes against property, but also female prostitutes, badgers, thieves, and murderers. Indeed, black women's crimes and experiences in the justice system offer important information about the quality of black women's lives as a whole, shedding much-needed light on the experiences of women who were often unable to leave behind firsthand accounts.

Arrest, conviction, and incarceration distinguish black female criminals from the general population of black women, but those circumstances do not negate their larger shared experience. Most incarcerated black women typified the city's larger black female population in marital status, education, and employment. Further, black female violence and the surrounding circumstances offer illustrative points for comparison. The inner worlds that criminal records unearth confirm much of the existing historical research on black women's lives, as well as showcase important contradictions to commonly held beliefs. In this instance, the arrest, trial, and sentence of Henrietta Cook offer valuable information on notions of sexual propriety, the corporeality of bloody murder, and the peculiarities of race, gender, and criminal justice. But gleaning this information is not without challenges. Making the most of prison records, which are often dry intake rosters, incomplete transcripts and court papers, and prison administrators' one-sided observations of inmate behavior means employing a comprehensive methodology that combines traditional archival research with an expansive, and at times elastic, analytical framework.[6]

In this sense, the analysis must incorporate several key factors. It is important to read race, gender, and sexuality in critical ways—particularly how these elements are being constructed during the period of study. Using traditional sources such as prison records and news accounts is also essential. These sources provide basic information that helps to fill in research gaps, and these records also usually contain descriptions about the women's behavior and violence, descriptions that can be interpreted as texts. Equally important is the need to suspend judgment; the researcher must resist the urge to either demonize or instantly martyr the subjects. Exploiting contradictions and collisions in the documents are extremely important for historians, because these sites offer rich material for excavation and interpretation. At the same time, however, one must allow for ambiguities and paradoxes—people are complicated and not often purely linear or rational. Comparing evidence with the broader historiography to reveal consistencies and contrasts affords a more nuanced view, and unraveling information to understand how events unfolded. In other words, understanding the conditions or motivating factors that contributed to or preceded the crime is fundamental for this type of historical investigation.

For our purposes, then, and in keeping with the notion of unraveling historical events, the story of the infant corpse and his accused mother really begins a few years before Martin and Welsh's fateful introduction, in the latter part of 1904. That is the year that fifteen-year-old Henrietta Cook left her parents' home in Gloucester County, Virginia, to live with her sister, who had migrated and found work in Ardmore, Pennsylvania.[7] Cook's migration tale is somewhat unique, in that she was fairly young for the typical black female migrant, and going to a suburb roughly ten miles outside of the city highlights the existence of a less-explored black community.[8] Staying only a short time, Cook returned to her home in Virginia for several months in 1905 before again migrating to Ardmore. By the summer of that year, she had secured work at Bryn Mawr College. Although the record does not state the nature of work explicitly, it is likely that she performed in some type of maintenance capacity, given her age and her later work as a domestic in Philadelphia.[9]

Notes of testimony also reveal that Cook met Franklin King, the father of her child, when she returned from Virginia in 1905. The two dated while she worked at Bryn Mawr, and Cook testified that "he went with me as a single man."[10] She testified to having had sexual intercourse with King in March of 1906; he was her first and only lover.[11] After she missed her monthly "sickness," she realized that she was pregnant but claimed that she did not know her due date. She also learned that King could not marry her because he was married already. These details, however, did not stop the pair from renting a room in Rachel Martin's home in Philadelphia in early October, two weeks before the birth. By that time, Cook had left her job at Bryn Mawr and found work as a chambermaid at a boardinghouse at 1505 Race Street in October of 1906.[12] Several months pregnant at that point, Cook used her servant's uniform, particularly the apron, to camouflage her growing belly.[13]

On October 19, 1906, she went into labor; however, at work she complained only of feeling ill and wondered aloud to her co-workers if the clam chowder and omelet she ate had upset her stomach. Cook, camped in the water closet at 1505 Race Street, delivered a son sometime between 3:00 and 6:00 P.M. Although she would later claim ignorance as to what was happening, Cook's actions indicate that she suspected her time was near; she carried a dress suitcase to work and had kept it in the yard by the water closet.[14] After giving birth, she placed the infant in the case. Cook then returned to the kitchen, where Laura Bell, a cook at the boardinghouse, noticed that her "feet were bloody. She was dripping blood as she walked."[15] Bell urged Cook to go home, suspecting what had happened. Before leaving, Cook asked for a broom and a bucket of water, presumably to clean the outhouse.

Then, after giving word that she would not be in tomorrow, and apparently without an umbrella in the "pouring down rain," Cook left work, walked to Seventeenth and Market streets, and took a Porter car home with the dress suitcase in tow.[16] Inside the case, the infant lay wrapped in a petticoat with a cloth tied around its neck and stuffed in its mouth. Although she claimed that the child was stillborn, Cook testified that she did this because she "thought it might holler going up in the car if it had been alive."[17] At home, she sat for a time with Rachel Martin; sometime between 9:00 and 10:00 P.M., when Martin had gone outside to run an errand, Cook threw the infant down the cesspool.[18]

That night Cook may have believed that her actions would go undiscovered, but based on the testimony from neighbors, police, and her co-workers, it appears that her capture was likely just a matter of time.[19] Two witnesses in particular would provide damming testimony regarding the infant's mortality. Ten-year-old Georgianna McGowan and Mrs. Annie Peterson, both staying at 1528 Capitol Street that night, would each testify to hearing strange sounds coming from the toilet. The outhouse consisted of a common tank between the two properties, 1526 and 1528, with a divided structure built on the top. McGowan testified that she had been frightened when she went to the toilet because she heard something or someone cry.[20] Peterson, too, had heard the cries that night, but thought a sick cat was dying; because she had been ill, Peterson did not go to check. However, she did inform Kate Welsh about the matter the following morning, fearing the dead animal might smell. Welsh went to Martin's house, and the two got a poker and sifted through the tank. They discovered a petticoat covered in blood. At that point, Martin went to a local store and phoned for the police.[21]

As it turns out, police and detectives had been working the case from a number of angles. Close to the time that officers fished the infant's body from the cesspool at 1526 Capitol Street, authorities had an independent report about the blood-stained water closet at 1505 Race Street. Laura Bell herself also searched the privy and the yard after Cook departed and had found and preserved the afterbirth. She presented it as evidence to Special Officer William Minnis when he arrived later that morning on October 20, 1906.[22] This much of the story can be pieced together based on the testimony given at Cook's trial.

However, once she was in police custody, details surrounding Cook's case become somewhat murky, as Cook and the authorities involved gave conflicting testimony. This particular discrepancy not only gives us a glimpse of the case from two differing viewpoints, but also gestures toward the broader impact that racism played on the justice system. In this instance, police investigators claimed that Cook made statements that amounted to a confession, which they wrote up and she signed.[23] Cook, who had to be taken to Pennsylvania Hospital later that day, alleged that the detective had questioned her and then made her sign a form without reading it before she received medical treatment.[24] Whether Cook lied to interrogators or Detectives Miller and Ipe took liberties with her answers is difficult to determine, but the police statement was rife with inaccuracies. For example, the statement referred to Henrietta Cook as "Marietta Evans" and listed her as having been married to a Charles Cooper of Charlesburg, North Carolina. It further charged that she said that the "child was alive when born."[25] The defense asserted that Cook told authorities that she did not know it was a crime to throw out an infant that was already dead.[26]

Although it is impossible to definitively say which version is more accurate, historically contextualizing the evidence can help to determine whether any of the information fits in with broader historical trends. Whereas defendants probably routinely tried to change their stories after giving police statements, allegations of coerced or false "confessions" against the Philadelphia police department were not uncommon. Existing evidence suggests that blacks especially suffered abuses during police interrogations. In this sense, Cook's charge appears to fit into a larger historical pattern. For example, in 1887 an African American man charged that police investigators terrorized him. He claimed he confessed "to save myself from being deviled to death."[27] In 1911, Bessie Banks, an African American woman charged with the murder of a white man, testified that officers both threatened and terrified her. She was at one point interrogated by detectives in masks, men who were "all looking her over." As Banks put it, "I was forced to confess that lie on myself."[28] Such examples lend credence to the notion that Cook may have been the victim of unethical police practices.

Further, a similar tactic appears to have been employed in the case of a woman charged with the murder of an infant in 1906. During the murder trial of Katie Cincard, a German immigrant who would later plead not guilty, Officer Harry Lehr testified that after his German-speaking partner interviewed Cincard, they wrote up what amounts to a confession statement and had her sign it. The validity of the statement might have been more rigorously challenged in court under normal circumstances, but because the Commonwealth could not produce the *corpus delecti*, Judge Ralston instructed the jury to "acquit the prisoner and render a verdict of not guilty."[29] In Cincard's case, however, in addition to the absence of a corpse, the alleged crime took place months before the authorities were involved. Moreover, the midwife, the only person who could offer corroborating evidence, had fled the country. That Cincard was arrested, indicted, and tried at all is somewhat surprising under the circumstances. As the judge explained, "before a prisoner's confession can be introduced into evidence it must be shown that the crime was committed."[30] This crime serves as another point of a comparison; it provides more evidence of possible unethical police tactics and suggests that white ethnics also could be vulnerable to the vagaries of criminal justice.

Whereas Henrietta Cook's case did not suffer from a lack of physical evidence, it nonetheless contained opaque elements. For example, although Cook appeared in court on October 31, 1906, charged with "infanticide in killing one male child," and was most likely held at the Philadelphia County Prison, she does not appear in any of the existing female entry or discharge dockets.[31] Further, she appears only in the *Prisoners for Trial Docket* on October 31, 1906, where it notes that she was discharged "At Court" on May 10, 1907.[32] Yet the records of her indictment show that Cook had been before a grand jury, apparently without representation, and had been indicted on murder charges on November 26, 1906.[33] Almost a month later, on December 20, 1906, she appeared before Judge Ralston to enter a plea of not guilty. At that time, Cook's court-appointed attorneys, Joseph Gaffney and William Spencer, accompanied her—this information comes from a handwritten note on the original bill of indictment.[34] Having been assigned to the case a day before, the attorneys also received a continuance.[35]

Cook's case apparently remained in limbo until her attorneys were able to make payment arrangements. Perhaps fortuitously for Cook, an act "to provide for the assignment of counsel in murder cases, and for the allowance of expenses and compensation in such cases" was approved on March 22, 1907. The act noted in section 2, "This act shall apply to cases now pending."[36] Shortly thereafter, on April 12, 1907, Cook's attorneys filed an affidavit of destitution on her behalf, which allowed them to bill their fees to the Commonwealth. Less than a month later, Cook would have her hearing on May 9, 1907.

Cook's testimony demonstrates her efforts to clear herself of wrongdoing at the same time that it sketches the tightrope that early-twentieth-century black women walked vis-à-vis respectability, sexuality, and reproduction. In particular, her account reveals a surprising blend of naiveté and cynical awareness. Although she took the dress suitcase to work on the day she gave birth, presumably to transport the infant, other actions suggest that she did not know quite what to expect. For example, Cook testified that while sitting on the toilet, "It went into the bowl, whatever it was." She then got up and "broke the cord" with her hands—this might explain Laura Bell's description of her hands being covered in blood.[37] These acts gesture toward a paradoxical blend of hard realism and childlike innocence. Cook prepared for hiding the infant but either forgot or did not know to bring a knife or scissors—something that would have allowed her to simply cut the umbilical cord. Such instruments would have been readily available given her access to the kitchen where she worked and the fact that she had spent a good part of her day there with Laura Bell.

Further, Cook's relationship with Franklin King demonstrates the more paradoxical aspects of human nature, as it portrays both a desire for respectability and youthful gullibility. Cook testified that King was her first and only sexual partner and that "he made some effort" to get her into bed. After dating her for a few months, King claimed to be taking her to a theater, but the two ended up in a house where they shared a room. She also testified under oath that "he had promised to marry me."[38] Her testimony suggests both ambivalence about engaging in sexual intercourse and willingness to do so if it would prompt a proposal. In one sense, her story affords a glimpse into the kind of sexual bartering that young single black women engaged in with potential lovers and offers a point of comparison with white working-class girls' sexual negotiations as documented by Kathy Peiss in *Cheap Amusements*.[39]

But also, Cook's testimony was not unlike that of Annie Cutler's in 1885. Cutler, an African American also tried for murder, explained to the court that the victim, her ex-lover William Knight, had "ruined her" and had not followed through on his promise of marriage. In Cutler's case, Knight had gotten another woman pregnant and married her instead. Blinded by guilt, jealously, rage, and shame, Cutler shot Knight dead on a city street in front of horrified onlookers.[40] Similarly, it was only after Cook was "in trouble" that she learned that Franklin King "could not marry," as he had misrepresented his single status.[41] She took the room with him at Martin's because, as she explained to King, "I could not go home to my mother in the state I was in."[42] The similarities may well point to either a pattern of sexual maneuvering among black women during the late nineteenth and early twentieth centuries or a pattern of black women using this narrative of being sexually "led astray" as way to reconcile their sexual escapades once the liaisons landed them in criminal court.

If taken at face value, both accounts demonstrate how black women traded in sexual intercourse in the hopes of attaining respectability through marriage. At the same time, the cases can diagram the pitfalls that an unexpected pregnancy could cause. In Cutler's case, the pregnant woman apparently trumped the deflowered one; in Cook's case, having been deflowered by someone already married, she found herself ruined and, more importantly, facing dishonor. She testified that she hid the infant from her co-workers "because [she] did not want to be disgraced."[43] In this respect, Cook's actions were not unique to black women during this period, as many women who committed infanticide essentially sought to escape the same thing. Catherine Cowley, a white widow, also threw an infant she bore out of wedlock down a cesspool in 1912. Josephine Darmska, a European immigrant, buried her newborn in the backyard, hoping to cover up an illicit "connection" with the child's father in 1907.[44]

But what is unique about Cook's case is that we get to hear her own words on the matter. Although black female sexuality has long been the subject of historical texts, it is almost exclusively written on, dissected, and discussed from the vantage of others. As Hortense Spillers notes, "Black women are the beached whales of the sexual universe.... Their sexual experiences are depicted, but not often by them, and if and when by the subject herself, often in the guise of vocal music, often in the self-contained accent and sheer romance of the blues."[45] Cook's experience and her actions offer a bald sense of the sexual anonymity that the city offered female migrants, and of how they understood those opportunities within the larger context of social mores and accepted notions of sexual purity. She and King relied on the anonymity of the urban environs to sneak off to a rented room to have sex and later to reinvent themselves as a married couple. Based on her actions, it also seems that Cook believed that the city would provide the kind of cover she needed to hide all evidence of her pregnancy.

However, just as we obtain a glimpse of how black women potentially deployed sex, we also see how they could have been unwittingly duped and exploited for it. In Cook's case, after her arrest, Franklin King disappeared. Apparently, he not only lied about his marital status, but he also did not visit her in the hospital or while she was in prison. Imagine the sting Cook must have felt answering, "Yes, sir" to the question by the court, "He ran off and left you did he?" Or the following question by her own attorney: "You have never seen him since you were arrested that day?"[46] This aspect of the case, as well as Cook's testimony, suggests that sexuality could be black women's undoing—in personal relationships and potentially in the courtroom. For example, both Cook and Cutler were careful to assert their virginity before their respective ill-fated sexual encounters, almost in an attempt to stave off negative assumptions about their morality. Further, both women endeavored to show that they remained otherwise pure afterward. Cutler refused to see any men after her ordeal with Knight, and even after she was imprisoned, she refused visits from the men who petitioned the courts for mercy on her behalf.[47] Cook, too, told the court that even though they secured the room at Martin's and pretended to be husband and wife, she let King stay over only a few nights a week, and during those times she refused to have sex with him.[48]

Cook's disclosure, however, came during her cross-examination, when the prosecutor asked whether she continued to engage in sexual intercourse with King after she knew he was married.[49] In this sense, her response was to both assert her morality and probably to avoid being further maligned by having willingly engaged in adultery. It also would have served her best interest to appear, aside from having premarital sex, as upstanding as possible. She needed the jury to see her as basically good in order to believe her version of events—specifically, that the infant was stillborn. According to her testimony, the newborn did not move or make any sound. And while Bell and Martin testified to not having heard an infant, the fact that Cook had tied muslin around its neck and fitted it into its mouth suggests otherwise.[50]

Yet beyond simply being a tactic deployed to counter specific evidence in her case, projecting virtue proved essential to black female defendants, both as a means to convey legal innocence and as a measure to counteract the negative attributes assigned to blackness in general. In selecting a jury for black female defendants, the primary concern for defense attorneys was whether the men could be impartial on a case involving a "colored" defendant. In Cook's trial, of the thirty-seven potential jurors questioned, a few men admitted their doubts. Men such as twenty-two-year-old Fred D. Osman, a former student of the University of Pennsylvania's Medical Department, explained that he was prejudiced against African Americans. When pressed by the court as to whether his bias would prevent him from rendering an impartial verdict, he said believed he "could [serve] as a matter of duty." He was, however, rightly excluded, as was Joseph Fertig, who stated of blacks that he "could never trust them" and doubted their veracity. John McGuigan told the court that he did not "care a whole lot" for blacks. He, too, was dismissed.[51] Similar concerns about white jurors' impartiality on black defendants' cases surfaced during the voir dire of both Bessie Banks and Helen Thomas, a black woman accused of murder in 1908. As a potential juror in Thomas's case explained, "I have had a good deal of experience with negroes, and I think their morals are not as good as those of white people."[52]

Typically, in cases involving white female defendants, the sole concern appears to have been whether the jurors could render a guilty verdict in capital cases. Even in cases where the defendants had recently immigrated and required translators, the fundamental concern remained whether white men could sentence white women to death, or as one prosecutor phrased it, "If you were accepted as a juror in this case . . . and the evidence warranted a verdict of guilty of murder in the first degree, which would mean the hanging of this woman, would you render such a verdict?"[53] Ultimately, the different concerns underscore much of the larger historical work that has demonstrated the ways that white women, native-born and immigrant, benefited from a certain chivalry in the justice system—a chivalry not easily extended to black women.[54]

The particular inner workings of racial inequities in the justice system notwithstanding, Cook's case and her particular crime, infanticide, provide fertile ground for the historian. In this instance, the case essentially depicts a collision between the private worlds of black women and the larger public. Contested terrain often yields some of the richest insights about the primary subjects, as well as the world in which they live. Moreover, the corporeality of the female world appears to have operated as a specific bond between women of different ages and stations. For example, Bell testified that she tried to aid Cook: "I asked her was anything wrong with her to tell me because I was a woman like her and maybe I could help her."[55] Further, it was the kind of situation that Bell endeavored to keep away from men's eyes for as long as possible. On the day of the birth, Bell repeatedly expressed concern about an older black man seeing Cook's stained clothes and the blood in the water closet. She told the court, "I seen her tracks, she was tracking across the floor. Having a man in the house I told her she better get her things and go home."[56] Blood and afterbirth—such sights were typically for women's eyes only. With the crimes before the courts, however, this private world was often laid bare in rudimentary terms.

In an environment where menstruation constituted a *monthly sickness*, mediating the gruesome discoveries of discarded newborns cast unlikely types of men and women in intimate contact with one another.[57] Police officers testified to not simply fishing out and in some cases unearthing dead newborns, but also to washing blood and refuse off the corpses. Some investigators testified to being sickened by the sights. Others recounted the discoveries with utter detachment, as Officer James Cowan did in 1912, in *Commonwealth v. Louella Jennings*. Jennings was also charged with throwing her newborn into a cesspool. Cowan explained to the prosecutor, "I simply went down there and recovered the body and I brought it up in a paper and put it in the patrol-wagon and sent it down to the Morgue."[58] Cowan's statement seems to mask the horror of such a scene.

And, indeed, some of the scenes were truly horrific—sites depicting the almost unspeakable extremities of fear, shame, and half-crazed desperation. Cook's actions gesture toward these circumstances, but other cases proved even more harrowing. The 1908 case against a young Polish servant, Katie Chizawska, depicts a sickening tableau. After giving birth to what she claimed was a stillborn, Chizawska dismembered the infant and stuffed six or so pieces of it into a nearby drainpipe. According to the attending physician's testimony, "The head was off, and I think that was split in half. The chest was open. The arms were off, and I think the hips and the two legs were intact."[59] In this sense, the crimes provide ample information to be explored and analyzed as texts. If nothing else, the lengths to which these young women would go toward concealing the births highlight the near fanaticism about the appearance of chastity and respectability. They also tell a profound tale of isolation and alienation. In Chizawska's case, she seems to have feared the possibility of losing the only home she had known since arriving in the United States. Her employer testified that when she asked Chizawska why she concealed the pregnancy, the girl wept on her shoulder and said, "Mrs. White so good to Katie, Katie can't tell her."[60]

That desperation and powerlessness was usually reflected in the kind of press coverage the cases received. Typically, black women either suffered harsh treatment in news coverage or received little coverage at all; however, white women, depending on their ethnicity and the circumstances, would generally receive a measure of sympathy.[61] But beyond providing a cultural reading of how the crimes and perpetrators were regarded, press accounts also help to corroborate criminal records and can fill in otherwise ambiguous information. For example, though trial testimony makes it clear that Peterson and Welsh were white, it does not definitively give us an insight into Laura Bell's race.[62] Black women typically worked as cooks, but white women did, as well. Census data might be helpful here if Bell lived or worked at 1505 Race Street for at least five years, but given that most domestics stayed at jobs for an average of just over one year, the chances of this are unlikely. In this instance, press coverage would be ideal. Unfortunately, though jury selection alluded to Cook's crime being covered in the papers, preliminary searches have yielded little, save an account announcing the verdict.[63]

Ultimately, the jury found Henrietta Cook not guilty.[64] Although this outcome may seem surprising, Pennsylvania had a fairly substantial history of leniency in these kinds of cases. As G. S. Rowe points out, in the eighteenth century, "Determining the condition of the baby at birth proved difficult for coroners and juries and, consequently, for prosecuting attorneys."[65] This dilemma seemed to coincide with an increasing mainstream sympathy for accused women, which often resulted in a high rate of acquittal. Moreover, the ongoing difficulty in proving an infant's mortality operated as a mainstay for defense attorneys. For example, Cook's defense, which consisted of her testimony and two from physicians, also hinged on whether the infant was alive when he went into the cesspool. The defense charged that the official examination of the lungs was flawed because the coroner's office did not perform the "hydrostatic test," whereby doctors put the lungs in a pail of water. According to testimony, "If the lung floated upon the surface of the water it would indicate that air had been received into the lung, it would indicate that the child had breathed."[66] Further, that there was no waste in the child's lungs or internal organs also cast doubt on whether it was living—enough doubt for the jury to disregard the testimony of witnesses who heard the infant cry, as well as the cloth that had been tied around its neck.

Like Cook, Katie Chizawska was found not guilty. However, in Chizawska's case, the court's inability to believe that a woman could do such abominable harm to her young seems to have prompted the not-guilty verdict. As Judge Ralston instructed the jury in Chizawska's case, "It would be such a horrible and unnatural thing for a mother to cut up her own when it was alive, that you will consider this in considering the probabilities."[67] However, such instructions were in stark contrast to those he gave to Cook's jury. Judge Ralston acknowledged that "one's sympathy cannot help but go out to her." However, he added that since Cook had been living as an honorable wife at Martin's home, with no one the wiser, she would not have had "to suffer the disgrace that the child was illegitimate." Under these circumstances, that Cook still concealed the pregnancy was "indicative of what her general condition of heart was with regard to the fate of the living or dead infant."[68] Nevertheless, these words apparently held no sway with the jury. The physician's testimony, and perhaps some measure of sympathy among the jury, ultimately led to Cook's release.

In this sense, Cook's case may attest to the fact that being barred from the benefits of true womanhood did not automatically condemn black women, though ample evidence shows how it could weigh heavily against them. After her trial, Henrietta Cook was discharged from the court and, to a large extent, from historical consciousness. Yet her case, with its drama, gore, and provocative intersections, demonstrates the wealth of information that can be mined from the macabre when the researcher combines archival research with an expansive interpretive analysis. Creating and deploying such a methodology enables historians to delve more deeply into texts and histories that otherwise might be disregarded. At the same time that this approach allows us to resurrect the historical experiences of poor and working-class black women like Cook, it demonstrates how those experiences can enrich our understanding of respectability, sexuality, and reproduction in the Progressive Era. Further, by using comparative measures to flesh out the details surrounding Cook's crime, her case effectively unearths information about white women and white ethnics who were her contemporaries, and it adds texture to larger studies of African American women.

NOTES

1. *Commonwealth vs. Henrietta Cook, No. 625, November Sessions, 1906*, 47; *Philadelphia County Prisoners for Trial Docket, 1790–1948* (vol. 4-19-1906 to 10-31-1906: 512), October 31, 1906.

2. Edward P. Omasta purchased the property from Catherine O'Gormon, June 1903, and he sold it to Julia Almeida, November 1907. Philadelphia City Archive, Registry Department, Bureau of Surveys, for 1526 So. Capitol Street.

3. *Comm. v. Cook,* Special Officer William Minnis, 47; Rachel Martin, 84, 87.

4. *Comm. v. Cook,* Minnis, 54; Kate Welsh, 80.

5. See Evelyn Brooks-Higginbotham, "Beyond the Sound of Silence: Afro-American Women in History," *Gender & History* 1, no. 1 (1989): 50–67, especially 50, 52; Michelle Mitchell, "Silences Broken, Silences Kept: Gender and Sexuality in African-American History," *Gender & History* 11, no. (November 1999): 443–44, especially 434, 439. bell hooks critiques the concentration on the heroic aspects of black history—she charges that this focus ultimately dehumanizes blacks by negating their trauma. See *Talking Back: Thinking Feminist, Thinking Black* (Boston: South End Press, 1989), 178. Patricia Scott Bell also calls attention to these biases in black women's history: see "Debunking Sapphire: Towards a Non-Racist and Non-Sexist Social Science," in Gloria T. Hull and Barbara Smith, eds., *All the Women Are White, All the Blacks Are Men, but Some of Us Are Brave: Black Women's Studies* (Old Westbury, N.Y.: Feminist Press, 1982), 87. Although several works explore the experiences of blacks and women in the justice system, only a few concentrate on black women or include significant discussions about their history: Leslie Patrick-Stamp, "Numbers That Are Not New: African Americans in the Country's First Prison, 1790–1835," *The Pennsylvania Magazine of History and Biography (PMHB)* 119 (1995): 95–128; G. S. Rowe, "Women's Crime and Criminal Administration in Pennsylvania, 1763–1790," *PMHB* 109 (1985): 335–68; Roger Lane, *The Roots of Violence in Black Philadelphia, 1860–1900* (Cambridge, Mass.: Harvard University Press, 1986); Nicole Hahn Rafter, *Partial Justice: Women, Prisons, and Social Control* (New Brunswick, N.J.: Transaction, 1990); Cheryl D. Hicks, "'In Danger of Becoming Morally Depraved': Single Black Women, Working-Class Black Families, and New York State's Wayward Minor Laws, 1917–1928," *University of Pennsylvania Law Review* 151, no. 6 (June 2003): 2077–2121; Anne Butler, *Gendered Justice in the American West: Women Prisoners in Men's Penitentiaries* (Urbana: University of Illinois Press, 1997); L. Mara Dodge, "Whores and Thieves of the Worst Kind": A Study of Women, Crime, and Prisons, 1835–2000* (Dekalb: Northern Illinois University Press, 2002); Kali Nicole Gross, *Colored Amazons: Crime, Violence, and Black Women in the City of Brotherly Love, 1880–1910* (Durham, N.C.: Duke University Press, 2006).

6. Much of the historical material consists of rosters with an inmate's name, race, age, crime, date of sentence, and length of sentence. Occasionally these sources include more detailed physical descriptions, noting height, weight, eye and hair color, and distinguishing marks. Transcripts, when available, and news accounts help to round out information from the rosters. Other documents, such as the bills of indictment, outline court appearances, witnesses, and attorneys, while daily journals from the prisons may have information about a prisoner's behavior during incarceration.

7. *Comm. v. Cook,* Henrietta Cook, 137–38.

8. Du Bois discusses the demographics of black southern migrants, and Cook mentions that her sister would not let her work in the city because she was too young. See W. E. B. Du Bois, *The Philadelphia Negro: A Social Study* (1896; reprint, Philadelphia: University of Pennsylvania Press, 1996), 47, 56; *Comm. v. Cook,* Cook, 138.

9. *Comm. v. Cook,* Cook, 141.

10. Ibid., 140.

11. Ibid., 146, 148–50.

12. Ibid., Laura Bell, 97; Cook, 141; Martin, 85, 87.
13. Ibid., Bell, 102, 107.
14. Ibid., 97–99, 106. I use Bell's testimony because Cook contradicts herself—see pages 142 and 152.
15. Ibid., Bell, 99.
16. Ibid., Bell, 106; Cook, 142.
17. Ibid., Cook, 145.
18. Ibid., Martin, 84–85; Cook, 142–43.
19. Ibid., Detective Joseph Miller, 123–24.
20. Ibid., Georgianna McGowan, 61–64; Officer Thompson Black, 75–77.
21. Ibid., Mrs. Annie Peterson, 67–71; Welsh, 80–81; Martin, 90.
22. Ibid., Bell, 100–101; Miller, 122–24.
23. Ibid., Miller, 124–29, 136.
24. Ibid., Cook, 144.
25. Ibid., Miller, 134.
26. Ibid., Cook, 144.
27. "The Murder Mystery: Wilson's Statements Puzzle the Detectives," *Philadelphia Evening Bulletin*, February 26, 1887.
28. *Commonwealth v. Bessie Elizabeth Minor Banks, No. 307, August Sessions, 1910, January 6, 1911*, 77–78, 79–81, 145–47.
29. *Commonwealth v. Katie Cincard, October Sessions, 1906, December 5, 1906*, 3, 16.
30. Ibid., 16.
31. *Prisoners for Trial Docket*, October 31, 1906. Cook did not appear in the *Prison Female Entry Docket, 1905–1929; Discharge Book, Female 1895–1911; Prison Discharge Book, Female, 1/1895–4/1918*. Cook might have had some kind of bail arrangement, but nothing indicating this surfaced in the record.
32. *Prisoners for Trial Docket*, 10/31/1906.
33. Bills of Indictment: *November Sessions, No. 625, Commonwealth v. Henrietta Cook, Murder, True Bill, John Kaufmann, Foreman*, November 26, 1906.
34. Ibid., *Comm. v. Cook, Murder, True Bill*.
35. The form request for a continuance is tucked into the folder of the original bill of indictment. See *Comm. v. Cook, Murder, True Bill*.
36. A copy of the act is attached to a decree and Cook's affidavit of destitution. See *Comm. v. Henrietta Cook, Murder, True Bill*.
37. *Comm. v. Cook*, Cook, 142, 158; Bell, 99.
38. Ibid., 148.
39. Kathy Peiss, *Cheap Amusements: Working Women and Leisure in Turn-of-the-Century New York* (Philadelphia: Temple University Press, 1986); Gross, *Colored Amazons*, 90–93; Joan Jacobs Brumberg, "'Ruined' Girls: Changing Community Responses to Illegitimacy in Upstate New York, 1890–1920," *Journal of Social History* 18, no. 2 (Winter 1984): 247–72, especially 248–50. This notion of the pleasures and pitfalls of young women's sexuality at the turn of the century is also discussed in Mary E. Odem's work; see *Delinquent Daughters: Protecting and Policing Adolescent Female Sexuality in the United States, 1885–1920* (Chapel Hill: University of North Carolina Press, 1995), 55–57.
40. Gross, *Colored Amazons*, 91–93.

41. *Comm. v Cook*, Cook, 149–50.
42. Ibid., 150.
43. Ibid., 153.
44. *Commonwealth v. Catherine Cowley*, No. 117, October Sessions, 1906, November 27, 1906; *Commonwealth vs. Josephine Darmska*, No. 287, July Sessions, 1907, September 23, 1907, 74.
45. Hortense J. Spillers, *Black, White, and in Color: Essays on American Literature and Culture* (Chicago: University of Chicago Press, 2003), chapter 6, "Interstices: A Small Drama of Words," 153; Darlene Clark Hine, "Rape and the Inner Lives of Black Women in the Middle West: Preliminary Thoughts on the Culture of Dissemblance," in *Words of Fire: An Anthology of African American Feminist Thought*, ed. Beverly Guy-Sheftall (New York: New York Press, 1995).
46. *Comm. v Cook*, Cook, 140.
47. Gross, *Colored Amazons*, 93.
48. *Comm. v. Cook*, 147–48, 150–51.
49. Ibid., 147.
50. Ibid., 142.
51. Ibid., Selection of the Jury, 11–13, 19–21, 41–42.
52. *Comm. v. Banks*, 1–14; *Commonwealth v. Helen Thomas and Mame Brown*, No. 375, October Sessions 1908, January 4, 1909, V-7.
53. *Commonwealth v. Sarah Jones*, No. 608, May Sessions, 1905, February 8, 1906, v-28 and the *Prisoners for Trial Docket* (2/27/1905–9/13/1905) 178; *Comm. v. Cincard*, v-1 to v-12, 3; *Comm. v. Cowley*, 1-a to 22-a. In one instance, when a defense attorney tried to question a juror about any potential prejudice against foreigners or Polish people specifically, the prosecutor's objections were sustained and the questions were withdrawn; see *Comm. v. Darmska*, Calling of the Jury, B.
54. Rafter, *Partial Justice*, 155; Patrick-Stamp, "Numbers That Are Not New," 101–3. For sentencing disparities, see Lane, *Roots of Violence*, 108; and Marcia Carlisle, "Disorderly City, Disorderly Women: Prostitution in Ante-Bellum Philadelphia," *The Pennsylvania Magazine of History and Biography* 110, no. 4 (October 1986): 549–68, especially 563–64.
55. *Comm. vs. Cook*, Bell, 101.
56. Ibid., 102, 106.
57. Ibid., Bell, 101; Cook, 146.
58. Officer James Cowan, *Commonwealth v. Louella Jennings*, No. 74, October Sessions, 1912, October 31, 1912, 1–2.
59. *Commonwealth v. Kate Chizawska*, No. 450, January Sessions, 1908, February 17, 1908, 11.
60. *Comm. v. Chizawska*, 37.
61. Gross, *Colored Amazons*, chapter 4.
62. *Comm. v. Cook*, Minnis, 57.
63. "Acquitted of Murder Charge," *Philadelphia Inquirer*, May 10, 1907.
64. Ibid.; *Comm. v. Cook, True Bill, Murder*.
65. G. S. Rowe, "Infanticide, Its Judicial Resolution, and Criminal Code Revision in Early Pennsylvania," *Proceedings of the American Philosophical Society* 135, no. 2 (June 1991):

200–232, especially 203, 205; Broder notes that baby farming shocked Philadelphians in a way that "individual cases of infanticide had not." See Sherri Broder, "Child Care or Child Neglect?: Baby Farming in Late-Nineteenth-Century Philadelphia," *Gender and Society* 2, no. 2 (June 1998): 128–48, especially 129, 132, 134–35.

66. *Comm. v. Cook,* Dr. Randle C. Rosenberger, 162, 163–64, 172.

67. *Comm. v. Chizawska,* 44.

68. *Comm. v. Cook,* 183–84.

PART 2

INTEGRATING VARIED SOURCES
FOUND INSIDE AND OUTSIDE
OFFICIAL ARCHIVES

5. SPINNING AND WEAVING THE THREADS OF NATIVE WOMEN'S LIVES IN COLONIAL MEXICO

Lisa Sousa

In 1746, Spanish officials investigated reports of a riot in the Nahua community of Ocuila.[1] According to numerous witnesses, men and women of the community were outraged when they heard the announcement of the Real Audiencia's (high court's) judgment that awarded disputed lands to the Jesuits. The community had been engaged in several costly legal suits with the Jesuits over lands and water, and the women who had prayed to the community's patron saint, San Antonio, to protect their resources from the Jesuits felt especially betrayed. Upon hearing the pronouncement, the people became agitated and several women began to throw rocks. Soon the church bells were tolled, calling people to the center of town. As tensions escalated, the women of the community stormed the Jesuits' refectory, destroying the kitchen and smashing the dishes and other belongings found there. All of the eyewitnesses attested to the leading role that women played in the uprising.

As I began researching the history of indigenous women in early Mexico for my doctoral dissertation and my current book project, I was excited to find many similar archival accounts from the sixteenth through the eighteenth centuries, suggesting that the women's actions in Ocuila in 1746 were not extraordinary.[2] Throughout the colonial period, indigenous women confronted and fought with outsiders to protect the people and resources of their communities in central and southern Mexico. The archival records also attest to a broad range of women's less remarkable activities and reveal their vital, daily participation in the social, economic, and spiritual life of their communities. In colonial documents women appeared as social actors who forged networks within and among households. They emerged as market vendors, some with significant investments in native and Spanish goods.

They could be seen as tribute-paying commoners, spinning yarn, weaving cloth, grinding corn, making tortillas, and providing service in the homes and on the lands of indigenous nobles and Spaniards. And they stood out as wives who demanded that their husbands fulfill their marital obligations.

Fortunately for historians, indigenous women of early Mexico are not missing from the historical record, nor are they silent in the sources.[3] On the contrary, native women are everywhere—in criminal records, in civil documents, in formal texts, and in pictorial manuscripts. Little has been written on indigenous women's history because previous generations of historians have not made them a priority, not because there is a lack of sources.[4] After a short time in the archives in Mexico City and Oaxaca City, I realized that the challenge would not be in locating documents concerning women, but rather in making sense of the fragmented and sometimes contradictory evidence regarding their roles and status. Each new source seemed to raise more questions than it answered and to lead to new lines of inquiry. I developed a methodology that I describe as spinning and weaving the threads of native women's history, in which I integrate historical and philological evidence from a broad variety of sources, including archival documents, formal texts, and images, that when read against one another shed light on multiple views and conflicting perspectives of gender rights and obligations. This article begins with a discussion of these sources for the study of Nahua women and then uses my findings on women's work and duties to illustrate the benefits and challenges of using a great variety of sources and approaches.

SOURCES AND METHODS

When Spanish conquerors invaded central Mexico in 1519, they brought with them an incredible legalistic tradition. A variety of documents and manuscripts from the earliest colonial period survive in Mexican, American, and European archives, libraries, and museums, and they reveal the emergence of a unique society and culture as indigenous, Iberian, and African people interacted and commingled. The vast majority of these records were written in Spanish; however, many thousands also exist in the native languages of Mexico.[5] In the early colonial period, Spanish friars worked with native male elites to develop a system for writing the Nahuatl language using the Roman alphabet. The friars' principal concern was the development of written materials to aid them in the evangelization of native neophytes, and together with their aides they produced Nahuatl-language sermons, catechisms, and doctrinals, among other ecclesiastical texts. But soon indigenous scribes were writing all types of Nahuatl-language records concerning daily life in their communities, and across the course of the colonial period they left hundreds of mundane documents. When analyzed from a philological perspective, the surviving native-language texts and documents reveal indigenous ideology and organizational structures that are obscured in the Spanish-language record. Although native noblemen produced the majority of native-language writings during the period, many sources involve men and women of all social ranks. Let us consider some of the many genres of Spanish and indigenous-language writings on Nahua women in early Mexico.

CRIMINAL RECORDS

Native women appear in the colonial Mexican criminal records as plaintiffs, witnesses, and defendants. As plaintiffs, they sued local natives and Spaniards over all types of crimes, including theft, mistreatment, and assault. Women also brought charges against their husbands for wife beating and adultery. In most cases in which women were plaintiffs, they represented themselves in court. Only in lawsuits involving a minor or a severely injured woman did her parents, husband, or other relatives file charges on her behalf. As defendants, women appear in the criminal records charged with assault, adultery, and, as in the case that opened this essay, of the women who destroyed the Jesuits' kitchen, they were tried for leading and participating in riots. I use criminal cases in which spouses filed complaints against their husbands or wives to reconstruct gender roles and marital expectations, and legal suits involving riots and agitating against local authorities to illuminate women's leadership in local political and economic struggles.

My book project draws upon more than 150 cases from Nahua communities of central Mexico dating between the mid-sixteenth through the mid-eighteenth centuries in the Criminal section in the Archivo General de la Nación (AGN) in Mexico City. While cases that directly involved women as either plaintiffs or defendants yielded significant evidence about gender roles, sexuality, and marriage, incidental information also proved to be invaluable. Ultimately, I read and took notes on every case that fit the regional and temporal dimensions of my study. I became less interested in a quantitative analysis of crimes in which women were victims and more interested in uncovering the subtle attitudes and gestures that profoundly shaped social interaction and gender ideology in colonial Mexico. Indigenous officials, plaintiffs, defendants, and witnesses recounted details of daily life as they recalled what they were doing, or whom they were with, when a crime occurred. For example, testimony concerning criminal cases that took place in the market frequently mentioned female vendors, which contributed to my overall assessment of the range of women's economic activities. Women also often described how they were at the market or laundering clothes with their mothers, sisters, or *comadres* when they witnessed a crime, which allowed me to reconstruct women's networks. Even cases against Spaniards could reveal interesting information on women, as, for example, when Spanish men and women were accused of consulting with indigenous women who were healers and prognosticators. The incidental information in stories of past events and indiscretions revealed local attitudes and values, residence patterns, and social networks that are essential to the study of Nahua women's status in colonial Mexico.

CIVIL RECORDS

The Archivo General de la Nación and the special collections of international libraries and museums preserve many genres of civil records, including testaments, land documents, tribute disputes, and censuses, in which indigenous women appear, and many of these sources were written in the Nahuatl language.[6] In their testaments women addressed their Christian faith, requested masses and proper burial, disposed of their earthly possessions, and spoke frankly of family and friends who had treated them with love and respect.[7] They also sometimes reflected bitterly on those who had disappointed, abandoned, or betrayed them. Land documents attest to women's rights to possess property and can be used to trace changes in women's land tenure over time. Tribute disputes often included complaints about the exploitation of women's labor and highlight the significance of women's contributions to the community. Censuses provide evidence of female heads of household and reveal residence and marriage patterns, information that is essential to understanding the tenor of daily life for Nahua women and for assessing their status.[8] I rely on these various types of civil records, mainly located in the Tierras section of the AGN, as well as a number of published Nahuatl-language primary source collections, to uncover women's economic activities, contributions to tribute labor, social networks, and roles in the household. [9]

FORMAL TEXTS

Spanish- and Nahuatl-language formal texts, which include life-cycle speeches, ethnographic descriptions, and printed church publications, such as doctrinals and confessional manuals, are particularly rich for the investigation of gender ideology, marriage, and sexuality. One of the most important sources on Nahua women is the Florentine Codex, a sixteenth-century twelve-volume encyclopedia of Nahua society, culture, and history written in parallel columns of Nahuatl and Spanish by native noblemen working under the supervision of Fray Bernardino de Sahagún and illustrated by indigenous artists with hundreds of images. Among the most useful material in the Florentine Codex are the life-cycle speeches in Book 6 and the descriptions of different social types and artisans in Book 10. Scholars have relied most heavily on the Midwife's Speech, which was made to a newborn girl. During the ceremony, the infant was ritually bathed and her umbilical cord was buried near the household hearth. The text explains that the midwife's act "signified that the humble woman would nowhere wander. Only inside the house was she to dwell, only inside the house was her home; it would not be necessary for her to go anywhere else. And this meant that her duty was preparing drink and food. She was to prepare beverages, to make food, to grind maize, to spin, and to weave."[10] Most scholars have interpreted this speech as evidence of a distinction between public and private spheres and of women's relegation to the home.

I approach these sources as prescriptive texts that reveal values essential to reconstructing indigenous ideology. As the quote from the Midwife's Speech demonstrates, formal speeches clearly delineate activities of men and women, suggesting an underlying parallelism or complementarity in gender relations. On the other hand, the descriptions of social types and artisans obscure the clear differences between men and women by suggesting that the same traits and characteristics were ideal in both groups. Thus even the information in the idealized sources can complicate the one-dimensional view of women's roles and status in speeches and rituals as complementary.

IMAGES

Indigenous peoples of Mesoamerica developed elaborate pictorial, and in some cases glyphic, writing systems in preconquest times. Their writings survive on stone sculptures, on ceramics, and in codices, screenfold manuscripts that were painted on fig bark paper or deer hide covered with plaster. The codex could be folded to show individual scenes or stretched out to display a lengthy sequence of events. A reader would have narrated the scenes using music, song, and dance, or would have interpreted sections of the codex used for prognostication. These sources provide information on women and other relevant subjects, including the genealogies of rulers, ritual practices, cosmology, and tribute arrangements.[11]

The pictorial writing traditions persisted into the colonial period and were sometimes combined with the introduced system of native-language alpha-

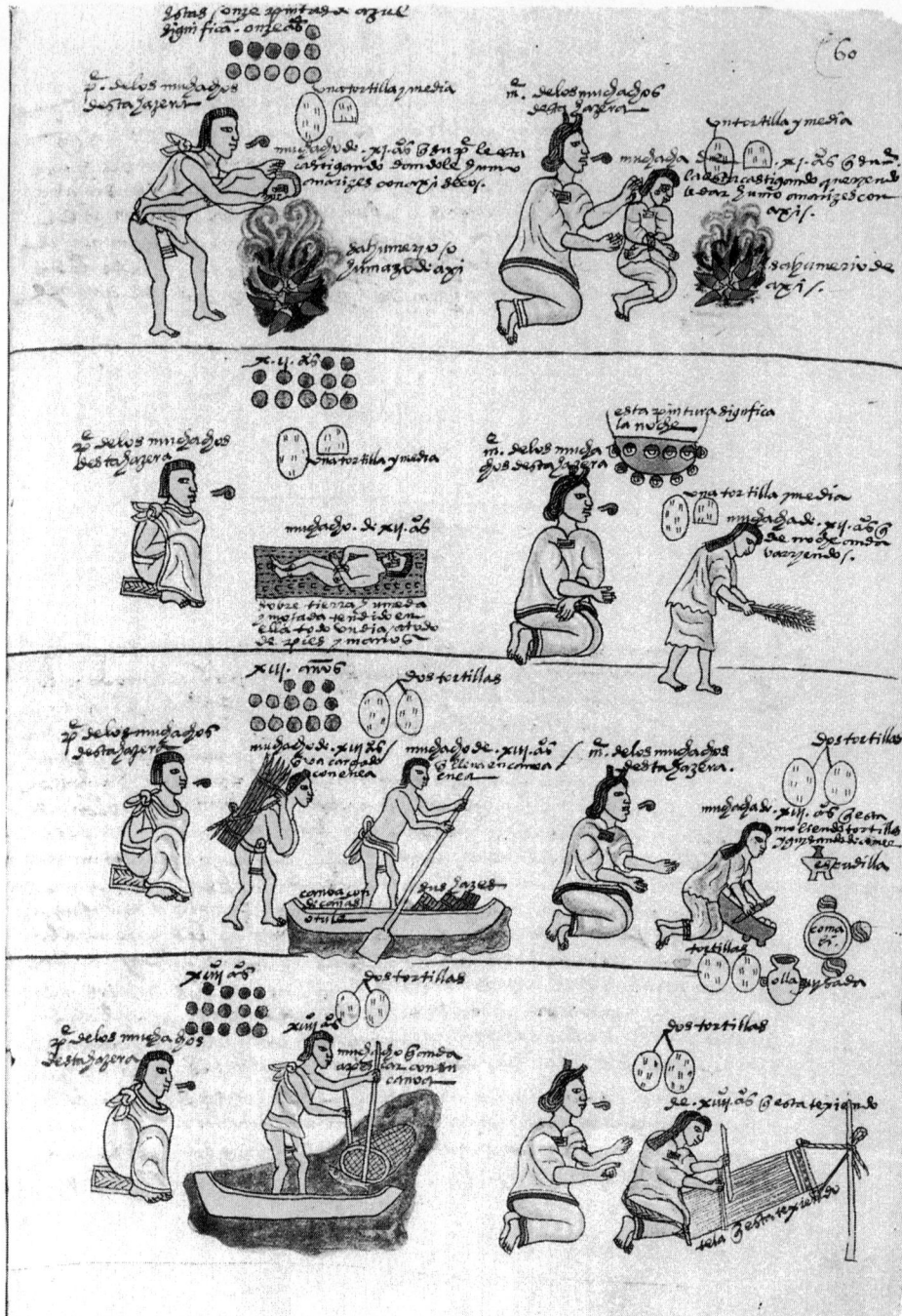

betic writing over the course of the sixteenth century. Illustrations drawn by native artists frequently show women performing a wide range of activities and ceremonies; often these roles are not recorded in the alphabetic record.[12] Furthermore, indigenous artists drew upon a rich visual language to convey gender and moral concepts in preconquest and colonial times. I analyze the historical content of the images, as well as the spatial relationships between individuals, their relative size, and their posture and the significance of material objects in the illustrations, which following Mesoamerican conventions all convey information about gender and social relations.

The narratives in the archive articulate a variety of perspectives that sometimes complement and other times contradict the prescribed gender roles and behavior of formal sources. Formal texts represent conservative, idealized roles that fall short of providing a comprehensive view of women's activities, and yet these sources reveal ideals and values essential to understanding indigenous ideologies. Preconquest and colonial pictorial manuscripts provide yet another dimension to topics represented in the many genres of alphabetic writing. I liken my methodology to a Nahua woman's work of spinning and weaving. The sources are the raw materials, *noichca*, "my cotton," which I sift and sort and spin into threads of evidence. I weave the many different threads into patterns and create multicolored fabrics, narratives that tell a coherent, complex story of Nahua women's lives.

WEAVING TOGETHER THE SIGNIFICANCE OF WOMEN'S LABOR

The topic of women's work illustrates how I bring various types of sources to bear on one important aspect of gender relations. Studies of native women in preconquest and colonial Mexico have paid little attention to labor. Scholars' heavy reliance on and literal interpretation of sources such as the Midwife's Speech in the Florentine Codex have left the impression that women's duties were limited to child care, weaving, and cooking, and that women's responsibilities were secondary to men's. Interpreting women's work through the framework of public and private distinctions, historians have considered the tasks of weaving and cooking as "domestic" duties, and they have

OPPOSITE: Figure 5.1. Mothers and fathers training and disciplining their daughters and sons (*Codex Mendoza*. Facsimile with commentary by Frances F. Berdan and Patricia Anawalt. 4 vols. Berkeley: University of California Press, 1992, folio 60. The original manuscript is held in the Bodleian Library, MS. Arch Selden A. 1, folio 60. Reproduced with permission from the University of California Press and the Bodleian Library, University of Oxford.)

not viewed women's labor within the broader context of community and Spanish-native relations.

The significant discrepancy that I found between the roles in formal texts and archival records like the account of the Ocuila uprising led me to consider a series of questions in assessing the status of women in Mesoamerica. Was women's production solely for household consumption—or in other words, were native women merely housewives? What symbolic and economic values were placed on goods produced by women? Did Nahuas really make a distinction between public and private spheres? Was the division of labor rigidly maintained? A number of broader issues concerning the community and colonial rule also emerged. How did communities respond to colonial economic and political pressures and changes? Rather than focusing on the primacy of political structures, I wanted to know how communities were created by social, gender, and economic relations within and among households.

By using a combination of archival documents, formal texts, and pictorial records, my study shows that native women performed many different types of labor in the colonial period. Furthermore, although the idealized sources present a rigid division of labor, other records revealed many instances of men and women's duties overlapping. In addition to the traditional female tasks of weaving and cooking, women performed a number of agricultural tasks, including planting, weeding, and harvesting, and raising animals, work that is often associated strictly with males. For example, one criminal record revealed that Juana Xochitl, a Nahua woman of Acatepec, owned and farmed an orchard of cacao trees.[13] In another archival narrative involving an assault, several witnesses testified that María Jeronima and her uncle went to help Juan Miguel and Agustina María sow corn.[14] A third case, concerning charges of adultery, discusses how a Nahua woman named Petra María helped Joseph Antonio work his wheat field.[15] As a final example, an investigation of the death of a man described how he had worked with his wife performing agricultural and domestic labor on the Teotihuacán ranch of a Nahua noblewoman named doña Leonarda.[16] Testaments corroborate this type of evidence by showing that women owned, bequeathed, and inherited land and agricultural tools.

The rich and unpredictable incidental information in criminal records also sheds light on daily life and shows that women did not assume sole responsibility for maintaining the household or raising children. In fact, women and men worked together to maintain the household; both fetched water and firewood, swept the patio of the household complex, and laundered clothes.[17] This evidence complements the information in early colonial pictorial manuscripts that show mothers and fathers sharing the responsibility of raising and disciplining their children and training them in gender-specific duties. Images in the Codex Mendoza, a preconquest-style central Mexican pictorial manuscript with Spanish glosses, chronicle in highly idealized terms the training of Nahua boys and girls from the ages of three to fourteen, showing their progression from year to year. Each scene depicts either a father with his son or a mother with her daughter instructing the child in gender-specific tasks suitable for his or her age and level of development. The woman teaches her daughter first to spin thread, then to grind maize, and eventually to weave cloth on the backstrap loom. The father trains his son to carry loads, to sweep, to navigate a canoe, and to fish (see Figure 5.1). Thus the responsibility of raising children did not fall solely upon women. In fact, it is interesting to note the omission of any reference to caring for children as one of women's responsibilities in the idealized roles outlined in formal speeches such as those preserved in the Florentine Codex. The Codex Mendoza also sheds light on the way in which children were corrected. The manuscript depicts a mother and father punishing a daughter and son, respectively, for misbehaving or for performing their duties poorly. The top two panels of Figure 5.1 show parents holding their children's faces in chili smoke, the father making the son lie in water all day with his hands and feet tied, and the mother forcing her daughter to awake and sweep in the middle of the night. The format of the image suggests a structural equivalency or parallelism in the authority of mothers and fathers in the Nahua household in raising and disciplining their children.

The images and text of the Florentine Codex have been critical to my study of women's work as artisans and midwives. Archival sources rarely refer to female artisans beyond weaving, although according to colonial speeches and the Florentine Codex, women's crafts included featherworking (also done by men and considered among the most prestigious of crafts), dying rabbit fur, and embroidering.[18] I analyzed Nahuatl-language terminology used to discuss craft production and found that the descriptions of both male and female artisans include constructions built on nouns such as *toltecatl* ("[elite] artisan") and verbs such as *tlananamactia* ("to make things meet or match"), *tlapalhuia* ("to paint or dye something"), and *tliloa* ("to outline in black"). Thus the philological evidence suggests that little distinction was made between female and male craftspersons or their labor and its value.

Midwives do appear as expert witnesses in criminal cases of rape and assault, but the archival records are silent on their rituals or healing methods. However, the Florentine Codex provides lengthy descriptions of the midwife and her interaction with a pregnant woman and her family, and these can be used to reconstruct some of the ceremonies and practices around pregnancy and birth. Philological evidence attests to the midwife's high status. For example, she is referred to in the texts as *in amantecatl* ("the wise one"), *in toltecatzintli* ("the skilled one"), and *amiamantecaoan totecuio* ("you [pl.] artisans of our lord/lady"), terms that associate her with elite artisans. She is also addressed with such honorific titles as *tlaçotitlacatzintli* ("precious person"), *totecuio* ("our lady"), and *cioapilli* ("noblewoman"). Ironically, the descriptions of the midwife undermine the prescribed confinement of women in the household in the Midwife's Speech to the infant girl. These examples show how I have used a combination of sources to uncover the range of women's economic activities and their significance. I have used similar methods to reconstruct women's contributions to the community tribute labor system.

Archival records show that women worked lands belonging to and served in the homes of local nobles, secular Spaniards, and ecclesiastics. Often women performed tasks for tribute, such as weaving cloth, grinding maize, preparing tortillas, and cooking food, that corresponded to the gendered division of labor. For example, several pages of the Codex Mendoza prominently display elaborately woven textiles produced by women among the precious items and agricultural goods that had been paid in tribute to the Aztec empire in preconquest times. The continued importance of women's labor in colonial times is revealed in a mid-sixteenth-century pictorial that was painted on behalf of the Nahua community of Tepetlaoztoc and submitted as evidence in a legal suit over tribute abuses against their *encomendero* (Spaniard who held a grant to collect tribute in goods and labor from a native community) and his agent.[19] The manuscript shows women who ground maize and men who worked as porters to meet their tribute obligations. Other pages in the manuscript show the enormous amounts of cloth paid in tribute, illustrating the exploitation of women's labor in colonial times.[20] A 1593 Nahuatl document on tribute arrangements in Quautla from the Tierras section of the AGN combines pictographic and alphabetic writing, confirming the significance of women's contributions to tribute labor by the end of the sixteenth century. An image depicts don Francisco de la Cueva, the indigenous hereditary ruler of Quautla, seated on the *petlatl icpalli*, a high-back reed mat throne, the Mesoamerican symbol of authority.[21] Before him are fields of maize, beans, chili, and other plants that were cultivated on his behalf by the community. Also shown are a man and a woman who are to serve him for a week, indicated by seven suns over their heads. Sharing tribute obligations, men and women of the community rotated the posts on a weekly basis. Legal suits on behalf of the community addressed the exploitation of native women and men and reveal the community's high regard for and dependence upon the contributions of all its members, male and female. Tribute labor also gave women's production a public dimension. Clearly women's labor, even when performed within the household, was not necessarily for domestic consumption. Rather, women's tribute labor bound the household to the community socially and economically.

As I observed the full range of women's activities, I still wondered what significance women's labor had beyond its economic value. I began to read my sources for the symbolic significance of cloth, food, and drink in Nahua society and for the ways these items were exchanged to build social, sacred, and political relations. For example, ethnographic sources make repeated references to sharing food as an essential part of all relationships, human and divine. Thus Mesoamericans spoke of making offerings to their gods as "feeding" the deities. Just as the exchange of food between humans and deities was required to maintain life, the sharing of food among humans was essential for a civilized existence. Virtually all Nahua rituals involve feasting and drinking as a social and sacred act. Eating and drinking together symbolized the creation of family and social bonds. In preconquest times, when Nahua parents placed their children in temple schools, they showed their good faith by sponsoring a feast for the people who trained the children: "They drank and ate; there was the mutual giving of gifts in the spirit of friendship" ("*atli, tlaqua: nel motlauhtia in netlacamatcapan*").[22] The Nahuas, like other Mesoamericans, ascribed a great deal of importance to speech and associated food and drink with eloquent speech, which was considered the epitome of refinement. One Nahua proverb recorded in the sixteenth century articulates the relationship between food and speech: "Only by drink and food did words of wisdom emerge, so that no one might live in evil. Not without purpose did they drink and eat" ("*in çan atica i çan tlaqualtica, in onca quiçaia in nezcaliliztlatolli, inic aiac tlauelilocanenca, amo çan quinenquaia, amo ça quinemia, in atl in tlaqualli*").[23] Food and drink stimulated speech and enriched social interaction. As these examples show, I often found evidence of the significance of women's work in texts that were not specifically focused on women or their labor.

As in preconquest times, the sharing of food and drink continued to be a highly symbolic social and political act during the colonial period, and grinding maize and cooking continued to be major forms of tribute labor. Reading multiple sources and developing this understanding of the economic, social, and political significance of women's work allowed me to appreciate the gendered act of resistance performed by the women of Ocuila who destroyed the Jesuits' refectory in 1746. The kitchen was the scene of their tribute service, and by destroying it they defied their obligation to work there. Their act also signaled the end to feeding the friars, or in other words, the termination of their duties of sustaining and caring for the Jesuits, responsibilities that were central to the reciprocal relations between the community and the Company of Jesus.

By shifting the focus away from formal political institutions that excluded women and toward social and economic relations at the household level, women's activities take on great significance. To uncover informal relations and the internal dynamics of the household and community requires a great deal of investigation and the use of various sources read in conjunction with and against one another. The multiple perspectives provided by the sources reveal consistencies as well as contradictions concerning women's roles. By drawing upon all these sources, which provide different perspectives on native women's lives and activities, I am able to spin a variety of threads that I can then weave into a complex assessment of native women's status in colonial Mexico. The study of women not only adds to history, but changes our understanding of native society and culture under colonial rule.

NOTES

1. Archivo General de la Nación (AGN), Criminal, 18:3, Ocuila, 1746.

2. My current book project is a social and cultural history of native women in highland Mexico from roughly 1520 to 1750 that examines marriage, sexuality, household and community relations, the construction of gender, and the organization of labor among the Nahuas ("Aztecs") of central Mexico; the Mixtecs of the Mixteca Alta in northwestern Oaxaca; and the Zapotecs and Mixes of the Sierra Zapoteca in eastern Oaxaca. Despite differences in language and sociopolitical organization among the many native groups of this region, Mesoamericans shared countless defining social, cultural, and political traits. For the sake of simplicity, I focus here on the documents for Nahua women's history.

3. Several pioneering studies of indigenous society and culture in Mexico that influenced the formation of my project include Charles Gibson, *Tlaxcala in the Sixteenth Century* (New Haven, Conn.: Yale University Press, 1952) and *The Aztecs under Spanish Rule: A History of the Indians of the Valley of Mexico, 1519–1810* (Stanford, Calif.: Stanford University Press, 1964); Arthur J. O. Anderson and Charles E. Dibble, trans., *Florentine Codex: General History of Things of New Spain*, 13 parts (Salt Lake City and Santa Fe: University of Utah Press and School of American Research, Santa Fe, 1950–82); James Lockhart, *Nahuas after the Conquest: A Social and Cultural History of the Indians of Central Mexico, Sixteenth through Eighteenth Centuries* (Stanford, Calif.: Stanford University Press, 1992); Frances Kartunnen and James Lockhart, *The Art of Nahuatl Speech: The Bancroft Dialogues* (Los Angeles: UCLA Latin American Center Publications, 1987); S. L. Cline, *Colonial Culhuacan, 1580–1600: A Social History of an Aztec Town* (Albuquerque: University of New Mexico Press, 1986); S. L. Cline and Miguel León-Portilla, *The Testaments of Culhuacan* (Nahuatl Studies Series 1, Los Angeles: UCLA Latin American Center, 1984); Susan Kellogg, *Law and the Transformation of Aztec Culture, 1500–1700* (Norman: University of Oklahoma Press, 1995); and William B. Taylor, *Drinking, Homicide, and Rebellion in Colonial Mexican Villages* (Stanford, Calif.: Stanford University Press, 1979).

4. With a few notable exceptions, the great interest in the history of indigenous peoples in Latin America is fairly recent. It has been only since the mid-1980s that ethnohistory has developed as a major subfield in Latin American history. One of the few works to focus on indigenous women in New Spain is Susan Schroeder, Stephanie Wood, and Robert Haskett, eds., *Indian Women of Early Mexico* (Norman: University of Oklahoma Press, 1997).

5. Archival documents are known to exist in several major native languages of Mexico and Guatemala, including Nahuatl, Mixtec, Maya, Zapotec, Cuicatec, and Cachiquel.

6. In the United States, the special collections at the following institutions have especially important collections of Nahuatl-language archival materials and printed texts: John Carter Brown Library at Brown University, the Newbury Library at the University of Chicago, the Bancroft Library at the University of California, Berkeley, the Charles E. Young Research Library at the University of California, Los Angeles, and the Huntington Library in San Marino, California.

7. For more on testaments, see Susan Kellogg and Matthew Restall, eds., *Dead Giveaways: Indigenous Testaments of Colonial Mesoamerica and the Andes* (Salt Lake City: University of Utah Press, 1998).

8. See S. L. Cline, ed. and trans., *The Book of Tributes: Early Sixteenth-Century Nahuatl Censuses from Morelos* (Los Angeles: UCLA Latin American Studies Center Publications, Nahuatl Studies Series, Number 4, 1993).

9. See the following collections of native-language primary sources for examples: Arthur J. O. Anderson, Frances Berdan, and James Lockhart, eds. and trans., *Beyond the Codices: The Nahua View of Colonial Mexico* (UCLA Latin American Studies Series, no. 27. Berkeley: University of California Press, 1976); Cline and León-Portilla, *Testaments of Culhuacan*; James Lockhart, Frances Berdan, and Arthur J. O. Anderson, eds. and trans., *The Tlaxcalan Actas: A Compendium of the Records of the Cabildo of Tlaxcala (1545–1627)* (Salt Lake City: University of Utah Press, 1986); Matthew Restall, Lisa Sousa, and Kevin Terraciano, eds. and trans., *Mesoamerican Voices: Native-Language Writings from Colonial Mexico, Oaxaca, Yucatan, and Guatemala* (Cambridge: Cambridge University Press, 2005).

10. Fray Bernardino de Sahagún, *Historia universal de las cosas de Nueva España: Codice Laurenziano Mediceo Palatino 218, 219, 220* (Florence: Giunti, 1996), Book 6: 147v–48.

11. Fewer than twenty preconquest codices survive, and the majority of these are from the Mixtec region. Especially significant for my study are the Nahua manuscripts Codex Borgia, Codex Laud, and Codex Vaticanus B. For discussions of preconquest writing systems see Lockhart, *Nahuas after the Conquest,* 327–30; Joyce Marcus, *Mesoamerican Writing Systems: Propaganda, Myth, and History in Four Ancient Civilizations* (Princeton, N.J.: Princeton University Press, 1992); Kevin Terraciano, *The Mixtecs of Colonial Oaxaca: Ñudzahui History, Sixteenth through Eighteenth Centuries* (Stanford, Calif.: Stanford University Press, 2001), 16–18; and Elizabeth Boone, *Stories in Red and Black: Pictorial Histories of the Aztecs and Mixtecs* (Austin: University of Texas Press, 2000).

12. Betty Ann Brown, "Seen but Not Heard: Women in Aztec Ritual—The Sahagún Texts," in Janet C. Berlo, ed., *Text and Image in Pre-Columbian Art* (Oxford: B.A.R. Press, 1983), 119–53.

13. AGN, Criminal, 686:3, Acatepec, 1558.

14. AGN, Criminal, 140:4, Malinalco, 1626.
15. AGN, Criminal, 730:9, Tacuba, 1752.
16. AGN Criminal, 10:13, San Juan Teotihuacan, 1757
17. For cases of women collecting firewood, see AGN, Criminal, 10: 3, Temascalapa, 1641, and examples of men washing clothes in the river can be found in AGN, Criminal, 641:27, Ciudad de México, 1581 and AGN, Criminal, 139:17, Malinalco, 1757.
18. Kartunnen and Lockhart, *The Art of Nahuatl Speech*, 153.
19. *Códice de Tepetlaoztoc* (Códice Kingsborough), Edición facsimilar (Toluca: El Colegio Mexiquense, 1994), 12, lamina B.
20. See, for example, ibid., 12, lamina A of the manuscript.
21. AGN, Tierras, 1871:1, Quautla, 1593.
22. Sahagún, *Historia Universal,* Book 6:176v.
23. Ibid., Book 9:25v.

6. EXCAVATING RADICAL WOMEN IN PROGRESSIVE-ERA CALIFORNIA

Sherry J. Katz

In 1948, at age seventy-five, Frances Nacke Noel reflected on her long career as a social activist. Noel expressed frustration at losing the energy to pursue the social justice causes she had championed for most of her adult life. "There is so much to be done and it makes one restless to be no longer young and strong to go in line with leadership. However I have already, in a quiet way done a few things which may bear bigger fruit than one expects. . . . So I am keeping at it to the best of my strength and ability."[1] Although she worked in the latter part of her life (she died in 1963 at age ninety) in environmental conservation and public safety, Noel's primary, and most passionate, commitment was to the empowerment and emancipation of women, especially working-class women.

Noel had come to the United States from Germany in 1893 as a young "adventure loving woman" with training in an early period of the kindergarten movement. After developing dual commitments to feminism and socialism in the mid-1890s, Noel settled in California in the early twentieth century. There she joined an active network of radical women similarly dedicated to advancing "underminingly ameliorative" reforms designed to empower women and the working class and to create a genuinely redistributive state that would prefigure socialism. These women spanned several generations, and while most came from relatively privileged, native-born, and Protestant backgrounds, they shared deep and life-changing identifications with the laboring classes, especially with wage-earning women.[2]

At the heart of their vision of a "Cooperative Commonwealth" was women's freedom, and essential to that freedom was women's economic independence, to be achieved through a combination of wage earning, full political participation, state remuneration for child rearing, and access to birth control. Both their commitment to women's economic independence and its centrality in their multilateral program for women's emancipation were unusual among women reformers at the time. Yet from 1890 to 1920, Noel and her colleagues actively championed these goals—through campaigns for woman suffrage, female unionization, protective labor legislation, mothers' pensions, legal contraception, and the gender integration of political parties and the state. Adept at coalition building, and especially at facilitating class-bridging alliances among women, they established a distinct, independent, and effective socialist-feminist presence in the socialist and women's movements and in broader progressive coalitions.[3]

Reconstructing the political and personal lives of California's socialist-feminists is not an easy task. While Noel (and her son) left behind two small manuscript collections and a brief oral history interview, most of her socialist-feminist colleagues did not deposit their organizational records or personal papers in archives. But Noel's collections and historian Mari Jo Buhle's pioneering study, *Women and American Socialism,* did provide windows into the world of socialist-feminist activism.[4] From these important threads, I was able to construct a research methodology appropriate for tracing the paths of radical women whose distinctive political ideas and reform proposals ultimately rested in the margins of both politics and scholarship.

I developed what I am calling a method of "researching around our subjects," in order to reconstruct and interpret their lives.[5] This process involved mining the small number of manuscript collections and oral histories of my subjects, and then working outward in concentric circles of related sources—from socialist movement newspapers and manuscript collections; to the varied materials of the specific feminist, labor, and social reform campaigns and organizations in which socialist-feminist activists played key roles; to the collections of individuals and organizations they collaborated with in the mainstream women's movement and in progressive reform coalitions; to government documents in which they made appearances; and to reportage in the local, state, and national press. Integrating these layers of materials enabled me to construct the political trajectory and impact of socialist-feminists, but it is still a very partial portrait, full of silences and unanswered questions. In particular, my ability to probe their personal lives and the relational aspects of their political careers is limited by a source base heavy in newspaper reportage and scattered organizational remains, with little complementary biographical material. In this essay, I will discuss the ways I utilized different kinds of materials in piecing together the whole fabric of early-twentieth-century socialist-feminism in California. I will also consider some significant limitations of the sources in this field.

My "researching around" methodology is not unique. In fact, this method may be widely practiced by women's historians, especially those working to excavate "marginalized" or little-known women who left few of their own records (for example, many ethnic-racial and working-class activists). Yet there appear to be only a handful of explicit discussions of this type of research strategy in the women's history literature. Historian Nell Irvin Painter's description of her work on Sojourner Truth certainly suggests a "researching around" methodology. Painter lacked archival collections on her subject, and further, she faced an "extreme version of the usual lack of sources" because of Truth's illiteracy. "Understanding her activities and thoughts in the decades in which Truth flourished meant combing through antislavery newspapers and the personal papers of her colleagues and friends . . . and several obscure autobiographies." Painter argued, however, that her task was not "quantitatively different" from that of other women's historians, as many "achieving" women lacked their own archives because their papers were destroyed or lost or because no one considered them "important enough to warrant an archive."[6] I am naming this essential research strategy, detailing important sources for recovering radical women, and advocating this practice for the reconstruction of marginalized political voices.

Excavating left-wing women is vital to our understanding of women's political diversity. Without such research, the radicalism that has often been foundational to feminism remains invisible. As historian Ellen DuBois argues, socialist-feminism, as a distinctive political tendency, can be traced back at least to the mid-nineteenth century and "has consistently been a radicalizing force in the larger history of feminism" within the United States and internationally.[7] Yet radicalism, including socialist-feminism, has often been, as historian Linda Gordon writes, "lost, erased, or distorted" in U.S. history writing, as left-wing proposals are viewed merely as "defeated alternatives" with "little political possibility" of enactment (dismissed in part, I would add, because of assumptions about the potency of anticommunism in American politics).[8] Although socialist women rarely achieved all that they envisioned, their contributions to the women's movement and social reform were certainly central to contemporary struggles and are relevant to feminists in our own time.

In *Dual Commitments: Socialist-Feminism in Progressive Era California*, a book-length manuscript-in-progress, I argue that socialist-feminists played unique and critical roles in some of the key transformations of turn-of-the-century America—the rewriting of the social contract to account for industrialization, the expansion of the social welfare functions of the state, and the transformation of gendered political behavior. The impact of California socialist women on social reform and the expansion of an activist state are major themes of the book. As a rich historical literature now demonstrates, social policy making operated on two gendered tracks during the Progressive Era, with women reformers playing an instrumental role in conceptualizing and constructing the early welfare state. What has never been shown is the influence of socialist-feminist politics, in particular, on proposed reforms, reform coalitions, and state policies. I argue that the remarkable activism of socialist-feminists helps explain why California was one of the most prominent sites of nuanced debate and early enactment of gender-specific social welfare legislation in the Progressive Era, including protective labor legislation for women and mothers' pensions.[9]

Another central theme of my research, undocumented in the historiography up to now, involves the efforts of California socialist-feminists to shape the gendered integration of partisan politics, a relatively new development at the time. The impact of women on political parties and partisan alignments represents an important aspect of recent research in U.S. women's history. Operating as an independent political tendency within the Socialist Party, radical women attempted to "redefine the political" as they worked to merge the traditions of white middle-class women's political culture with those of male partisan politics. Socialist-feminists championed the full integration of women in electoral politics, the incorporation of gender-specific concerns in the agendas of parties and the state, coalition building in social policy making, and an independent style of partisanship, one that made loyalty to party contingent on support for women and their political priorities.[10]

My search for California's socialist-feminists began with my discovery of a taped interview with Frances Noel recorded in 1952 by labor historian Irving Bernstein in the Special Collections Department at the University of California, Los Angeles (UCLA), along with eleven small boxes of manuscript materials deposited around the time of Noel's death a decade later. I also stumbled upon another collection of Noel materials held privately by historian Knox Mellon. These materials were critical in shaping my interest in studying California's socialist-feminist network and in suggesting a research path.[11]

I do not know how Bernstein came to interview Noel, but he was clearly interested in her role in the Los Angeles labor movement in the early twentieth century (and she was, indeed, one of the most prominent and outspoken women in organized labor at that time). It was amazing to hear her voice—strong, with a distinctive German accent—as she engaged in a tug-of-war on tape with her interviewer. Bernstein wanted her to stick to the history of labor and socialism in Los Angeles (and her participation in those movements), while Noel kept fighting time and again to come back to the topics of women and feminism. Her socialist-feminist ideals, and their importance in her political activism, came through clearly. Noel was most proud, she remembered, of her efforts on behalf of working women and for the creation of cross-class alliances among women in the service of social reform. She spoke of campaigns for woman suffrage, birth control, and social welfare, and of efforts to integrate women into the labor movement and Socialist Party. I was taken with her passion, tenacity, and continuing commitment to gender and class issues.[12]

Noel's UCLA manuscript collection reinforced what I learned from her taped interview. The collection put her interest in wage-earning women at the center, and it was organized around Noel's involvements in the women's, labor, socialist, and progressive movements. The collection's letters, writings, and organizational materials also made it clear that Noel was part of a lively and active network of like-minded socialist-feminists and helped me to identify their main Progressive Era campaigns. These materials also suggested the promises and difficulties of their efforts to work within the male-dominated Socialist Party and labor movement, and their complex relationships to the mainstream women's movement. I am not sure I was quite conscious at the time of how important all of these building blocks would be to my broader research, but in retrospect, this collection clearly grounded much of my subsequent work. While the collection helped direct my research, it also proved frustrating. The eleven small boxes offered incomplete organizational records, although they did provide some newspaper clippings and drafts of flyers and speeches. And the correspondence was relatively sparse, providing very few clues about her personal or family life.[13]

Mellon's collection of Noel materials consisted of several large boxes. I came upon this collection, as researchers sometimes do, by accident. Mellon had worked in the 1970s with urban and architectural historian Dolores Hayden on historic preservation. Hayden, one of my mentors at UCLA, believing that Mellon might have conducted some research on Noel, decided to introduce us. Mellon had interviewed Noel's son, Francis, for a research project on socialist Job Harriman, and Francis Noel had given Mellon his mother's remaining papers. Some of these were duplicates of materials in the UCLA collection, but I also found new correspondence, newspaper clippings, and a photo album. The new materials tended to be more personal—a number of letters and the photo album allowed me a few glimpses into Noel's family life and some of the friendships and activities that sustained her. The photo album, for example, suggested the centrality of the wilderness to Noel's life and spirit, as it documented numerous hiking trips with her husband, son, extended family, and close friends.[14]

What these small and fragmented collections imparted to me as a researcher was the necessity of examining every possible type of extant material that might shed light on how Noel and her colleagues operated politically and influenced social reform. At this early stage in my research, I had identified a substantial number of Progressive Era socialist newspapers and journals (many originating in California and focusing on the state's radicals), and I began my broader search there. My dissertation advisors believed that I should read these selectively, choosing time periods relevant to specific campaigns for the vote, female unionization, social welfare legislation, and birth control. The Noel collections, Buhle's book, and previous scholarship on California radicalism certainly provided key issues and dates.[15] But I sensed that a more thorough search was needed. And so I embarked on an extended journey into these weekly newspapers and monthly magazines, including the *Los Angeles Socialist/Common Sense, People's Paper, Socialist Voice, World, California Social-Democrat, Wilshire's Magazine, Western Comrade,* and *Socialist Woman/Progressive Woman.* These sources proved to be a gold mine for my research. Most of the publications made considerable space available to socialist-feminists. The *Los Angeles Socialist* even published a women's column for about half of its eight-year run. During at least two of those years (1902–4), socialist-feminists clearly controlled the column, with Mary Garbutt serving as editor.[16] Interestingly, earlier treatments of California radicalism that had also utilized these sources but were written prior to interest in women's history largely ignored women's participation and gave no hints of this substantial socialist-feminist presence.[17]

In these publications, the voices of many of the leaders of California's socialist-feminist network could be heard. What was particularly exciting was their engagement in an extended conversation about the core issues of socialist-feminist theory and practice. In fact, the newspaper reportage and correspondence had the feel of letter writing. Their dialogues proved especially important, since I lacked extensive collections of letters or complete organizational records. The newspapers and journals provided access to socialist-feminist discussions and musings that could not be found anywhere else. Clearly, socialist-feminists used these publications to share their experiences in different parts of the state and to knit together local groups of radical women into a statewide network of socialist women's clubs (which went through several formal organizational incarnations). Through the radical press, they conceptualized a socialist-feminist vision for women's emancipation and debated strategies for advancing this vision.[18]

Through these exchanges, I saw the construction of what I call a "dual political strategy" of separatism and integration that socialist-feminists used to create a distinctive presence, and exert substantial influence, within the Socialist Party, the women's movement, and the larger sphere of social reform. Josephine Cole, a prominent and sophisticated leader, complained that "man Socialists seem to consider the political movement a man's movement, one in which women need not be considered except as passive beneficiaries, or at most, obedient helpers."[19] As they sought a place in the socialist movement, Cole and her colleagues demanded both gender equality and respect for women's socially constructed differences. To foster their participation in the party as equals, they built autonomous women's organizations (under the umbrella of the Woman Socialist Union [WSU] of California) in which they could develop their individual and collective political skills and voices. Organizational independence, they believed, would also provide the strategic leverage necessary for socialist-feminists to incorporate women's distinctive political issues and styles into the party, with the ultimate aim of creating a truly gender-integrated socialist movement.[20] In fact, Cole proposed that the very articles I was reading in the socialist press had been published because socialist-feminists "succeeded in getting an allowance of space in our Socialist papers" for women's issues and activities due to the fact they had their own organization.[21]

The incorporation of these independent-minded women into the party was not smooth, and the socialist press also provided important windows into conflicts over women's presence in the party. These conflicts arose most clearly when socialist-feminists sought to integrate feminist political issues such as woman suffrage or gender-specific organizing strategies intended to reach women and children. In 1907 the Los Angeles WSU organized a meeting on woman suffrage for the party local. This meeting generated weeks of heated exchanges in the socialist press, as Mary Garbutt and her female colleagues felt that they had been "sat down upon vigorously" for raising this issue. "To ridicule the women who are working for their enfranchisement shows a want of sincerity at least, if not direct antagonism to woman's emancipation. How can we look for fidelity to the principles of woman's economic and political freedom under Socialism, when any effort to secure them in part now is hooted at."[22] In response to the charge that "woman suffrage [was] merely incidental" to the socialist program, socialist-feminists argued that working for the vote was indeed a key issue of emancipation and should be a political priority for the party.[23] After California women won the right to vote in 1911, socialist-feminists would more fully develop a new concept of partisanship. Their independent style of politics would link loyalty to party with organizational commitments to feminist principles and goals.[24]

Exchanges in the socialist press also helped socialist-feminists construct a "dual strategy" with respect to their involvement in the mainstream women's movement. Many state leaders articulated the need for a distinctive socialist-feminist presence in the women's movement, developed through a combination of organizational autonomy, integration, and efforts to build cross-class alliances. Cole proposed a "program for those of us who are vitally interested in the woman question. Let us bring together the various organizations of women into one strong woman's movement. Who so well trained to do this as the Socialist woman, standing upon a platform broad enough to embrace the thought of the suffragist, the trade-unionist, and the temperance worker."[25] Ethel Whitehead argued that socialist women could develop a "voice" and "a good strong delegation" within women's groups only with their own "Socialist Woman's organization."[26] Georgia Kotsch added that socialist-feminists could not "fall in unreservedly and contentedly with this general woman movement," for they had a "special mission" to perform in raising consciousness about "material conditions," working-class women, and the central relationship of economic independence to women's rights.[27] Socialist-feminists' major involvement in the women's movement prior to 1912 focused on the struggle for woman suffrage; in the second decade of the twentieth century, they turned to social welfare policymaking in campaigns for mothers' pensions and protective labor legislation, and to the legalization of birth control.

My research on socialist-feminist involvement in the suffrage movement began with the Noel collections and the socialist newspapers, but I eventually relied heavily on suffrage movement materials and mainstream press coverage. The suffrage materials did not, unfortunately, constitute a complete organizational record and were scattered across the state. These materials included various movement publications (especially suffrage newspapers covering western activism), scrapbooks compiled by mainstream suffrage activists, and manuscript collections in California repositories—most consisting of the personal papers of suffrage activists (several of them socialist-feminist, but most mainstream) and a few featuring suffrage movement materials exclusively. I remember being astounded, when I first read the *Yellow Ribbon*, the official organ of the California Equal Suffrage Association (CESA) from 1906 to 1908, to see many socialist-feminists featured prominently as California suffrage leaders.[28] I was able to piece together from all of the diverse sources that at least thirty-six socialist-feminists led local suffrage organizations between 1902 and 1911 and that they maintained a continuous presence on the CESA's executive committee during this period. In fact, socialist-feminists created an influential constituency within the broader suffrage coalition. They helped expand the movement's base among the working class, devised new arguments linking economic and political emancipation, and introduced modern methods of "militant" agitation, including open-air meetings and street speaking. Their grass-roots activism in working-class communities proved critical to the success of California's 1911 suffrage amendment, a victory that ignited expectations nationwide.[29]

One particularly important figure in the California suffrage movement, and in the preservation of suffrage materials, was socialist-feminist Alice Locke Park, who served as the head of the CESA's literature committee from 1906 to 1911. From this position, Park produced leaflets directed at working-class and wage-earning women and highlighted socialist-feminist contributions to the state's suffrage movement via articles in the suffrage press.[30] Park's "collecting zeal," and her belief in the importance of history, also led her to carefully compile suffrage materials in order to preserve the historical record of the state's suffrage coalition. In 1918, Park complained to a colleague that she was one of the few activists to save suffrage materials, and the only one to do so somewhat systematically. "I kept more than most suffragists not only because of my appreciation of literature, but because we had no headquarters at all until toward the end. . . . I knew my stuff would be wanted some day—I even thought I might some day write the California chapter in the final suffrage story." Park continued to collect suffrage materials from all over the world for almost three decades after the national suffrage amendment was ratified in 1920.[31]

Although other California suffragists did save critically important materials that eventually made their way into the archives, Park was responsible for creating key collections and depositing them in a number of libraries across the state. In fact, Ellen DuBois suggests that Park helped pioneer the archiving of women's history materials when she gave some of her personal papers to the Huntington Library in San Marino in the 1930s. In 1941, Park (with the assistance of Una Winter) donated a broad collection of suffrage materials named for Susan B. Anthony (featuring many items from the California campaign) to the Los Angeles Public Library; this collection later joined Park's papers at the Huntington Library. Several other collections of Park's materials, relevant to many aspects of socialist-feminism (and other social movements), are now housed at Stanford University, the Hoover Institution Library and Archives, and the California State Library in Sacramento.[32]

After winning the right to vote in 1911, socialist-feminists focused on achieving other aspects of their multilateral program for women's emancipation, through activism geared toward legislation and policymaking. In hopes of achieving greater economic independence for women and laying the groundwork for socialism, they played key roles in campaigns for protective labor legislation, state provision of mothers' pensions, and the legalization of birth control. The California women's movement as a whole also embraced legislative activism after 1911, and socialist-feminists often worked for social welfare reform as members of women's clubs and organizations (grounded, as always, in their own networks).³³

As I researched the socialist-feminist contributions to social welfare policymaking, I explored many new layers of primary materials. In examining the campaign for mothers' pensions, progressive reform and mainstream women's movement publications and manuscript collections came to the fore, including *The California Outlook* and *The Woman's Bulletin*. For protective labor legislation, I consulted labor movement records and publications, as well, especially the California State Federation of Labor *Proceedings* and labor council publications from San Francisco (*Labor Clarion*) and Los Angeles (*The Citizen*). For both of these topics, state government documents and contemporary compilations of the work of the California legislature proved useful.³⁴

These diverse documents made clear how involved socialist-feminists were in mainstream women's organizations and their social welfare campaigns, especially after 1911 and in Southern California. It is impossible from extant records to trace the precise anatomy of the popular campaign for mothers' pensions in 1912 and 1913, but it is evident that radical women helped to draft a number of the twenty proposed bills on the subject. Caroline Foster, a socialist-feminist prominent in the Friday Morning Club of Los Angeles (one of the most influential women's clubs in the state), chaired its mothers' pension subcommittee, worked on several pension proposals, and may have been involved in negotiating the final bill. The unique contribution of socialist-feminists to the campaign, and to our broader understanding of the mothers' pension movement in the United States, was in engendering a vigorous debate about the meaning of mothers' pensions as a social welfare policy. I discovered and reconstructed this thoroughgoing debate not through organizational records, for only a few fragments exist; rather, I examined key progressive and women's movement journals, the socialist press, and coverage in a number of daily urban papers.³⁵

Mainstream clubwomen argued for minimalist programs designed to support the children of impoverished "worthy" widows and to protect society from their possible "delinquency" and "immorality." Socialist-feminists, by contrast, proposed broad and well-funded mothers' pensions for all impoverished self-supporting women with small children, challenging distinctions between the worthy and unworthy poor and framing such support as a right of the indigent and a responsibility of the state. A number of them went even further in arguing for mothers' pensions as a means to compensate women for their socially important childrearing services and a mechanism for furthering women's economic independence. Socialist-feminist arguments reverberated in the controversy in the spring of 1913 over the competing bills drafted by women's groups, juvenile court judges, and state agencies. Mainstream reformers worried that the radicalism of some bills might lead to guaranteed government support for the poor or to the funding of "all mothers, regardless of circumstances." Although the bill enacted by the legislature (one of the first in the nation) was probably the most limited of all the proposals, the nuanced discussion of this new social policy in California, in which socialist-feminists articulated the most radical approaches, may have implications for our understanding of the mothers' aid movement nationwide.[36]

As we have seen, the method of "researching around my subjects" enabled me to analyze socialist-feminists' activism, and explain their larger political significance, by weaving together layers of diverse primary sources. But because my sources tended to be incomplete, fragmented, and without corroborating personal detail, I have had to choose how to work with the list-like quality of the materials. I decided to privilege those episodes for which I could combine sources in such as way as to explore, in some depth, the beliefs, activities, and contributions of radical women. But I am troubled by my inability to develop other aspects of their work for which there is simply not enough data for an "imaginative reconstruction."[37]

Understanding the complexities of my subjects' lives presented even greater challenges. Simply constructing a demographic portrait of the leadership cadre was problematic because of the absence of strong biographical materials. While the life stories of Frances Noel, Alice Park, and several other socialist-feminists could be gleaned from their manuscript collections, the life courses of other leaders proved elusive. For about forty leaders, I located some information about age, nativity, family background, employment history, adult family structure, and their paths to socialist-feminism. Many types of sources were used in this process, and once again newspapers played a central role, especially the socialist press. The *Socialist Woman/Progressive Woman* ran a series of biographical sketches on socialist-feminist leaders, and several of my subjects were the focus of those pieces, Mary Garbutt and Ethel Whitehead among them. Articles about socialist-feminists running for political office frequently highlighted their backgrounds. Obituaries written by longtime comrades proved helpful. And numerous articles and letters to the editor by socialist-feminists contained bits and pieces of demographic data (regarding themselves and their co-workers). I also used manuscript census materials (when I knew the head of household), death certificates, and city directories. Occasional letters found in the manuscript collections of others sometimes contained demographic details. Several radical women authored books, and these sometimes provided personal information. A few of the more elite or socially prominent women (or their spouses) appeared in contemporary biographical dictionaries.[38]

The most surprising sources of biographical information were short written portraits produced by the Works Progress Administration (WPA) in the 1930s as part of its Federal Writers Project. I found these in the Los Angeles Public Library, where they enjoyed broad public access after WPA writers completed them as part of a "City Officials" local history project. Some of the writers documented their subjects' lives and public careers through research in local newspapers and municipal records. Remarkably, Estelle Lawton Lindsey, elected as a radical, labor, and women's club candidate to the Los Angeles City Council in 1915 (and the first city councilwoman to serve in any major city in the United States), was interviewed for her 1936 sketch. These WPA-funded local research projects, conducted in many cities during the 1930s, may offer valuable biographical material for other historians of activist women.[39]

One of the most frustrating aspects of working with my sources has been the absence of personal material for most of my subjects—letters, diaries, oral histories, and other sources that provide windows into the feelings and personal details of their lives. The paucity of collections of intimate and self-conscious materials means that my understanding of their personal struggles and choices, and even of their political relationships, remains limited. In particular, I have been hindered in adequately developing the dynamic connections between their personal lives and their political activism (between the private and public). How did the married women and mothers in this group (who constituted the majority of these activists) blend activism, paid work, and household responsibilities? How did their efforts to combine these aspects of their lives, these dilemmas of modern womanhood, shape their focus on women's economic independence and the political priorities that flowed from that issue? What sustained them in their political activism—family, friends, comrades, other sources of support? How did they cope with "a degree of ostracism" or "otherness" they must have felt in working within larger movements and coalitions in which their political views did not predominate? How did they feel about their political careers and choices over time?[40]

I am indebted to historian (and mentor) Regina Morantz-Sanchez for helping me name this problem—what she termed a "disembodied" quality in the research materials.[41] And I have begun to wonder recently if it would be possible to uncover more of the personal in the manuscript collections at my disposal. I was more focused on political questions when I did my original research; perhaps I neglected some of the more personal materials and the possible linkages between private and public. To begin this process, I went back to Knox Mellon's collection of Noel materials. There I rediscovered a letter from Noel to her close friend Ethel Duppy Turner dated October 19, 1911. Noel described in some detail her activism in the last months of the woman suffrage campaign, when she was out speaking or at planning meetings most evenings and traveling to many parts of Southern California in the final push for the vote. She made it clear that her feverish activism was made possible because of support from her husband, son, and friends. Noel wrote that she "adore[d]" her husband, P. D. (also a socialist and labor activist), for his assistance and patience with her political work. She called her son, Francis (about seven at the time), a "dear sensible kid" who "went to all and everybody, and made himself at home." He "traveled alone in street cars from one end of the city to the other to meet me or P. D. or to meet with folks where he could spend the afternoon." He also went on a three-day camping trip with family friends. Here we catch a glimpse of the ways radical women constructed complex support systems in order to sustain their demanding public careers.[42]

This letter also provided a rare extant discussion of Noel's feelings about her political activism—in this case working with women of different classes and political orientations. While socialist-feminists certainly believed they had a special role to play in bridging the class divide and helping women from different walks of life work together for common goals, it has been difficult to find references to what such activism meant to them personally. Noel wrote enthusiastically that she took "genuine pleasure" as she observed women from different classes come "so closely in contact." The campaign, she believed, had done more to "kill snobbishness than we can dream of."[43]

Another letter in the Mellon Collection revealed the experience of illness and recovery, in which Noel's love of the outdoors, her humor and imagination, and her underlying passion for feminism helped sustain her spirits. Noel wrote to her sister-in-law in 1913 about recent surgery for breast cancer, an event she reported confiding to only two local friends. Noel confessed that she had been anxious, not "just for myself to be butchered and disfigured," but also about the possibilities of long-term disability. However, she had "a jolly group of nurses" at the hospital, and they all had "such fun together" that she missed their humor when she came home. Once home, she experienced many "crying spells" because she "felt so blue," but it helped to pull herself "out by the boot straps as the saying goes" and concoct "a lot of foolish plans for this and that just to forget" herself. Her recovery sped up once she could take her "blessed walking exercises," which "revived" her spirits completely. Noel could not resist playing on feminist themes as she joked about her illness. "Well it's done now, and all I can hope for is that the dear god, who so generously damned all women when he chased Eve out of paradise, will call it square with me and not keep adding insults to injury."[44]

These personal materials, coupled with the rarity of such sources in the archives, suggest how socialist-feminists understood the relationship between the personal and the political. Noel's admission that she told few friends about her breast cancer seems to represent a suppression of the private, and especially the painful, aspects of their lives. Perhaps part of their ethic at the time, then, was to save more political than personal materials. Or perhaps they (or their heirs) acted to keep the private out of the public record of their political careers. Conversely, Noel's discussion of how family and friends supported her activism does provide a window into the ways socialist-feminists combined the political and the personal in their daily lives.

The method of "researching around our subjects" has proved a painstaking but rewarding strategy for reconstructing the public careers of socialist-feminists and shedding light on their important contributions to Progressive Era social reform, including the construction of the early welfare state and the gendered integration of partisan politics. Yet the limitations of these rich but incomplete and fragmented sources shape the story I wish to tell, providing only a partial view of their political commitments and relationships, their social backgrounds, and their personal lives. Further excavation of personal correspondence, photographs, and other private materials may help me construct a more integrated understanding of the personal and the political in the lives of these radical women. This seems particularly appropriate, as their own multilateral program for women's emancipation, with women's economic independence at the center, demanded the rethinking and restructuring of women's relationship to both public life and private matters.

NOTES

Thanks to Mary Elizabeth Perry, Glenna Matthews, Mary Felstiner, Wendy Sarvasy, and the editors of the *Journal of Women's History* for their insightful comments and suggestions on earlier drafts of this essay. I acknowledge the kind permission of Johns Hopkins University Press to publish this modified version of the essay, which appeared earlier in the *Journal of Women's History* (vol. 20, no. 1, Spring 2008).

1. Frances N[acke] Noel to Ed Heim, October 5, 1948, box 11, folder 18, Frances Noel Papers (Collection 814), Department of Special Collections, Charles E. Young Research Library, University of California, Los Angeles, hereafter Noel Papers.

2. For Noel's characterization of herself, see Frances Noel's handwritten obituary for P. D. Noel, [1943], Knox Mellon Collection, a collection of Frances Nacke Noel materials held privately by historian Knox Mellon, hereafter Mellon Coll. The phrase "underminingly ameliorative" comes from Sara [Bard Field] to [Charles Erskine Scott Wood], April 8, 1913, box 270, Charles Erskine Scott Wood Collection, Huntington Library, San

Marino, Calif., hereafter Wood Coll. For Noel's life course and the demographic portrait of California socialist-feminists, see Sherry Katz, "Frances Nacke Noel and 'Sister Movements': Socialism, Feminism, and Trade Unionism in Los Angeles, 1901–1916," *California History* 67, no. 3 (1988): 181–89; Sherry Katz, "Socialist Women and Progressive Reform," in William Deverell and Tom Sitton, eds., *California Progressivism Revisited* (Berkeley: University of California Press, 1994), 118–19.

3. Sherry Jeanne Katz, "Dual Commitments: Feminism, Socialism, and Women's Political Activism in California, 1890–1920" (PhD dissertation, University of California, Los Angeles, 1991); Sherry J. Katz, "Redefining 'the Political': Socialist Women and Party Politics in California, 1900–1920," in Melanie Gustafson, Kristie Miller, and Elisabeth I. Perry, eds., *We Have Come to Stay: American Women and Political Parties, 1880–1960* (Albuquerque: University of New Mexico Press, 1999), 23–32.

I am grateful to historians Joanne Goodwin and Glenna Matthews for suggesting (in various informal conversations) that the centrality of socialist women's commitment to women's economic independence set them apart from other women reformers of the Progressive Era. For more on radical women's fierce commitment to women's economic independence, see Nancy F. Cott, *The Grounding of Modern Feminism* (New Haven, Conn.: Yale University Press, 1987), 13–50; Mari Jo Buhle, *Women and American Socialism, 1870–1920* (Urbana: University of Illinois Press, 1981), especially chapters 1, 2 and 5; Jacquelyn Dowd Hall, "O. Delight Smith's Progressive Era: Labor, Feminism, and Reform in the Urban South," in Nancy A. Hewitt and Suzanne Lebsock, eds., *Visible Women: New Essays on American Activism* (Urbana: University of Illinois Press, 1993), 166–98, especially 179–85.

4. Frances Noel, "Recollections," interview conducted by Irving Bernstein, November 4, 1952, Miscellaneous Manuscripts Collection (Coll. 100), Department of Special Collections, Charles E. Young Research Library, University of California, Los Angeles, hereafter Noel Interview; Noel Papers; Mellon Coll.; Buhle, *Women and American Socialism*. Although socialist women did not use the term "socialist-feminists" to describe themselves, I believe, along with Ellen DuBois, that this phrase captures their unique political commitments. And, like DuBois, I am hyphenating this term to suggest that their political outlook resided "precisely at the point of the hyphen that separates and connects 'socialism' and 'feminism.'" See Ellen Carol DuBois, "Woman Suffrage and the Left: An International Socialist-Feminist Perspective," *New Left Review* 186 (1991), adapted in Ellen Carol DuBois, *Woman Suffrage and Women's Rights* (New York: New York University Press, 1998), 253.

5. I am indebted to my colleague Julyana Peard for this phrase.

6. Nell Irvin Painter, "Writing Biographies of Women," *Journal of Women's History* 9, no. 2 (1997): 160. Also see Elisabeth Israels Perry, "Critical Journey: From Belle Moskowitz to Women's History," in Sara Alpern et al., eds., *The Challenge of Feminist Biography: Writing the Lives of Modern American Women* (Urbana: University of Illinois Press, 1992), 83–88, and articles assessing the research possibilities of newly opened archives on U.S. feminists at Smith College in *Journal of Women's History* 14, no. 2 (2002).

7. DuBois, "Woman Suffrage and the Left," 253.

8. Linda Gordon, *Pitied but Not Entitled: Single Mothers and the History of Welfare, 1890–1935* (New York: The Free Press, 1994), 3. Historians of socialist women have also noted a tendency to marginalize women in the historiography of the Left. See Buhle,

Women and Socialism, xiv, and June Hannam and Karen Hunt, *Socialist Women: Britain, 1880s–1920s* (London: Routledge, 2002), 11, 16–17.

9. Katz, "Socialist Women." For the concept of gendered tracks, see William H. Chafe, "Women's History and Political History: Some Thoughts on Progressivism and the New Deal," in Hewitt and Lebsock, eds., *Visible Women,* 101–18.

10. Katz, "Redefining the Political." For the recent focus in U.S. women's history on women and gender in partisan politics, see Nancy Cott et al., "Considering the State of U.S. Women's History," especially comments by Kathryn Kish Sklar and Ellen DuBois, *Journal of Women's History* 15, no. 1 (2003), 147–54.

11. Noel Interview; Noel Papers; Mellon Coll.

12. Noel Interview.

13. Noel Papers, including the collection's finding aid.

14. Information on the origins of Mellon's collection of Noel materials came from discussions we had in 1983; see photo album and other materials in Mellon Coll.

15. Noel Papers; Mellon Coll.; Buhle, *Women and Socialism;* Ralph Edward Shaffer, "A History of the Socialist Party of California" (MA thesis, University of California, Berkeley, 1955); Ralph Edward Shaffer, "Radicalism in California, 1869–1929 (PhD dissertation, University of California, Berkeley, 1962).

16. I read the most complete extant runs available for the *Los Angeles Socialist/Common Sense* (Los Angeles), November 2, 1901–August 7, 1909; *People's Paper* (Santa Barbara and Los Angeles), December 6, 1902–July 8, 1911; *Socialist Voice* (Oakland), August 6, 1904–June 1, 1907; *World* (Oakland), May 22, 1907–April 13, 1917; *California Social-Democrat* (Los Angeles), July 15, 1911–July 29, 1916; *Wilshire's Magazine* (Los Angeles), January 9, 1900–February 1915; *Western Comrade* (Los Angeles), April 1913–June 1918; and *Socialist Woman/Progressive Woman/Coming Nation* (Chicago and Girard, Kans.), June 1907–July 1914. I also mined many other socialist periodicals, including *Appeal to Reason, American Socialist, Chicago Daily Socialist, International Socialist Review, Party Builder,* and *Socialist Party Monthly Bulletin.* Hannam and Hunt discuss the importance of socialist periodicals (and especially their women's columns) to their research on British socialist women; see Hannam and Hunt, *Socialist Women,* 61.

17. See Shaffer, "Socialist Party," and Shaffer, "Radicalism."

18. Katz, "Dual Commitments," chapters 2–3, especially 167–68.

19. J. R. Cole, "New Wine in Old Bottles," *Wilshire's Magazine* 5 (June 1903): 75.

20. Katz, "Dual Commitments," chapter 3. For an excellent discussion of the ways many Progressive Era women's-rights activists combined equality and difference arguments, see Cott, *Grounding of Modern Feminism,* 18–34.

21. Josephine R. Cole, "Women's Unions," *Appeal to Reason,* June 13, 1903; letter from J. R. Cole, *Common Sense,* June 10, 1905.

22. Mary E. Garbutt, "Thinks Criticisms Were Unjust" [letter to the editor], *Common Sense,* March 9, 1907.

23. Alfred E. Sanftleben, "To My Critics," *Common Sense,* March 30, 1907; Josephine R. Cole, "In Defense of Woman Suffrage" [letter to editor], *Common Sense,* March 9, 1907; and Garbutt, "Thinks Criticisms Were Unjust." For more on conflicts over women's presence in the party, see Katz, "Dual Commitments," chapter 3.

24. Katz, "Redefining the Political."

25. Cole, "Women's Unions."
26. Ethel Whitehead, "Appeal to Socialist Women in the State of California," *Common Sense*, October 31, 1908.
27. Georgia Kotsch, "The Mission of the Socialist Woman," *Progressive Woman* 5 (August 1911): 13–14.
28. *Yellow Ribbon/ Western Woman* (San Francisco), October 1906-January/Feburary 1908. See also the *Woman's Journal*, 1888–1916, and the *Western Woman Voter*, 1911–13. Key collections containing suffrage materials include the Susan B. Anthony Memorial Collection (Ephemera), Huntington Library, San Marino, Calif. (HL); Alice (Locke) Park Collection, HL, hereafter Park Coll.; Caroline Maria (Seymour) Severance Collection, HL; Elizabeth Morrison (Boynton) Harbert Collection, HL; Friday Morning Club Scrapbooks Collection, HL, hereafter FMC Scrapbooks; Wood Coll.; Woman's Suffrage Scrapbook, compiled by Mrs. M. A. Holmes, Pasadena Historical Society, Pasadena, Calif., hereafter Suffrage Scrapbook; Amy C. Ransome Collection, Special Collections Department, University of Southern California, Los Angeles, Calif.; Alice Park Manuscripts, Department of Special Collections and University Archives, Stanford University, Palo Alto, Calif.; Alice Park Papers, Hoover Institution Library and Archives, Stanford University; Minutebook of California Equal Suffrage Association, Inc., 1904–10, California State Library, Sacramento, Calif.; Keith-McHenry-Pond Family Papers (Mary Keith), Bancroft Library, University of California, Berkeley (BL); Hester Harland Papers, BL; McLean Family Papers, BL.
29. Sherry J. Katz, "A Politics of Coalition: Socialist Women and the California Suffrage Movement, 1900–1911," in Marjorie Spruill Wheeler, ed., *One Woman, One Vote: Rediscovering the Woman Suffrage Movement* (Troutdale, Ore.: NewSage Press, 1995), 245–62.
30. Katz, "A Politics of Coalition," 252, 258.
31. For Park's "collecting zeal," see Ellen DuBois and Karen Kearns, *Votes for Women: A 75th Anniversary Album* (San Marino, Calif.: Huntington Library, 1995), 38, 41, 43; for the Park quote, see Alice Park to [Sarah J.] Eddy, December 3, 1918, box 5, Park Coll.
32. Ellen Carol DuBois, "Making Women's History: Historian-Activists of Women's Rights, 1880–1940," *Radical History Review* 49 (1991), reprinted in DuBois, *Woman Suffrage and Women's Rights*, 210–38, especially 228; DuBois and Kearns, *Votes for Women*, 38, 41, 43; Una R. Winter, ed., *Alice Park of California, Worker for Woman Suffrage and Children's Rights* (Upland, Calif.: [n.p.], 1948), 7–8, box 8, Park Coll. See note 28 for the Park collections.
33. Katz, "Dual Commitments," chapters 6–8; Katz, "Socialist Women," 117–43.
34. I consulted, for example, *The California Outlook* (Los Angeles), January 6, 1912-June 5, 1915; *The Woman's Bulletin* (Los Angeles), June 1912-April 1915; California State Federation of Labor, *Proceedings* ([San Francisco]: California State Federation of Labor) for 1909–16; *The Citizen* (Los Angeles), 1907–16; *Labor Clarion* (San Francisco), 1904–13; California Board of Control, Children's Department, *Report[s]* (Sacramento: California Printing Office) for 1914, 1916, and 1919; and Franklin Hichborn, *Story of the California Legislature* (San Francisco: James H. Barry), for 1911, 1913, and 1915.
35. Katz, "Dual Commitments," chapter 6, especially 510–26, 541–42n32, 553n61. Key primary sources included *The California Outlook; The Woman's Bulletin; California Social-Democrat; Los Angeles Record;* FMC Scrapbooks; Suffrage Scrapbook; John Randolph

Haynes Papers, Department of Special Collections, Charles E. Young Research Library, University of California, Los Angeles, hereafter Haynes Papers.

36. Katz, "Dual Commitments," chapter 6; Katz "Socialist Women," 121–27. For the quotes, see Estelle Lawton Lindsey, "Associated Charities Is Heartily in Favor of Mothers' Pension Law," *Los Angeles Record* [1913]; and E. A. Dickson, "'Mothers' Pensions'—Being a Survey of Constitutional Limitations upon Proposed Legislation," [*Los Angeles Examiner?*] February 13, 1913, box 161, Haynes Papers. National studies of mothers' pensions include Gordon, *Pitied but Not Entitled;* Molly Ladd-Taylor, *Mother-Work: Women, Child Welfare, and the State, 1890–1930* (Urbana: University of Illinois Press, 1994); Theda Skocpol, *Protecting Soldiers and Mothers: The Political Origins of Social Policy in the United States* (Cambridge, Mass.: Harvard University Press, 1992).

37. Many readers of my dissertation helped me to understand the difficulties of the list-like materials; see especially an anonymous reader's report from 1993 (in my possession). The quote is from Carl Becker, "Everyman His Own Historian," *American Historical Review* 37 (January 1932): 233–34, cited in Gerda Lerner, *Why History Matters: Life and Thought* (New York: Oxford University Press, 1997), 117.

38. For a discussion of the biographic difficulties and the sources utilized, see Katz, "Dual Commitments," 106–12. For the specific sketches, see Agnes Halpen Downing, "Mary Alderman Garbutt," *Socialist Woman* 2 (June 1908): 2, and A[gnes] H[alpen] D[owning], "Ethel Whitehead," *Socialist Woman* 2 (August 1908): 2.

39. Estelle Lawton Lindsey sketch, compiled by Clare Wallace, December 18, 1936, for the Works Progress Administration Project: City Officials, California Biography File, Los Angeles Public Library.

40. For the "ostracism" language, see Georgia Kotsch, "The Mission of the Socialist Woman," 13.

41. Gina [Morantz-Sanchez], letter to author, July 15, [1991] (in the author's possession).

42. [Frances Nacke Noel] to E[thel Duppy Turner], October 19, [19]11, Mellon Coll.

43. Noel to Turner, October 19, 1911, Mellon Coll.

44. Frances [Nacke Noel] to G[race Noel], [1913], Mellon Coll.

7. RECOVERING WOMEN'S VOICES IN COMMUNIST POLAND

Malgorzata Fidelis

Anyone who looks closely at women under communism in Eastern Europe is sure to encounter two contradictory images. In the popular press and scholarly literature alike, women were presented as either the beacons of communist liberation or the desperate victims of communist social exploitation. East European newspapers and other popular publications were rife with the liberation image, especially during the Stalinist period of 1948–56. This image was immortalized in political art by the "woman on the tractor," which illustrated two major aspects of women's emancipation under communism: paid employment and equal rights, symbolized by access to traditionally male jobs. According to this propaganda, the communist state liberated women from capitalist exploitation and offered personal fulfillment through employment and political activism.[1]

The second image presented a sharp contrast to such propaganda. In postcommunist popular and scholarly writings, women were often depicted as the victims of communism and postcommunism. In this view, communist emancipation was a sham that exploited female productive and reproductive labor. Women in Eastern Europe were overworked, burdened by the double duties of work outside and inside the household. Consequently, they became alienated and cultivated their maternal and familial identities in opposition to the production-oriented regime.[2] This victimization continued after the collapse of communism in 1989, when women were hurt, as evidenced by high unemployment statistics, job discrimination, domestic violence, and sex trafficking.[3]

What can one make of these two incongruent representations of women's experiences in post-1945 Eastern Europe? How can one recover women's voices from under the piles of propaganda materials, statistical numbers, and emotional (even if justified) interpretations of women's victimization under communism and postcommunism?

I address these questions in my own work, which focuses on women industrial workers in the context of postwar reconstruction and socialist state building in Poland. Most of my documents came from party and official trade union archives. They became accessible to researchers only after the collapse of communism in Eastern Europe in 1989. I was one of the first to look at the records of the Women's Sections of the Polish United Workers' Party (*Polska Zjednoczona Partia Robotnicza*, or PZPR), the ruling party in communist Poland. Even though the party archives are now open, scholars are hard-pressed to find documentation of women's voices untainted by party-state perspective. This essay focuses on a collection of readers' letters to the popular women's magazine *Girlfriend* (Przyjaciółka) in the late 1940s and early 1950s and oral history interviews. I found the letters as part of the party documentation and conducted oral interviews in 2002. Together, these materials provide new insights into women's lives that cannot be gained from institutional records and statistical studies alone.

A large portion of my current manuscript, titled *Women, Communism, and Industrialization in Postwar Poland*, focuses on how the communist regime understood gender differences and how it formulated policies aimed at the equality of the sexes. I consider diverse state actors—the Politburo, the trade union leaders, and local party officials—critical in shaping the work environment and gender relations in postwar Poland. I examine social responses to state policies, as well. These responses proved influential in how the new policies unfolded in everyday life. For example, pressures from local communities prompted the state to retreat from some of its more radical projects, such as promoting women to male-dominated skilled and managerial occupations. While archival collections allow me to examine institutional and ideological developments related to women's work, they alone cannot answer the crucial questions regarding women's identities and experiences.

Little research on women and communism outside the Soviet Union and East Germany exists in the historical literature.[4] Indeed, sociologists, anthropologists, and political scientists have produced most works on women in post-1945 Eastern Europe. The majority of this literature focuses on the transition from communism to liberal democracy, especially the so-called backlash against women exemplified in the new postcommunist elite's emphasis on women's maternal and domestic roles.[5] In comparison to the vast body of historical literature on women and gender in Western Europe and the United States, East European historiography on this subject is almost nonexistent. The scarcity of secondary sources makes the primary research particularly challenging.

Though reading the variety of material ranging from economic plans and political speeches to secret police reports and sociological research was painstaking, I sustained my efforts of traveling from one archive to another in search of women's voices. Eventually, I decided that I should use traditional and nontraditional sources. By traditional sources, I mean documents generated by party-state institutions that any historian of the communist era is bound to use. My goal was to extract any rare documents, or sections of documents, that contained statements by or about women that described women's perceptions of state policies or their experiences of everyday life. In addition to these conventional materials, I decided to create my own sources by conducting oral interviews with women who had worked in the specific workplaces I studied.

As I began my research, I expected to find women's stories about the difficulties of everyday life in the context of political repression and endemic material shortages. Instead, I found complex and lively characters who actively shaped their identities through their interaction with state institutions. By carefully reading letters and listening to women's stories, I discovered not only the richness and diversity of women's experiences, but also the complex relationship between individuals and a totalitarian state.[6]

The letters and interviews point to women as active historical subjects rather than passive recipients of communist messages and policies. They also reveal that women's identities under communism cannot be understood apart from state-sponsored identities, such as those of labor heroines or dutiful workers and household managers. This does not mean that women uncritically accepted state-imposed models. Rather, they negotiated and redefined them in the context of traditional cultural values, new policies, and everyday experiences. For example, they often became accomplished and dedicated workers but resisted joining the party and openly criticized policies they found harmful to the workers and their families. In this sense, the letters and oral interviews reveal not only experiences of women, but also their agency. They illuminate the ways in which individuals and groups interacted with a totalitarian state and point to women's attempts to influence those policies that they perceived as incongruent with the communist promise of equality and justice.

WOMEN AND COMMUNISM IN POLAND: HISTORICAL BACKGROUND

Equality of the sexes was one of the main tenets of communist ideology. The founding fathers of communism, Karl Marx and Frederick Engels, recognized the subordinate position of women in capitalist societies. They advocated the incorporation of women into economic production as part of uplifting the working class and creating a new classless society. Bolshevik leaders in revolutionary Russia implemented these ideas by establishing the legal equality of the sexes, extending mass employment to women, and conducting political indoctrination to make women, traditionally connected to the domestic sphere, into equals to male workers and political activists.[7] At the end of World War II, Soviet leaders backed by the victorious Red Army carried these revolutionary ideas to East European states.

In 1945 the communist-dominated coalition government in Poland abolished remnants of interwar discriminatory legislation and established equal legal rights for men and women. After the imposition of one-party dictatorship in December 1948, equal legal rights and compulsory civil marriage were confirmed by the Constitution of the Polish People's Republic of 1952. The constitution also granted women equal pay for equal work and equal rights within the family.[8] Furthermore, the Family Code of 1950 demanded that both women and men contribute to the work within the household and to raising children. In contrast to prewar law, mothers now acquired custody rights and single mothers earned the right to child support from the father or the state.[9]

The Polish Family Code, however, placed significant restrictions on women's freedoms. The laws were modeled on contemporary Soviet regulations and reflected Stalinist amendments to the revolutionary Soviet legislation of the 1920s. As in the contemporary Soviet Union, divorce was difficult to obtain and abortion remained illegal, except when a women's life was in danger or when the pregnancy resulted from rape or incest.[10] In this way, the communist state promoted both productive and reproductive roles for women as equally important.

During the rapid Stalinist industrialization of the Six-Year Plan (1950–55), Polish communists launched a powerful campaign to promote women's mass employment. Legal equality, mass female employment, and political education of women were revolutionary changes imposed on a predominantly agricultural and Catholic Polish society that was also traditionally anti-Russian and anti-Soviet.[11] How women adjusted to these rapid social and economic transformations is a critical historical question.

LETTERS TO *GIRLFRIEND:* BETWEEN TRADITION AND CHANGE

The bulk of the primary material on gender policies in postwar Poland are found at the Archive of New Documents (*Archiwum Akt Nowych*) in Warsaw in the records of the Polish United Workers' Party (*Polska Zjednoczona Partia Robotnicza*, or PZPR), the ruling party in communist Poland. At first glimpse, party documents seem to rarely reflect female voices or individual concerns. Even the meetings specifically devoted to women's issues or the extensive collection of the documents of the PZPR Women's Section focus primarily on party membership, party women's activism, employment statistics, and implementing specific communist policies. Thus even the archival documentation that is specifically devoted to women must be sieved through and often read against the grain to retrieve women's voices.

The communist archives teach us that collections consciously devoted to preserving documents about women do not necessarily reflect a range of women's identities and perspectives. It is difficult to talk about women as a marginalized group in communist societies, because significant efforts were made to incorporate women into economic and political life. Rather, women, much like workers and peasants, functioned in party documents as an ideological category. The category of "woman" denoted primarily a member of a gender group oppressed by the capitalist system and on the way to inevitable emancipation by the workers' revolution. In the process of constructing this idea of womanhood, the communist state reinvented gender differences and recreated the inferior status of women in society in new ways and on new terms. Working with communist sources thus requires taking apart layers of state agenda to see women as historical actors in their own right.

One place where women express agency is in letters to the popular magazine *Girlfriend*, which are part of the archival collection of the Women's Section. This separate women's chapter in the Polish party existed from 1948 to 1952. Women's letters are featured in the typed reports prepared by *Girlfriend*'s editor-in-chief, Anna Lanota, and sent to party headquarters. As historian Sheila Fitzpatrick has noted, communist regimes suppressed uncensored people's views in public, but at the same time they were "extremely anxious to know what people were thinking."[12] As a result, editors of newspapers and periodicals were obliged to regularly report summaries of readers' correspondence to the Party Central Committee. The letters I analyzed are thus selective because they focus on issues that were of interest to the party. Nevertheless, they provide genuine voices of working women with no interference from censorship. Lanota provided extensive summaries of topics and concerns expressed in these letters. Most of the surviving reports came from 1949 to 1950, the time of transition from the relatively pluralist society of 1945–48 to a Stalinist dictatorship.

My interpretation of women's letters and other documents was guided by my understanding of totalitarianism as a system that was shaped not only from above, but also from below. The state's intrusion into the private lives of citizens is at the core of most discussions of gender and communism in

Eastern Europe. But as historian and sociologist Jan Gross suggests in the context of the Soviet conquest of eastern Poland in 1939, the fusion of the public and the private under communism "occurs not because of the confiscation of the private realm by the state but primarily because of the *privatization of the public realm.*" During the brutal Sovietization of Poland's Western Ukraine and Western Belarus, individuals and groups often used the new state "against other members of society" in pursuit of their own social and economic interests.[13] To maintain its monopoly of power and ensure "that *no one else* can get things done," the communist state had to work through and with individuals.[14]

Although Gross's analysis refers to the Stalinist system in the extreme circumstances of war and occupation, the communist monopoly of power ensured that the state remained the only entity through which people could channel their concerns and receive assistance during peacetime. Curiously, this state monopoly of power empowered individuals in unexpected ways. "Precisely because totalitarianism depends for its success on spoiling individuals—on sowing mistrust and demoralization, or by outright killing—the refusal of a single individual to share these ways represents a decisive challenge to the regime."[15] Letters to *Girlfriend* testify to the powers of individual women to challenge the authority of the state and negotiate their own place in a communist society.

After its creation in 1948, *Girlfriend* was by far the most popular periodical in communist Poland. It was first created as a weekly for women blue-collar workers, in particular. Its wide readership, however, included women from all social strata, as well as men. In the 1950s, *Girlfriend* published two million copies that sold out quickly without satisfying the popular demand.[16] Large numbers of readers' letters testified to the magazine's enormous popularity. In 1949–50, *Girlfriend* received between 250 and 550 letters daily.[17] Correspondence from women workers and workers' wives constituted 65 percent of those letters.[18] The magazine published a small fraction of these letters (five to six per issue). Although this essay discusses unpublished material, similar letters, with the exception of those pertaining to religious practices, appeared in the magazine. They were usually accompanied by an extensive editorial commentary instructing readers on the correct interpretation of the problems discussed.

As with all other newspapers and magazines, *Girlfriend* was printed by a state publishing house and served the political goals of the communist regime. It was, in particular, designed to promote new roles for women as socialist citizens. But even a cursory look at the magazine reveals a curious mixture of old and new ideas. During the Stalinist industrial drive, the magazine was at the forefront of promoting female mass employment and encouraging male-dominated occupations for women. But often the same issue featured traditional female roles by providing advice on cleaning, cooking, and child rearing as exclusively feminine domains. It also featured fashion and templates for sewing clothes at home.

This mixture of new and traditional ideas about womanhood made *Girlfriend* especially appealing to women of diverse social strata and political views. To women who subscribed to Polish and Catholic traditions that emphasized women's maternal identity, it provided assurance of their feminine distinctiveness. To women who were progressive and interested in social advancement, *Girlfriend* promoted equal rights and condemned traditional assumptions about the necessity of confining women to the domestic sphere. In addition, the emphasis on everyday life and regular featuring of readers' correspondence made the magazine seem less explicitly ideological and propagandistic than other contemporary publications. This quality was significant in building credibility in a society generally hostile to the communist system and wary of Soviet political domination.

The letters illuminated aspects of women's identities, such as religious identities, that were rarely mentioned in party documents and official publications. The Catholic religion was particularly important for women in their familial and patriotic roles. The bond between Catholicism and Polish national identity was strengthened in the nineteenth century during the partitions of Poland to Russia, Prussia, and Austria.[19] In the countryside, Catholic beliefs and rituals were the backbone of women's roles as guardians of morality and community traditions.

Many women protested against communist attempts to eradicate religion from public life. For example, they criticized the removal of religious instruction from schools and the elimination of religious songs and live broadcasts of Sunday holy mass.[20] Few of these women, however, expressed their concerns in a hostile manner. Rather, women claimed to be confused by antireligious policies. They wrote to the magazine asking for further explanation and help.

The best illustration of this confusion and frustration with the regime's policies was a letter from a group of oil miners' wives from the town of Gorlice in southern Poland: "Give us advice on how to act, when they are taking away religious icons and even crosses from schools," they wrote. "We feel sad, when we read that there is a freedom of religious beliefs, but what we see is quite the opposite. We don't know what to think about it, and would like to ask you to reply as soon as possible. We go to work with the word 'God Bless You,' and we say these words to our husbands, who are going to the mine, because only this one word gives them courage to fulfill the [production] norm."²¹ In this letter, religious and communist ideas are intertwined. The miners' wives were a group of traditional women, and like coal miners' wives, they rarely entered wage work. Instead, they devoted themselves to their husbands, households, and children. These women claimed to be surprised and confused when the workers' state attempted to shatter miners' most cherished traditions.

Another woman expressed alienation from the new system after experiencing antireligious agitation by the League of Women, an official women's organization, at a local meeting in her town. Up until this experience, this woman and her husband had supported the communist system and considered joining the party. The author of the letter juxtaposed how her understanding of patriotism differed from that of the communist state: "When my husband, brother, and father fought for the Fatherland, I prayed to God to save them, and to return our Fatherland free to us; and now in this Fatherland, they persecute religion; they say that people should not go to church and that we should not teach children prayers. . . . I decided not to go to any party meetings anymore and won't let my husband attend these meetings either, where there are more lies than truth."²²

Letters like these clearly indicated that *Girlfriend*, a state-run magazine, succeeded in gaining the trust of its female readers. Women believed that the editors must be, as they often claimed, on the side of women. In fact, *Girlfriend* offered contradictory messages about religion. While the magazine did not abstain from endorsing the "secularization" promoted by the Stalinist regime, it nonetheless provided advice on how to celebrate religious holidays, including dressing up children and arranging a party for the First Communion.²³

Women's letters about religion reveal the deep struggle of traditional Polish society with revolutionary social and political changes. As it turns out, many women did not necessarily consider their Catholicism opposed to the state until the Stalinist regime intensified its repressive policies toward the church. Eventually, Catholics had to accept the elimination of most of their religious symbols from public life. But the regime also made religious concessions. The Church remained the only independent institution in Poland outside of government control. This fact would prove instrumental in facilitating anticommunist opposition in the years to come, an opposition that eventually brought down the entire communist system.²⁴

Rather than succumbing to state propaganda, women contested the meaning of political messages they heard. Some women simply did not agree with the official exaltation of productive labor and the designation of homemakers as "nonworking women." One homemaker wrote: "Can we call a woman, whose family consists of six people, including three small children, and who is taking care of the household herself a nonworking woman, only because she cannot afford to hire domestic help?"[25] Other women noted that paid work that was to serve as the basis for gender equality was in fact unavailable to many women. A female reader from Kraków in her lengthy letter to *Girlfriend* vividly described her and other women's experiences of looking for work at the local employment office:

> I'll tell you about one such day of standing in line at Lubelska street—for instance on Saturday, May 7, 1949, I was standing all the time from 5 to 10, so I am standing like this every day and there is no work and there is still no work—people are standing there . . . young ones, old ones, mothers with kids, they're all standing around me. And this woman, she's got five kids and her husband has one of those seasonal jobs, so it's been all winter and he's still out of work and they've got nothing at home—no food—so she comes here—maybe she'll get something sooner, otherwise they're gonna throw her out of her place. . . . There're also these ladies standing here who found work by themselves, they came to Lubelska street for assignment—but they didn't get it, they're making problems for them just so that there should be more people with no work, so that there's more suffering, more complaining, more curses—because if there is some good position, some good job, then the party people get it, their friends, the ones they're looking out for—well, and there are the ones who give a bribe. And there're these women coming who already got an assignment and they're coming back, 'cause in the factory they say that they're not suited for the work, that they don't have the skills. . . . So the office clerk opens that little window—he's not listening to what people are saying, if they're pleading with him, he doesn't care about anything, only he says first, who has a letter, well, no one [does] . . . the window slams, again waiting, after a while the window goes up again, but only a crack, if the guy hears, "Excuse me, sir"—then it slams again, so now they're knocking on the window, he opens the window and says: "There is no work."[26]

This dramatic account of unemployed women facing an indifferent state bureaucracy revealed another contradiction in the state's approach to women: the communist regime glorified paid employment but fell short of providing it to everyone. Women were still less valued as workers than men. By pointing to contradictions in state policies, women challenged ideological underpinnings of the state and implicitly questioned the communist commitment to the workers' well-being and women's rights.

Multiple identities and diverse concerns emerge from women's letters to *Girlfriend*. One is tempted to stress women's attachments to traditional values, such as religion, but one cannot ignore the League of Women and female party members who actively sought to weaken or even uproot traditional understandings of gender roles. The deep rifts that existed among women depended on their social class, political beliefs, generation, place of residence, and personal experiences. Nonetheless, all of these women engaged in a dialogue with the state by voicing their concerns and asking questions.

Looking for women's voices in communist sources brings to light unexpected elements of the social and political context. In this sense, the letters are more than windows into women's lives: they provide glimpses into multiple dimensions of the communist system. We do not usually think about popular culture as a significant part of communist societies. Yet popular magazines played an important role in everyday life, because they facilitated interaction between state and society. Politicized popular culture, more often described in scholarly literature as propaganda, backfired and served as an important forum to channel voices of ordinary men and women, who were typically excluded from official discussions.

"NOT JUST HARD WORK": REMEMBERING COMMUNISM THROUGH ORAL HISTORY

Because of censorship and the preponderance of party-state perspectives in documents produced during the communist period, oral histories can serve as a compelling source of voices from below. In this section, I discuss the interviews I conducted with women workers from the linen factory in Żyrardów near Warsaw, and with women who worked in coal mines aboveground (in the sorting house and coal transportation) in and around the city of Katowice in Upper Silesia (southern Poland). The latter engaged in typical women's jobs in coal mines. They performed physically demanding, low-paying manual labor that placed women at the bottom of the hierarchy of mining jobs.

Conducting interviews was the most enjoyable part of my research. I traveled through central and southern Poland, learning the Silesian dialects and tasting local foods.[27] Since the bulk of my sources came from the archives, I used interviews only as supplementary material. Most interviews were arranged by friends and local researchers. I used two basic criteria while selecting interviewees: they had to be females who held blue-collar jobs at specific factories and mines I studied; and they had to have worked there in the 1940s and/or the 1950s.[28] My interviewees were eager to share their stories and frequently digressed on other interesting topics, most of them related to developments in contemporary Poland and local gossip.

Indeed, reflections on the present set the tone for the conversations about the past, at least at the beginning of each interview. Most women had positive memories of the communist period.²⁹ Women often expressed anger and bitterness toward the new postcommunist political elites and economic reforms that virtually eradicated industrial workers as a significant social group. Women were unhappy with high rates of unemployment, high prices of food items, and widespread corruption. In this context, they remembered communism as a time of stability.

When I entered the house of Pani Rozalia³⁰ in Żyrardów, three former spinners, now in their seventies, greeted me warmly. They invited me to a table with cookies, pretzels, and hot tea. Pani Rozalia, Pani Maria, and Pani Aniela represented three different types of personalities. Pani Maria was a leader. She was the one to organize this meeting at the request of my friend who lives in Żyrardów. Pani Aniela was the embodiment of calmness: "One needs to choose what one wants to stress about," she said. Pani Rozalia, the hostess, was the least outspoken and preoccupied with making her guests comfortable.³¹

Like typical female textile workers in Poland, all three women worked in the factory and raised families at the same time. Maria and Aniela had two children each, while Rozalia had three. All three women could not come to terms with the fact that the Żyrardów factories, in which they had worked for many years, were closed down during the economic reforms of the early 1990s. The meeting seemed to be guided by one implicit motto: in the old times, there was work; now there is none.

Catholicism was visible from the moment I entered most of my interviewees' homes. Pani Wanda, former seamstress and labor heroine from the Żyrardów sewing shop, displayed a collection of religious icons in her living room with a sizable portrait of Pope John Paul II in the center. Since this was Pani Wanda's name day, my friend and I brought her flowers and a box of chocolates. She invited us to a table full of appetizers: cold meats, pickles, and salads. She also poured three glasses of vodka with caramel, an old recipe, as she explained, that only older people in Żyrardów remembered. Pani Wanda was glad to have company. She had recently lost her husband, and her two daughters lived in other parts of Poland.

As in most of my interviews, I did not use a tape recorder while talking with Pani Wanda, but rather made copious notes during and immediately after the meeting. Women were more relaxed and open if the tape recorder was switched off. Pani Wanda often broke into tears as she recalled the times when she was a valued worker and a League of Women activist in charge of providing material help to female workers and their families. "My life was hard," she said, "but I always tried to help other people. I like helping people, because it breaks my heart to look at people's misery."³²

I experienced a similar warm welcome by women in Silesia. Born in 1920, Pani Anna, a former sorting-house worker in the "Wieczorek" mine in Katowice, was significantly older than most of my interviewees. She lived in an early-twentieth-century coal miners' cottage, the so-called *familiok*. In the early 1950s, she was a brigade leader and labor heroine: "They carried my portrait during the May Day parade," she recalled with pride.[33] Her husband worked on the surface in the same coal mine as she did, and they had two daughters.

The longest and liveliest interview I conducted was the one with Pani Zuzanna and Pani Janina. They both worked in heavy physical jobs on the surface in the "Kleofas" and "Murcki" coal mines near Katowice, respectively: they pushed carts loaded with coal. Pani Janina eventually married a male coal miner and became a full-time homemaker and a mother of three. Pani Zuzanna worked before and after marriage while raising two sons.[34]

Scholars have extensively studied issues of gender and memory.[35] They have devoted much attention to the question of whether oral histories of women are distinct from oral testimonies of men.[36] It is difficult to answer this question with regard to East European communism, because of the scarcity of oral histories collected there. From my preliminary observations, however, it was clear that some conventional arguments developed by Western scholars, such as the contention that women's testimonies tend to focus on domestic life, did not always apply to my subjects. The women I interviewed expressed strong work identities and were more willing to talk about their work experiences than their families or intimate lives. This pattern was prevalent especially in the industrial region of Upper Silesia.[37]

This did not mean, however, that women talked about their work in the same way as men. I was struck by their persistent emphasis on the significance of work aboveground to the process of coal extraction. The pace of work and the amount of coal delivered often depended on how fast the sorting-house women were able to do their jobs. Women's narratives of dedication and hard labor in managing the coal after it reached the surface asks for revising the established history of coal mining based on the superiority of underground work. In this sense, the testimonies did more than "fill the gaps" in archival and published sources. They provided a new perspective on coal mining, gender, and labor.

My approach was to let women talk as extensively and freely as possible.[38] Rather than leading them to answer my specific questions, I wanted to see what issues were important to them. I usually started by asking them how they began to work at a specific factory or mine. Their responses turned into fascinating stories about material hardships, looking for work, interactions with state bureaucracy, and experiences in the workplace. They described with incredible detail their work: the equipment they operated, the protective gear and work uniforms they wore, the daily schedule, the surroundings of their workplace, and their coworkers and bosses. Surprisingly, women stressed enjoyment associated with work. If they talked about hardships, they did so to emphasize the qualities of their characters rather than to condemn the political and economic system.

Work outside the home in both Żyrardów and Katowice shaped women's identities in powerful ways. Women discussed discomforts associated with their work: long hours of work (coal miners worked on Saturdays and sometimes Sundays during the early 1950s), conflicts with supervisors, and difficulties in obtaining privileges granted more frequently to male workers, such as new apartments. But all women I talked to warned me against interpreting their work experiences in a negative light. Pani Anna stressed that what she did in the mine "was not just hard labor."[39] The workplace was also a place where she found joy in accomplishing her tasks. It was a site of sociability. Women met husbands and lovers and bonded with other women in the workplace. "After the shift," another female worker, Zuzanna, recalled, "we [women] would take a shower. We all bathed together, young or old, thin or fat.... We would wash each other's backs, and then we would go shopping together and stand in line to get coffee. There was so much friendliness, and we had fun."[40]

Although most women, as most men, worked for economic reasons, once on the job, they tended to develop emotional attachments to their workplace. In addition, Zuzanna pointed to solidarity and mutual support among women. In her story, the shared experience of work held a potential for leveling differences based on age and other marks of external appearance. Even food lines, a dreaded feature of communist systems, were a source of forming positive social bonds with female coworkers.

Many women saw their wage work as advancement from poverty. Most women I interviewed came from poor villages and started to work as teenagers to help out the family. They were attached to their rural religious identities but did not have problems accommodating their beliefs to their productive roles and even political activism. Pani Wanda, for example, did not see her Catholicism as incongruent with her strong commitment to work and activism in the League of Women.[41] Most likely, this accommodation of religious identities was facilitated by party-state concessions to the overwhelmingly Catholic population. Thus the new arrivals from the countryside often became dedicated and valued workers. Like Pani Anna from Katowice, Pani Wanda and Pani Aniela from Żyrardów attained the status of so-called labor heroines for exceeding production quotas. This status gave them privileges, such as higher wages and sometimes new apartments.

Like female textile workers, female coal miners considered their work to be a significant source of self-esteem. Despite their low social status, women working on the surface developed their own work culture and codes of honor. They established boundaries regarding sexual behavior and acceptable interactions between females and males. If men transgressed those unofficial rules, women exacted punishment. "There was a window in our bathroom, and men climbed up to peep in," recounted Zuzanna. "If women caught the guy, they would push him under the shower and soak him completely. They would take away all his clothes and then release him home."[42] By punishing the trespasser, women asserted control over their space at the workplace. They reversed the roles of the voyeur and the exposed by undressing the man. They did to him what he intended to do to them: violate their intimate space and potentially their bodies.

According to the women I interviewed, wage work was a significant part of their identities. Despite difficult work conditions and familial responsibilities, women refused to reduce their work experience simply to the issue of hardship. Rather, the factory and mine provided opportunities for social advancement, interaction with other people, and enhancing self-esteem. Romanticizing the past was a significant component of women's memories, and this needs to be taken into consideration while assessing the experiences of women under communism. But one should be careful not to discount these sentiments as mere nostalgia.[43] Historical actors assign meaning to their experiences through working and reworking their memories. As these interviews demonstrate, the meaning that many women assigned to their work experiences involved acknowledging the harsh and demanding nature of their labor but ultimately defining wage work as heroic and personally rewarding. This is their history as told in their own voices.

CONCLUSION

The sources described here are mere archival fragments of the vast materials open to historians exploring women's lives under communism in Eastern Europe. The letters to *Girlfriend* and my oral interviews remind us that these women were agents, not passive recipients or victims of communist social and economic life. I believe that other East European countries hold collections of party documents containing women's voices much like the letters to *Girlfriend,* waiting to be unearthed by researchers. These hidden treasures illuminate more than women's experiences, because they offer new perspectives on the social and political conditions that shaped women's lives.

Recovering women's voices reveals the diverse experiences of womanhood under communism. The communist state demanded women's unique contribution to socialist society as both workers and mothers, such that they built a strong state while they nurtured the future communist generation. Although full-time employment placed additional burdens on women's everyday lives, such work also allowed them to escape poverty and discover new ways of life in an urban industrial setting. In addition, paid work gave women legitimacy as members of the workers' state. In the process, women exchanged ideas about the terms of their participation in the communist project with agents of the state, from factory managers to editors of the communist press.

How can historians accurately interpret the disparate images of women in post-1945 Eastern Europe? As my research shows, we should resist simple categories of liberation and exploitation. Instead, we must collect and examine women's personal testimonies from archival documents and oral interviews, in order to see clearly the complexity of women's experiences during this period. This research will strengthen other historical work on Eastern Europe, which is now exploring how both individuals and social groups shaped the political and social reality of the era.[44] Discovering and documenting women's experiences will help us to better understand the impact of totalitarian states on gender norms and, just as important, how gender ideology shapes the trajectory of totalitarian states.

NOTES

I would like to thank Andrea Davies Henderson, the editors of this collection, and the anonymous reviewers for their valuable comments and suggestions.

1. On employment policies and women in male-dominated jobs in postwar Poland, see Malgorzata Fidelis, "Equality through Protection: The Politics of Women's Employment in Postwar Poland, 1945–1956," *Slavic Review* 63 (Summer 2004): 301–24.

2. See, for example, Donna Harsch, *Revenge of the Domestic: Women, the Family, and Communism in the German Democratic Republic* (Princeton, N.J.: Princeton University Press, 2007), 1.

3. For feminist perspectives on postcommunism, see, for example, Tanya Renne, ed., *Ana's Land: Sisterhood in Eastern Europe* (Boulder: Westview Press, 1997). Kristen Ghodsee has recently disputed the dominant view on women as "losers" in the postcommunist transition. See Kristen Ghodsee, "Feminism-by-Design: Emerging Capitalism, Cultural Feminism, and Women's Nongovernmental Organizations in Postsocialist Eastern Europe," *Signs* 29 (2004): 727–53.

4. See, for example, Barbara Wolfe Jancar, *Women under Communism* (Baltimore: Johns Hopkins University Press, 1978); Tova Yedlin, ed., *Women in Eastern Europe and the Soviet Union* (New York: Praeger, 1980); and Sharon L. Wolchik and Alfred G. Meyer, eds., *Women, State, and Party in Eastern Europe* (Durham, N.C.: Duke University Press, 1985). The more extensive historical literature on women in East Germany is an exception because of the broader scholarly interest in social history of the GDR. See, for example,

Gunilla-Friederike Budde, ed., *Frauen arbeiten: Weibliche Erwerbstätigkeit in Ost- und Westdeutschland nach 1945* (Göttingen: Vandenhoeck and Ruprecht, 1997); Elizabeth D. Heineman, *What Difference Does a Husband Make? Women and Marital Status in Nazi and Postwar Germany* (Berkeley: University of California Press, 1999); and Harsch, *Revenge of the Domestic*.

5. See, for example, Susan Gal and Gail Kligman, eds., *Reproducing Gender: Politics, Publics, and Everyday Life after Socialism* (Princeton, N.J.: Princeton University Press, 2000); Barbara Einhorn, *Cinderella Goes to Market: Citizenship, Gender and Women's Movements in East-Central Europe* (London: Verso, 1993); and Nanette Funk and Magda Mueller, eds., *Gender Politics and Post-Communism: Reflections from Eastern Europe and the Former Soviet Union* (New York: Routledge, 1993).

6. Characterizing East European communist regimes as totalitarian is disputed in the historical literature. Some historians consider the Polish party-state authoritarian rather than totalitarian. I discuss my understanding of Polish Stalinism on page 9.

7. On gender roles in revolutionary Russia, see Elizabeth A. Wood, *The Baba and the Comrade: Gender and Politics in Revolutionary Russia* (Bloomington: Indiana University Press, 1997).

8. Hoover Institution Archive, Mikolajczyk, Box 151, "The Text of the Polish (Communist) New Draft Constitution," March 1952, 18.

9. Jan Winiarz, *Ochrona praw matki, dziecka i rodziny* (Warsaw: Wydawnictwo Prawnicze, 1954), 25–32.

10. See articles 231 and 232 in Józef Fajnberg and Mikołaj Leonieni, eds., *Kodeks Karny z orzecznictwem sądu powojennego według stanu prawnego na dzień 1 sierpnia, 1956* (Warsaw: Wydawnictwo Prawnicze, 1956), 221. On the Soviet abortion legislation in the 1930s, see Mary Buckley, *Women and Ideology in the Soviet Union* (Ann Arbor: University of Michigan Press, 1989), 128–37.

11. The Russian Empire, along with Prussia and Austria, participated in the partitions of the Polish-Lithuanian Commonwealth in 1772, 1793, and 1795. In the nineteenth century, the Polish population was subject to repression and intense Russification. Anti-Russian sentiments were strengthened in the twentieth century. In September 1939, the Red Army invaded eastern Poland as a result of the Ribbentrop-Molotov Pact, which divided Poland between Nazi Germany and the Soviet Union. The Soviets used terror, mass arrests, and deportations to impose their rule. See Jan T. Gross, *Revolution from Abroad: The Soviet Conquest of Poland's Western Ukraine and Western Belorussia*, 2nd ed. (Princeton, N.J.: Princeton University Press, 2002).

12. Sheila Fitzpatrick, *Everyday Stalinism, Ordinary Life in Extraordinary Times: Soviet Russia in the 1930s* (New York: Oxford University Press, 1999), 164.

13. Gross, *Revolution from Abroad*, 117.

14. Ibid., 234.

15. Ibid., 236.

16. Zofia Sokół, *Prasa kobieca w Polsce w latach 1945–1995* (Rzeszów: Wydawnictwo Wyższej Szkoły Pedagogicznej, 1998), 403.

17. Archiwum Akt Nowych (AAN), Polska Zjednoczona Partia Robotnicza (PZPR), Komitet Centralny (KC), Wydział Kobiecy (WK), 237/XV/31, Listy do redakcji "Przyjaciółki," Sprawozdanie za okres od 17 września do 1 listopada, 1949, k. 135; and

AAN, PZPR, KC, WK, 237/XV/31, Listy do redakcji "Przyjaciółki." Sprawozdanie za okres dwutygodniowy, March 12, 1949, kk. 34–46, 34.

18. AAN, PZPR, KC, WK, 237/V/180, Sekretariat, Redakcja "Przyjaciółka," Sprawozdanie za okres od 1 sierpnia do 10 października, 1950, kk. 1–18, 1.

19. The popular image of Polish women during the time of partitions is associated with the concept of *Matka Polka* (Polish mother and patriot), responsible for raising sons-fighters for national independence and maintaining Polish traditions and Catholic religion at home. For further discussion, see Katherine R. Jolluck, *Exile and Identity: Polish Women in the Soviet Union during World War II* (Pittsburgh: University of Pittsburgh Press, 2002), especially 87–89.

20. AAN, PZPR, KC, WK, 237/XV-31, Listy do redakcji "Przyjaciółki." Sprawozdanie za okres dwutygodniowy, March 12, 1949, kk. 34–38.

21. AAN, KC, PZPR, WK, 237/XV/31, Listy do Redakcji "Przyjaciółki." Sprawozdanie za okres dwutygodniowy, February 26, 1949, kk. 19–33, 22.

22. AAN, KC, PZPR, WK, 237/XV/31, Listy do Redakcji "Przyjaciółki." Sprawozdanie za okres dwutygodniowy, February 26, 1949, k. 23.

23. Mg. "Do Pierwszej Komunii," *Przyjaciółka*, June 6, 1948, 9.

24. On the church and state relations in communist Poland, see Hanna Diskin, *The Seeds of Triumph: Church and State in Gomułka's Poland* (Budapest: Central European University Press, 2001).

25. AAN, PZPR, KC, 237/V/180, Redakcja Przyjaciółki, Listy interwencyjne 1950–53, Sprawozdanie z listów czytelników, 1950, kk. 34–51, 49.

26. AAN KC PZPR WK, 237/XV-31, Listy do redakcji "Przyjaciółki." Sprawozdanie za okres sześciotygodniowy, June 1, 1949, kk. 66–80, 70–71. I would like to thank Marci Shore for help with translating this document.

27. Upper Silesia is a historic Polish-German borderland. Even today, many inhabitants have a strong sense of local rather than modern national identity. They speak a distinct Silesian language (a Slavic language with German borrowings).

28. For my book project I interviewed a total of nineteen women and one man. They came from three different industrial centers in Poland: Żyrardów, Zambrów, and Katowice/Upper Silesia. This essay discusses only a portion of these interviews.

29. The idealization of the communist era is common in present-day women's testimonies in Poland. See, for example, Dobrochna Kałwa and Ewelina Szpak, "'Die besten Tage meines Lebens . . .' Der Alltag in den Staatlichen Landwirtschaftsbetrieben aus Sicht der oral history," in *Geschlechterbeziehungen in Ostmitteleuropa nach dem Zweiten Weltkrieg*, ed. Claudia Kraft (Munich: Oldenbourg, 2008), 277–90.

30. "Pani" and "Pan" are the common forms of addressing women and men, respectively, in Polish society. The custom derives from the traditions of the Polish nobility in the premodern era that eventually spread to lower classes.

31. Aniela K., Maria M., and Rozalia L., interview by author, Żyrardów, October 19, 2002. All personal names have been changed.

32. Wanda L., interview by author, Żyrardów, October 19, 2002.

33. Anna J., interview by author, Katowice-Nikiszowiec, December 2, 2002.

34. Janina L. and Zuzanna M., interview by author, tape recording, Studzienice, November 22, 2002.

35. See, for example, Selma Leydesdorff, Luisa Passerini, and Paul Thompson, eds., *Gender and Memory* (New Brunswick, N.J.: Transaction, 2005); Sherna Berger Gluck, "Women's Oral History: Is It So Special?" in *Handbook of Oral History*, ed. Thomas L. Charlton, Lois E. Myers, and Rebecca Sharpless (Lanham, N.Y.: Altamira Press, 2006), 357–83; and Joanna Bornat and Hanna Diamond, "Women's History and Oral History: Developments and Debates," *Women's History Review* 16 (2007): 19–39. For my book I used oral testimonies only sporadically, as a supplementary source to archival materials.

36. Gluck, "Women's Oral History," 357–83. Recent approaches stress the plurality of voices among women. Scholars have identified other categories, such as social, ethnic, and cultural backgrounds, as significant in affecting the memory of the interviewee. See Selma Leydesdorff, Luisa Passerini, and Paul Thompson, "Introduction," in Leydersdorff, Passerini, and Thompson, eds., *Gender and Memory*, 1–30, especially 5.

37. A group of sociologists that conducted an oral history project in the 1990s regarding Upper Silesian identity found that men as well as women stressed the experience of work in their life stories. "One of the interviewed—an inhabitant of Siemianowice working in the confectioner's factory, tells us with great details about her relations with superiors, with colleagues from work, about conflicts occurring at work and solving them and only casually mentions such important matters for her as the birth of two daughters. Of course, we should not conclude that family life is neglected by the examined. One must notice, however, that in relations about work there are purely emotional plots which are missing in the stories about their adult family life. The latter are often told in a very objective, definite way, whereas for example stories about conflict at work are filled with colour and point to emotions." Krzysztof Łęcki, Kazimiera Wódz, Jacek Wódz, Piotr Wróblewski, "The Elements of the Social World of the Silesians," *Region and Regionalism, Prace naukowe Uniwersytetu Śląskiego* nr. 1469, Katowice 1995, 76–93, quotation on 87–88.

38. On different techniques in conducting oral interviews, see Susan Geiger, "Women's Life Histories: Method and Content," *Signs* 11 (1986): 334–51.

39. Anna J., interview.

40. Janina L. and Zuzanna M., interview.

41. Wanda L., interview.

42. Janina L. and Zuzanna M., interview.

43. Basia A. Nowak, "'There Is Nowhere to Turn to Today': Women Reinventing a Communist Past," *Ohio Slavic Papers*, "Beyond *Little Vera*: Women's Bodies, Women's Welfare in Russia and Central/Eastern Europe," vol. 7 (2008): 111–30.

44. See, for example, Padraic Kenney, *Rebuilding Poland: Workers and Communists, 1945–1950* (Ithaca, N.Y.: Cornell University Press, 1997).

8. ARCHIVAL THINKING AND THE WIVES OF MARCUS GARVEY

Ula Y. Taylor

Although most historians remember the 1980s as a Republican decade (marked by the presidencies of Ronald Reagan and George H. W. Bush), some of us recall it as the blossoming of African American women's history. I began college in 1980 and was fortunate enough to enroll in two courses that inspired my scholarly interest: one on the history of prostitution, taught by Professor Mary Elizabeth Perry, and one on twentieth-century women's history, taught by Professor Kathryn Kish Sklar. Prior to these classes, I had never imagined that I would become a professional historian. But the personal stories of African American women made me feel firmly connected to distant places and eras. As I read, I would often imagine the lyrical sound of these women's voices, the slight tilts of their heads. Once I read Rosalyn Terborg-Penn's seminal essay "Discontented Black Feminists," my conversion was complete.[1]

My entry into graduate school in 1985 provided me with the opportunity to be trained in the field of African American women's history and coincided with the rich period in the growth of that field. The publications of Deborah Gray White's *Ar'n't I a Woman* (1985); Jacqueline Jones's *Labor of Love, Labor of Sorrow* (1985); Paula Giddings's *When and Where I Enter* (1984); and JoAnn Gibson Robinson's *The Montgomery Bus Boycott and the Women Who Started It* (1987) further ignited my desire to relocate and dive into a *real* archive. For some reason, I linked the investigative dimension of historical writing with the physical movement away from my familiar surroundings. Perhaps I intuited that a spatial separation from the known would help to destabilize what John Towes has called our "false sense of proximity to the people of the past."[2] Nevertheless, given my personal spiritual disposition, I still wanted the archive to—in Towes's words—"conjure up the world of the departed spirits so that they may speak to the inhabitants of the present with their own voices."[3] I quickly found out, however, that individual and collective identities are difficult to summon when the material traces holding the clues to those past souls are limited, heavily tainted, or virtually nonexistent. And, as legal scholar Cheryl Harris points out, given the historical devaluation of black women, any political intervention was "subject to be overlooked, misheard, misinterpreted, misrepresented and ultimately misappropriated."[4] The crisis of archival recognition for African American women is further compounded by what Darlene Clark Hine brilliantly terms "the culture of dissemblance."[5] Hine explains that a history of sexual violence against African American women has influenced "the behavior and attitudes of black women that created the appearance of openness and disclosure, but actually shielded the truth of their inner lives and selves from their oppressors."[6] These efforts at a self-protection, along with the sheer difficulty of becoming a part of the public record, have placed African American women on the periphery of most historical documents at best, and, at worst, made them—to borrow a phrase from Avery Gordan—merely a ghostly haunt.[7]

Despite these conditions, as Deborah Gray White has pointed out, "intensive work in primary sources" is necessary if we want to understand the intricate ways that race, gender, class, and region have shaped African American women's lives.[8] Thus interviews with African American women, along with personal and public organizational papers, have become the most fruitful sources from which to cull evidence for a "speculative reconstruction" of their histories.[9] A close examination of such evidence from the past can also generate conversations that shed light on the contemporary era. At the same time, the interplay of the past with the present makes it difficult to set aside our own historical context as we ask questions of those documents and listen to the alleged archival replies. Herein lies the test, in my opinion, of a good historian: the ability to construct a recognizable past via not only a careful resuscitation of silenced voices, but a dissolving of one's own personal voice and political persuasion. I must confess, I am constantly straining not to heed my personal or political leanings as I intervene in historical processes. That is, given the record of vilification and abuse suffered by African American women throughout history, it's a struggle to critically engage documents with my head when my heart wants to protect and affirm these women whom I consider my foremothers. Moreover, although history is never fully written, too often African American women have only one or two scholars willing to closely examine their documents; thus the pressures to write a definitive work magnify. It's under these loaded and at times emotionally charged circumstances that I attempt to analyze documents intelligently and craft credible and persuasive narratives of past lives.

Focusing on two different kinds of challenges that one can encounter in archival research—the problem of finding "more" than one expected and the problem posed by finding "less"—represents a formulation that locates a range of archival possibilities and my personal research experience. In the case of Amy Ashwood Garvey, the record was so limited that I had to draw on other sources and methods to fill in a plausible picture. However, with the case of Amy Jacques Garvey, a vast record seemed to contradict what I was expecting to find.

The private papers of Amy Jacques Garvey, located at Fisk University in Nashville, Tennessee, were my first significant introduction into archival research. I was informed by the archivist that only a few scholars had actually checked these documents out for viewing, and most of those scholars were primarily interested in what the collection revealed about Amy Garvey's husband, Marcus Garvey, and their organization, the Universal Negro Improvement Association (UNIA). I spent close to eight months over a four-year period reading, organizing, and copying letters, editorials, newspaper articles, and personal notes. With each visit I became more overwhelmed by the sheer volume of the material. Jacques Garvey had been Marcus Garvey's private secretary before their marriage, and her determination to preserve their place in history was attested to by the quantity of documents she helped to generate and preserve. It was not until I began to reread the documents—interestingly enough, outside the library—that I finally found myself able to relax and apply the historical methods I had learned in graduate school. Specifically, as I spent more time with the material, I grew more familiar with Jacques Garvey's voice and more confident in my ability to read for what was absent in her documents as well as for what was present. Documents, no matter how massive and detailed, never present the whole story; therefore, it's important to struggle just as much with archival voids as we do with material traces.

The textual snapshots of Jacques Garvey's personality and political energy that began to emerge from my reading comingled with and refuted at times the then popular representations of Garveyism. Moreover, Jacques Garvey's editorials detailed what appeared to be contradictory instructions for women in the black nationalist struggle. Although fascinated, I was also frustrated because the documents did not reveal what I was looking to find: evidence in a contemporary form of a staunch black feminist living during the 1920s. I had initially visualized writing a book filled with female political comrades. Jacques Garvey, however, overwhelmingly addressed her political correspondence to men who she believed shared her Pan-African vision. Another desire for my manuscript included celebrating interesting friendships and support networks. My failure to discuss sisterly cadres hinged upon Jacques Garvey's archival canon, which pictured her as a social loner—and her nemesis happened to be another woman activist. Finally, given the importance of interviews, I became extremely disappointed when my repeated requests to those who knew her well went unanswered. But this frustration led to a breakthrough in my research: I was forced to figuratively remove myself from the documents.

Challenged by the archival evidence, I had to critically engage a set of ideas that ran counter to my personal longings and convictions. More specifically, I was pushed to understand how Jacques Garvey had navigated a path between her dual political commitments to a Pan-African agenda and to feminist ideas, on the one hand, and her personal commitment to meeting her husband's needs, as well as those for her own development and expression, on the other. As a result, instead of presenting a tidy narrative of Jacques Garvey's activism, one of seamless coherence that would not really reflect the full picture presented by the documents, I developed the concept of *community feminism* to better explain the core of Jacques Garvey's activist spirit in Harlem during the 1920s.

In essence, community feminists are women who focus their activism on assisting both the men and women in their lives—whether sisters or husbands, mothers or fathers, sons or daughters—along with initiating and participating in activities to uplift their communities. Despite this "helpmate" focus, community feminists are undeniably feminist, in that their activism reveals an acknowledgment of oppressive power relations, shatters masculinist claims of women as intellectually inferior, and seeks to empower women by expanding their roles and options. Community feminism allows for the multiple identities of black women, along with communitarian ideas (the rejection of self-interest and the autonomous individual in recognition of the self as collective, interdependent, and relational), to take center stage. Of crucial relevance to this concept—and woven throughout Jacques Garvey's documents—is the interplay between helpmate and leadership roles.[10]

While Jacques Garvey left a large cache of materials for historical consideration, Amy Ashwood Garvey—Marcus Garvey's first wife—did not. Too often, scholars of African American women's history are forced to ground their narratives within a highly fragmentary archival record, and Amy Ashwood Garvey is a good case in point. Given that the historical record is confirmed through archival evidence, a lack of such material can make African American women historical outliers. By analyzing and drawing on what we *do* know of a period and location, however, African American women historians are often able to fill in a historical picture, even when the primary materials are scant. Obviously, a lack of documents does not give a scholar the right to take intellectual shortcuts. On the contrary, it is usually under the most difficult archival conditions that one must call most creatively and rigorously upon historical methods and theoretical ideas. The task of researching the life and contributions of Ashwood Garvey challenged me to employ my historical imagination, deeply rooted in other textual scholarship on Garveyism and feminist theory, in order to compensate for the lack of records.

Although Amy Ashwood Garvey was married to Marcus Garvey for less than six months, she was an important early leader in the movement. Documents clearly substantiate her role in creating the UNIA's constitution, which integrated women into the organization's structure. The constitution stipulated, for example, that each local division was to elect a male and female president and vice president. We also know that she assisted in the early production and distribution of the organization's newspaper, the *Negro World*. Although she was noted as a captivating speaker, only a few documents report what she said publicly, and most of these focus on how she channeled her political energy into poetic recitation, using a hear-me-talking-to-you mode of lecturing common in church sermons to draw people's attention to her race-conscious ideas. As Garvey scholar Tony Sewell puts it, Ashwood's "strength was in being out there and talking."[11] Faced with such sparse textual evidence and the knowledge that Ashwood Garvey was nevertheless a compelling and effective speaker, I began to look closely at the world in which she moved for clues about her life and work.

Confident in knowing that Ashwood Garvey understood the importance of the Harlem streets for eloquent orators, political theater, and UNIA recruitment, I began to focus in on this urban space. Moreover, her documents (primarily through the UNIA constitution) revealed a certain kind of feminist sensibility. Whether it was community feminism, the lyrics sung by blues singers, or the editorials written by middle-class clubwomen, multiple forms of black feminisms were produced during the 1920s. Tapping into this well-situated history, I was able to think beyond Ashwood Garvey's personal documents and ultimately include her within the host of feminist narratives by expanding on the idea of street strolling.

After reading Joanne Grant's biography of Ella Baker, I found myself intrigued by how Baker had supplemented her formal education by strolling the streets of Harlem.[12] By pushing the activity of strolling to include a wider scope of ideas, I was able to demonstrate how Ashwood Garvey theorized a Pan-African struggle through public oratory and walking the "cultural superstructure" of Harlem. With its leisurely pace, I argue, strolling (a stylized version of walking) allowed organic intellectuals to take in whatever was being said from corner to corner. Like dance, street strolling was an elaborate cultural practice, a Harlem fine art. As I began to think about strolling as a structured movement, I could see that it included mastering a set of protocols. For example, one had to make contact with others, position one's body to hear (often more than one speaker at a time), and be able to quickly calculate the value of information one was encountering. Crowded, dynamic streets engendered a certain quickness of mind; thus street-strolling scholars like Ashwood Garvey had to master the intellectual skill of thinking on their feet. By gathering information from the ground and sharing it with others, strolling became a way of knowing.[13]

Although the archival record on Ashwood Garvey provides only snatches of her public discourse, clearly her impassioned messages helped to galvanize sidewalk loafers and other strollers to pledge dues-paying membership with impressive results: UNIA membership was estimated at 35,000 in Harlem alone.[14] Strolling the streets from Harlem to Brooklyn, walking door to door, extolling the merits of her Pan-African vision, Ashwood Garvey helped build an international grassroots army of foot soldiers.[15] Already assertive and confident, Ashwood became further emboldened, in part, through experiencing the contested street energy in Harlem.

After closely reading and rereading the documents of both Amy Jacques Garvey and Amy Ashwood Garvey, I was encouraged to develop the concepts of community feminism and street strolling. Another reader of the same documents will no doubt introduce new tropes that further complicate or perhaps even refute (though I hope not!) the historical narratives that I have written. This is as it should be, because although historians require documents to support their narrative, historical processes produce multiple narratives.

The reality of multiple narratives became strikingly clear to me as I began researching my new project, women in the Nation of Islam (NOI) under the leadership of the Honorable Elijah Muhammad from 1934 to 1975. The Nation of Islam's weekly newspaper, *Muhammad Speaks,* has served as my primary archive thus far. My overarching exploratory question in approaching these documents was simple: Why would anyone become a member of the Nation of Islam after the assassination of Malcolm X (El-Hajj Malik El-Shabazz) in 1965? More than any other leader, Malcolm X stood at the ideological vortex of the movement for black liberation. His fiercely smart rhetoric helped to shift the dominant political struggle from a strategy of civil rights liberalism to eclectic expressions of black nationalism. As the most charismatic and visible spokesperson for the Nation of Islam, Malcolm moved beyond the

Honorable Elijah Muhammad's call for economic self-sufficiency and his prophecy of divine intervention, eventually breaking away from the group altogether. What would have motivated a politically active black woman to join the NOI after it had lost its most vital leader? In essence, my exploratory question was an effort to complicate our understanding of African American nation building during the peak of the modern Black Power movement.

Muhammad Speaks was the NOI's main propaganda organ. Reading both hard copies and microfilm versions of the newspaper has allowed me to see it from literally two different angles. The microfilm enlargement process allows one to focus clearly on a specific article, but in doing so, one loses sight of the whole (the rest of the paper). For this reason, I prefer to sift through hard copies of the newspaper. Reading for the question of "why?" I found myself drawn to an occasional feature of the newspaper titled "What Islam Has Done for Me." This column, made up of members' testimonies, is clearly open to a number of interpretations; what I have found in these autobiographical stories is a series of conversion narratives.

Every autobiography is a personal effort to document, as Charles Griffin puts it, whom one "believes and wishes [one]self to be and to have been."[16] In the case of conversion narratives, literary scholars have pointed out how "personal mythmaking" is used to "testify to the sincerity and significance of one's conversion experiences."[17] In short, most conversion narratives are compellingly written autobiographical accounts that detail turmoil and hardship, gradual understanding, and ultimately deliverance into a group that shares common beliefs and goals.[18] Keeping all of these important cautionary markers in mind, I repeatedly found in these newspaper narratives evidence of women crossing political and social boundaries by converting into the NOI. One such example is an account by Anna Karriem, and it highlights why a politically active black woman would decide to pledge membership into the NOI after 1965.

In her narrative, Anna Karriem explains that she had been a devoted member of the Student Non-Violent Coordinating Committee (SNCC) between 1964 and 1967 and had worked to bring "political power" to black people in Alabama and Mississippi. On election day in 1967, however, she witnessed local registrars holding loaded guns to drive SNCC members who were supervising the process away from the polling areas, and she saw black sharecroppers "driven off of their land and forbidden to take anything with them" because they had voted for a black candidate. Karriem found herself, "along with other SNCC workers and members of the homeless families[,] driving stakes into the ground and building a wooden floor, so that we could set up tents to get out of the cold." After 1966, under the leadership of Stokely

Carmichael, SNCC had grown more militant in its efforts to obtain political and economic freedom for black people, and Karriem states that the group's members were "willing to arm themselves for revolution in the streets." But by teaching that "freedom comes from the barrel of a gun," SNCC leadership, Karriem argued, did not address "the outcome of armed revolution by Black people, nor did [Carmichael] teach Black people in Los Angeles in 1965 how to restore their burned homes and businesses in Watts." Karriem was also critical of Carmichael for not coming "around to teach the people" who had, in Detroit and Newark in 1967, revolted against "slum living and unemployment, how to do for self in the way of rebuilding their burned communities." "Black Power" too often led to "Black Deaths," she concluded. Karriem writes that she decided to accept Islam as taught by the Honorable Elijah Muhammad because she was tired of the "destruction caused by so-called Black leaders who expounded on ideas that [had] no foundation in reality." Muhammad taught converts that "ideology is the science of ideas; we have had four hundred years to come up with ideas."[19] Karriem also concluded that the NOI had moved beyond ideological rhetoric and calls for revolution; their efforts had yielded small businesses, schools, and farmland, and no one had been displaced in the process.

Certainly, Karriem's story fits the rhetorical form of the conversion narrative. It was through the NOI that she saw the political light and deliverance from a movement that in her words had led to "Black Deaths." Given my exploratory question of "why?" I came to see from documents like this one how the NOI's conservative vision of "action" took on revolutionary meaning within a context of effete political resistance and racist violence.[20]

As I proceed with my larger project on women in the NOI, my engagement with the conversion narratives will require the difficult task of assessing the historical accuracy of the experiences they represent as fact. It is important to acknowledge, however, that the rigor expected in terms of evaluating the accuracy of these narratives should also hold true for all archival documents. And perhaps, too, that the writer's *subjective* experience of the facts is as significant, in terms of understanding their motives, as the accuracy of the fact themselves.

I opened this essay with a testimony of my own conversion to the field of African American women's history. And just as one could question the veracity of Karriem's account, one could be skeptical of my story. But after confirming my enrollment at the University of California, Los Angeles (UCLA), and my signature in the archival ledger at Fisk University, one could conclude that the documents support the narrative. In fact, the more material traces available to anchor voices into the slippery web of the familiar, the more comfortable we are in accepting them as "nonfiction." As historians follow a trail of documents to evaluate the claims of an alleged experience, we should also think and theorize from these same documents not only to recover voices, but also to disrupt those canonical discourses that have too often rendered African American women invisible.

NOTES

I acknowledge the kind permission of Johns Hopkins University Press to publish this modified version of the essay that appeared earlier in the *Journal of Women's History* (vol. 20, no. 1, Spring 2008).

1. Rosalyn Terborg-Penn, "Discontented Black Feminists: Prelude and Postscript to the Passage of the Nineteenth Amendment," in *Decade of Discontent: The Women's Movement, 1920–1940,* ed. Lois Scharf and Joan Jenson (Westport, Conn.: Greenwood, 1983).

2. John E. Towes, "Historiography as Exorcism: Conjuring up 'Foreign' Worlds and Historicizing Subjects in the Context of the Multiculturalism Debate," *Theory and Society* 27 (1998): 540.

3. Ibid., 535.

4. Cheryl Harris, "Finding Sojourner's Truth: Race, Gender and the Institution of Property," *Cardoza Law Review* 18 (November 1996): 317.

5. Darlene Clark Hine, "Rape and the Inner Lives of Black Women in the Middle West: Preliminary Thoughts on the Culture of Dissemblance," in *Words of Fire: An Anthology of African-American Feminist Thought* (New York: The New Press, 1995), 380–87.

6. Ibid., 380.

7. Avery F. Gordon, *Ghostly Matters: Haunting and the Sociological Imagination* (Minneapolis: University of Minnesota Press, 1997).

8. Deborah Gray White, "Mining the Forgotten: Manuscript Sources for Black Women's History," *The Journal of American History* 74, no. 1 (June 1987): 237.

9. John E. Towes, "Historiography as Exorcism," 546.

10. Ula Yvette Taylor, *The Veiled Garvey: The Life and Times of Amy Jacques Garvey* (Chapel Hill: University of North Carolina Press, 2002).

11. Tony Sewell, *Garvey's Children: The Legacy of Marcus Garvey* (Trenton, N.J.: African World Press, 1982), 25.

12. Joanne Grant, *Ella Baker: Freedom Bound* (New York: Wiley, 1998).

13. Ula Taylor, "Street Strollers: Grounding the Theory of Black Women Intellectuals," *Afro-Americans in New York Life and History* 30, no.2 (July 2006): 153–71.

14. John Henrik Clarke, ed., *Harlem U.S.A.: The Story of a City within a City* (Berlin: Seven Seas,), 80.

15. Lionel Yard, *Biography of Amy Ashwood Garvey, 1897–1969: Co-Founder of the Universal Negro Improvement Association* (Washington, D.C.: Associated Publishers, 1990), 45.

16. Charles J. G. Griffin, "The Rhetoric of Form in Conversion Narratives," *Quarterly Journal of Speech* 76 (1990): 152–63, especially 152.

17. Ibid., 153.

18. William Lloyd Allen, "Hearing Baptist Spirituality in Some Conversion Narratives from the American South," *Baptist History and Heritage* 37, no. 2 (Spring 2002): 32.

19. Anna Karriem, "The Preacher of Pan-Africanism," *Muhammad Speaks,* April 16, 1971, 15.

20. Ula Taylor, "Elijah Muhammad's Nation of Islam: Separatism, Regendering, and a Secular Approach to Black Power after Malcolm X," in *Freedom North: Black Freedom Struggles Outside the South, 1940–1980,* ed. Jeanne Theoharris and Komozi Woodard (New York: Palgrave Macmillan, 2003), 177–98.

9. FINDING AN ARCHIVE IN KRISHNOBHABINI DAS'S *ENGLANDE BANGAMOHILA*

Nupur Chaudhuri

In 1885, Krishnobhabini Das wrote a travel narrative in Bengali titled *Englande Bangamohila* (A Bengali Lady in England).[1] She was not the first Bengali lady traveler, but she was the first Indian woman to write about travel experiences in England. On the surface the book was a travel narrative of socioeconomic, political, and cultural life in London and elsewhere in England, but in reality it contrasted the existing sociopolitical life of Bengal with that of England. In the process, it sought to create a new spirit of nationalism and feminism for the Bengali reading public. Krishnobhabini's concept of feminism was blended with nationalism that developed in the context of colonialism.

Through analyzing *Englande Bangamohila*, some of her poems, and a contemporary biographical sketch published in 1923, I have discovered Krishnobhabini Das's views on nationalism and feminism and have found how her domestic life encouraged her to make an attempt to create a different world. These writings have collectively become a corpus to construct Krishnobhabini's home life, which sheds light on the condition of the majority of nineteenth-century Bengali women irrespective of their class backgrounds. Thus her biography and her writings, especially her travel narrative, serve as an archive that illuminates nineteenth-century Bengali women. Her experiences at home and abroad made her aware of her double subjugation: oppressed as a woman and oppressed as a Bengali woman in a colonial context.

My motivation to study Krishnobhabini Das's biography, travel narrative, and other writings grows out of my wish to learn about the roots of Bengali women's involvement in nationalism and feminism and the environment in which these concepts germinated. Since the 1990s, both in India and in the West, feminist scholars have written about Indian women. Their works brought Indian women's history to the center stage of South Asian history and women's history. To change popular perceptions about South Asian women both in the Western world and in South Asia, these scholars had to emphasize that many of those Indian women were not passive subjects but activists.[2] Even in the subcontinent, only a few works have been published focusing on Indian women's ideas and concepts since the 1920s.[3] In the West, most of these works concentrated on the writings of Western-educated Indian women, many of whom wrote in English, as these works are more accessible to Western scholars. Only a handful of works have been published in English about women's writings in literature of regional languages.[4] My desire was to find the intellectual foundations of the activism of Bengali women, for which I had to turn to the narratives written in Bengali.

Those of us who have studied and published in women's history (both Western and non-Western women) have quickly discovered that sources of women's history are not neatly preserved in various archives. We have written women's history by creating patchworks of information from journals, diaries, published biographies, autobiographies, and even recipes and advertisements. To us they are all archives, as we have used these sources not only as the sites for information, but as the information that opens up the broader contours of social, political, and cultural landscapes of a particular society in a particular time frame. Following historian Antoinette Burton's example, I have read Krishnobhabini's sketchy contemporary biography, her travel narrative, and her poems as an "archival site and history-in-the-making."[5] Thus I have not found Krishnobhabini's voice as a fragmented voice but as an archive itself. These scattered sources outside the traditional archives provided information to understand the lives and experiences of Krishnobhabini and her contemporaries in Bengal. Her contemporary biography and her writings have collectively provided me with a glimpse into the world of Bengali women in the late nineteenth and early twentieth centuries. Her works also pointed out how Krishnobhabini and women like her had to negotiate their lives often in an unfriendly environment and how their struggles paved the way for reforms. Like historian Nwando Achebe, I believe that Estelle C. Jelinek's statement on autobiography is also applicable to life stories and biographies. According to Jelinek, "a good [life history] not only focuses on its author, but it also reveals her connectedness to the rest of society; it is representative of [her] times, a mirror of [her] era."[6] Moreover, because of her experiences in her domestic life, Krishnobhabini wanted to create a different world for herself through social and political reforms against Bengali patriarchy and against British imperial interest. In this respect, her experiences and narrative are similar to sociologist Meera Kosambi's nineteenth-century Maharastrian women.[7]

Women in late-nineteenth-century Bengal took an increasingly active role in promoting sociopolitical interests of the nation. Gifted with writing skills, some women used their writings as a tool to instill ideas of social reform and nationalism among the reading public of the time. But their writings at this time made up a very small fraction of the body of published materials. Moreover, these women authors were not prominent figures in contemporary society. Their works consequently attracted less attention from a later reading public separated in time by a generation or more. Social, cultural, and national observations expressed in these writings have not received the wide acceptance accorded others. To reconnect the current reading public with the successes and reputations of these women writers, two scholars have recently compiled a volume of biographies of them.[8]

This collection included Krishnobhabini Das's biography, which was originally published in 1923 in a Bengali periodical titled *Bharati* and was written by one of her contemporaries, Saroj Kumari Devi (1875–1926), a well-educated woman for her time period who published three books of poetry and several short stories in various periodicals.[9] Besides using Saroj Kumari Devi's biography of Krishnobhabini, I have also used information on Krishnobhabini from *Antopurer Atmokatha* (Chronicles of Home): *Selected Works of Krishnobhabini Das* (*Krishnobhabini Daser Nirbachita Probondha*), edited by Aruna Chattopadhya.[10]

BIOGRAPHY OF KRISHNOBHABINI DAS

Krishnobhabini Das's views on nationalism and feminism are rooted largely in her own lived experiences. Her personal experiences are unlike those of any of the Indian women who were subjects of study either by Burton or literary critic Inderpal Grewal.[11] Krishnobhabini was self-taught at home, while Pandita Ramabai and Cornelia Sorabji, subjects of Burton and Grewal's studies, were highly educated and had traveled within India and in Britain. Pandita Ramabai also travelled in various places in the United States. Ramabai went to England for medical education, and Cornelia Sorabji studied law in Oxford. Ramabai converted to Christianity, and Cornelia Sorabji was a Parsee. Krishnobhabini was not a traditional Hindu, but nevertheless she was a Hindu and she was very proud of being a Hindu. She wrote in Bengali, and she was known mostly in Bengal, while Pandita Ramabai and Cornelia Sorabji wrote in English, and for that reason more English-speaking people including Europeans and Americans were familiar with their writings and activities. Information on her life comes primarily from Saroj Kumari Devi's article and from *Selected Works* previously mentioned. Some additional information, especially her relationship with her husband and daughter, comes from her book of poems titled *Jiboner Drishyamala* (Scenes from Life). In 1910 she published this book and dedicated it to the memory of her husband.[12]

There is some discussion about the exact birthplace of Krishnobhabini. Here I am using the generally accepted birthplace for her. In 1864, Krishnobhabini was born in a well-to-do traditional family in a village in the Murshidabad district in northern Bengal. She was an only child. Before her marriage, she could hardly read or write. Krishnobhabini's writings have created a picture of domestic life of nineteenth-century upper-caste Bengali women from childhood to death.

During the nineteenth century, according to the Hindu law that existed in Bengal, women could not inherit their father's land, and they even had no right to their husbands' land. Thus the daughters of property owners had ambiguous class status, which became more complex when the concepts of home and land were added. Sometimes daughters were married by the time they were ten years old and without their consent. The married daughters were expelled from their paternal lineage and were placed in their husbands' lineage. Also, these daughters were forced to leave their parents' home and settle down at their husbands' home, where they felt as outsiders. Their lack of property ownership and sense of being outsiders made these women not full members of the caste or class. Moreover, deep-rooted traditions not only provided class and caste order, but also dominated women's lives irrespective of their caste and class.[13]

Sexual intercourse with the husband was consummated as soon as the girls became adolescents.[14] As a consequence, girls were married before their first menstrual period started. Following this norm, Krishnobhabini was married at the age of ten. Often parents, especially fathers, believed that it would be an act of piety if they could arrange their daughter's or granddaughter's wedding between the age of eight or nine before their first menstrual period. This arrangement of the wedding was known as *Gauridan*. This practice led Srinath Das, Krishnobhabini's father-in-law, to later arrange the wedding of Krishnobhabini's nine-year-old daughter and his granddaughter Tilottoma.[15]

Srinath Das, Krishnobhabini's father-in-law, was a successful lawyer in the Calcutta High Court and had many progressive, reform-minded friends, including Ishwar Chandra Vidyasagar (1820–1891), a social reformer. What is surprising here is that his education and friendship with Vidyasagar, a well-known figure for his attempts to reform nineteenth-century Bengali society for the betterment of women, did not change Srinath's traditional ways.[16] His sons did not follow their father's conservatism. Krishnobhabini's husband, Debendranath, received his BA degree in 1876 and went to England to stand for the Indian Civil Service (ICS) examination. Debendranath's elder brother, Upendranath, was a playwright and a producer. Because of his controversial and nationalistic plays, he was punished by the British Raj, which around this time passed laws prohibiting anti-British plays. In 1869, Upendranath contravened norms by marrying a widow and became ostracized by his parents, and he left for England. Another brother-in-law of Krishnobhabini was a successful lawyer and also edited a weekly Bengali periodical focusing on politics and literature.[17]

Her husband, Debendranath, helped Krishnobhabini to learn the English language. She was self-taught and did not receive any formal education. When Debendranath went to England in 1876, Krishnobhabini was five months pregnant with their second child and stayed with her in-laws. During her husband's absence, she lost her first child and gave birth to her second child—a daughter named Tilottoma. Her daughter was five years old when her husband finally returned from London. Being a traditional Hindu, her father-in-law, Srinath, believed that going to a foreign country and assimilating foreign dietary customs made a person inadmissible to enter a Hindu home. He did not, therefore, let Debendranath stay at home. He also asked Krishnobhabini to sever all connections with her husband. He told her that by opting to go with her husband, she would have to disassociate herself from society. Krishnobhabini rejected the advice and social pressures from her in-laws and rejoined her husband and created a home of her own liking in Calcutta. Her father-in-law demanded that their daughter Tilottoma stay with him and his wife. Fearing a negative impact on the life of their daughter for living in social isolation in Calcutta, separated from traditional Hindu society during her early years, they left their five-year-old child with her grandparents.[18]

Even though all of his sons broke with traditions and customs, Srinath Das remained unchanged. When Debendranath returned from England, Srinath forced Krishnobhabini to choose between her husband and her daughter. Being the head of the household (*karta*), Srinath could behave in this manner. As head of the household, he made all the decisions, and even his wife could not interfere. For the head of the household, properly administering the domestic arena showed his political and administrative abilities—abilities that Indian men could not show publicly in the colonial context.[19] Krishnobhabini's voice enables us to view these domestic norms from the perspective of a person whose action was unusual.

Regarding her decision to go with her husband, she wrote in a poem that if she went to her husband's home, then she had to disconnect herself from all of her relatives. She continued by asking what kind of a cruel man created this rule, which broke her heart, and at what point these kinds of rules would come to an end.[20] Perhaps she also believed that in this respect she was being a good wife as she was following her husband.

Since Debendranath could not adjust to the traditional Bengali lifestyle, he chose to go again to London in 1882, about five months after his return to India. But this time his wife went with him. Perhaps this time they could have taken the daughter with them, because the impact of Bengali social isolation would have been less in a foreign country, but owing to a lack of resources, they were forced to leave their daughter with her paternal grandparents under the rules of the caste and the class agenda of the family. In London, Debendranath passed his ICS examination, but because of his age he was unable to get a posting. He was a linguist, so he taught India-bound civilians Indian history and culture and he also wrote columns on India in various British periodicals. Krishnobhabini became an avid reader, and she spent a lot of time visiting various libraries, including the British Museum Library. *Englande Bangamohila* is not a memoir, because she never described her personal life in this particular text. It reads like a travel narrative. Krishnobhabini never revealed where in London she and her husband lived. Neither did she mention her daily life. She minutely described her travel from Kolkata to London by ship. She described the city of London, including the British Museum Library, at great length, and she mentioned that she discussed some of her ideas with a couple of trusted British friends. She visited Manchester. She did not write anything about her friends or acquaintances in England. Her contemporary sketchy biography is also silent on these matters. However, she knew of Pandita Ramabai, as she commented that "after coming to England our well-educated Ramabai rejecting Hindu religion converted to Christianity which ashamed all the Hindus."[21] It seems that Krishnobhabini felt that one should stay in the system to reform that system.

While they were in England, they were informed that the grandfather had arranged the marriage of their nine-year-old daughter Tilottoma for religious reasons. This news greatly upset Krishnobhabini. In spite of her belief in women's autonomy, she could not stop the wedding. Again, she expressed her feelings in a poem. She wrote that the sudden news of her daughter's wedding broke her heart. The groom was wealthy but not desirable as a son-in-law. She mentioned that her father-in-law did not pay any attention to any advice. According to Krishnobhabini, if she had known this was going to be her daughter's fate, she would have drowned her daughter.[22]

After their return to Calcutta in 1890, Debendranath started to teach. But they were still ostracized by Debendranath's father. The traditionalist in-laws of Tilottoma prohibited her from seeing her parents, Krishnobhabini and

Debendranath. Soon afterward, Tilottoma became quite sick following the loss of her first child at childbirth. Her husband now decided to marry for a second time. Krishnobhabini urged her daughter to leave her husband, but she refused to do that. A few years later, in 1909, Tilottoma died.[23]

In 1909, at the annual conference of the Indian National Congress in Allahabad, Sarala Devi Chaudhurani, a prominent Indian feminist and nationalist, formed the Bharat Stree Mahamandal (the Great Circle of Indian Women). Soon after the Allahabad session, Krishnobhabini returned to Calcutta from Allahabad and, with help from Sarala Devi, established three branches of the Bharat Stree Mahamandal in Bengal.

Krishnobhabini Das became the secretary of the organization in Bengal. This organizational activity was the cornerstone of her efforts to improve the lives of women in India and create a climate of modernization in India. Although she had no formal schooling, for her works in the society she was recognized with an appointment as an examiner at Calcutta University.[24] She believed that after receiving education, women opting not to work outside the home were selfish and petty. Maintaining that women by nature were not lazy and self-indulgent, Krishnobhabini advocated that women take an active part in many social projects, a legitimate sphere of activity for women, whose duty was to provide nurture and care. She wrote: "If making life meaningful is the main aim of life, then working for others and making life happy for them is the duty of every individual."[25] She regularly published in *Brahmobodhini Patrika*, *Bharati*, and other journals. Many of her essays have been republished in a collection of essays.[26] In her *Early Feminists of Colonial India*, historian Bharati Ray wrote, "Krishnobhabini Devi was known to the public as the beloved and revered Mrs. D. N. Das of the *Bharat Stree Mahamandal*."[27]

Krishnobhabini died on February 27, 1919, after having lost both her husband and her only child, Tilottoma, in 1909. On March 5, 1919, *The Bengali* wrote: "In her the East, while imbibing the good of both the East and the West, retains the stamp of oriental genius and character."[28] In the last ten years of her life, following the deaths of her husband and daughter, she spent her time devising programs to advance social progress for women, educating women, raising funds for homes for widows and prostitutes, and writing. The idea of helping the widows and prostitutes and raising funds are quite similar to those of Pandita Ramabai. However, it would be interesting to make a comparative study of feminism and nationalism between Krishnobhabini and Pandita Ramabai, but it is not within the scope of this essay.

Scholars have readily recognized Krishnobhabini as a leader of a women's movement during her time, emphasizing her work with Bharat Stree Mahamandal and orphanages. But expressions of national identity may also be traced in some of her writings. She was apparently attempting to energize the reading public to seek changes in society with a spirit of national pride.

KRISHNOBHABINI DAS AND NATIONALISM

Nationalism is a modern phenomenon. Philosopher and sociologist Ernst Gellner wrote that depending on time and place, nationalism has taken different forms and directions with totally different central points.[29] Literary scholar Ann McClintock has written that "nationalism is invented, performed and consumed in ways that do not follow a blueprint."[30] In *Construction of Race, Place and Nation,* geographer Peter Jackson and sociologist Jan Penrose have asserted that nationalisms can be revolutionary ideologies concerned with resisting domination, or dominant ideologies legitimizing the interests of established elites.[31] Both forms can be identified in India in the late nineteenth century. They looked simultaneously backward and forward in time, drawing on both "tradition" and modernization as sources of legitimation. In its different forms, Indian nationalism during the late nineteenth century emphasized tradition and the past, and/or the future and modernization.

In his *Nationalism without a Nation in India,* sociologist G. Aloysius argued that some Indians created three dimensions of cultural nationalism that included Vedic Brahminism, or a sense of historical and ethical destiny connected with the traditional social and religious ideologies of the ancient Vedic era, and a commitment to a pan-Indian territory. He described the third aspect of cultural nationalism as an antagonistic polarity with the West, Europe, British imperialism, and modernity.[32] Based on his studies of communists R. Palme Dutt and M. N. Roy, political scientist Sanjay Seth presented Indian nationalism during the period 1870–1905 as "moderate nationalism."[33] The majority of the Indian nationalists of that period felt that the main enemy was not British rule as such, but the backwardness of the people, the lack of modern development of the country, the strength of forces of obscurantism and ignorance.[34] Later generations of Indian scholars perceived these activists as nationalists because their reform impulse against "social conservatism and religious superstition" came in response to a colonial encounter.[35]

Gender issues were almost nonexistent in generic discussions of nationalism. The omission of women has also been common in many recent scholarly studies on Indian nationalism. Yet women played an important role in the discourse of nationalism. Historian Mrinalini Sinha, in her recent publication *Gender and Nation,* has demonstrated the ways women have contributed to the construction of nation by reproducing, transmitting culture, and maintaining national/ethnic boundaries.[36] Scholar of gender and ethnic studies

Nira Duval-Davis and sociologist Floya Anthias have emphasized that women played a distinct role in constructing and shaping some distinctive marks in national identities by being actively involved in the development of producing and reproducing, preserving and adjusting their roles in this construct of national characteristics.[37] In their article on Irish nationalism published in 1998, Breda Gray and Louise Ryan, both sociologists and women's studies scholars, underscored the interactions among feminism, national identities, and colonialism.[38] Anne McClintock has emphasized that women act out of conservative principles of continuity, while men act as the "progressive agent[s] of national modernity embodying nationalism's progressive or revolutionary principle of discontinuity."[39] Consequently, she has identified in nationalism "a natural division of gender." This could be an oversimplification of a complex issue, as Krishnobhabini Das's writings suggest. Krishnobhabini Das's appeal to Indians reveals that Indian nationalism is more multifarious than it has been commonly perceived.

In colonized countries, often the construct of feminism and nationalism has been created in the context of the imperial landscape. This conclusion has energized some scholarship that has shown the means by which women from one cultural sphere shaped and promoted their visions of feminism and nationalism in the light of their perceptions about the status of women in the other juxtaposed cultural sphere. Both Antoinette Burton's book *The Burden of Feminism* and my article "Issues of Race, Gender and Nation in *English Women's Domestic Magazine* and *The Queen*, 1850–1900," have shown that British women structured their visions of feminism and nationalism from a perception of Indian women as inferior.[40] Another light on cross-cultural influence on feminism and nationalism comes from the works of Antoinette Burton and Inderpal Grewal, who analyzed some Western-educated Indian women's lives in England and described how London became a contested and contacted zone for reshaping visions of feminism and nationalism in an imperial context.[41] Much research is needed to understand the depth and the breadth of the experiences and beliefs of lesser-known educated Indian women who spent some time in England. The constraints of the culture of women like Krishnobhabini, who created the prototype of nationalism and feminism, have yet to be thoroughly examined, because the individual experiences cannot be put in a monolithic frame.

Krishnobhabini published her travel narrative in Calcutta while she was in London. At the beginning of the book, her publisher commented that since the author was in England with her husband, proper proofreading of the text could not be done. In the preface of *Englande Bangamohila*, Krishnobhabini wrote that although she was unknown to the public and she was far away from her readers, she published this book to express all the new concepts she had developed as she became exposed to new things. By comparing the lives of free people of England with those of the subjugated people of India, she wanted to explain to the readers the reasons for English dominance over India.

In her preface, she particularly addressed female readers when she wrote: "Like you, I was also imprisoned at home, I had no connection with my country and with the world. I tried to keep myself occupied with a few subjects, but I couldn't. I was eager to learn about all the things connected to my country. If I heard that anyone was going to England or had returned from England, I was eager to learn from them about the foreign land. But unfortunately, subjugated Bengali women cannot fulfill their wishes, so I kept quiet. Perhaps you are also eager to learn about England, so to satisfy that curiosity I am dedicating this book to you."[42] Here she was addressing middle- and upper-class Bengali women. She continued that in the book she included both good and bad qualities of the British. She tried to forget that in foreign countries, especially in India, there was a negative transformation in English character. She tried to write objectively about the English, explaining there was so much difference between the Indians and the British, and the relationship between them was so fractious, that it was quite difficult for the Indians to describe the good qualities of the English.[43] This statement clearly showed her dislike of the transplanted English in the Indian subcontinent, while her admiration for the English living in the metropole was also quite obvious in this narrative. Her antagonistic feelings against the English in India were quite common among Indians.

In her narrative, Krishnobhabini explained that her reason for going to England "was to fulfill a dream of seeing a free country."[44] The experience Krishnobhabini gained from this travel became a turning point in her life. Leaving behind her familiar private or domestic sphere, she felt the journey to a new territory let her breathe an air of freedom and come out of a society-crafted cage that suffocated the life of an individual. Travel offered her a new perspective on freedom. Inderpal Grewal has claimed that this awareness among Indian women of being constrained is a sign of modernization.[45] Krishnobhabini was able to construct in her mind the contrasts between lives of individuals in India and those in England. Reflecting on the difference, she wrote, "England is the center for freedom, and our India is totally enslaved. I myself have observed that since I am breathing English air and living with free people, I am developing new ideas."[46] The seed of consciousness of nationalism had already begun to germinate. She conveyed this sense in *Englande Bangamohila* and in later published essays through which she tried to reach middle-class Bengali women and men. Her goal was to create an identity of nationalism among middle-class Bengali women and help develop a spirit of feminism through promoting women's education. She conveyed her own feelings in this book when she wrote: "[After coming here] I have seen many new things, learned about many new things, acquired knowledge on many new subjects. However, the more I see, the more I learn, the longer I stay here, the more I become disheartened when I think of India. The more I compare this country with India, the difference between these two countries becomes more and more clear and the wretchedness of India becomes apparent, which saddens me immensely."[47]

She emphasized that during the ancient period before the Greeks, Hindus were respected in the world for their civilization, religion, and education. Learning mathematics, astronomy, and philosophy from ancient Indians, other civilized nations constructed new plans, made new discoveries, and became world famous. Then she raised the question: "We are the children of those Indians, then why are we so backward?"[48] She blamed Indian women as partly responsible for this sorry state. She asserted that by encouraging their Hindu husbands to go to wars, and defending virtues of their own religion, those Hindu ladies in the past were not afraid to kill themselves in a blaze. She continued:

> Once their heroic assertions were echoed everywhere; because of their devotion to religion, to their husbands and heroism, they established the pattern of excellence. Today we, who are their daughters, are trampled as subjugated people.... Today where is the pride of Indian ladies for their religion and valor? Today the Indian men sit idly like cowards. Where is our excitement to provoke these men into action? If we are the children of those Hindus [from northern India], then why has our condition deteriorated so much?[49]

Here she is echoing the concept of cultural nationalism, as Aloysius did, in referring to past glories. Unlike many Indian nationalists, she evidently did not blame the British for the subjugation and wretched conditions of India. She found other causes for the misery of India. "Now, we don't have anything and it is our fault that we have lost everything. Like a cobra, disunity has destroyed us ... because of their unity these inhabitants from a small island [England] can defeat a bigger country like India and dominate over her. Because of our disunity, we are now becoming poorer, more timid and recognized as uncivilized."[50] Here she basically blamed Hindu men, especially Bengali men, for this disunity and loss of freedom, since Bengali Hindu women did not have any control over their lives and society. She continued, "Other free people consider subjugated Indians as uncivilized, weak, and cowardly. We, made of flesh and blood, have accepted these insults without any hesitancy, or we ignore them totally. Isn't it our fault? Bengalis, in spite of being the most intelligent and educated among all Indians, are extremely cowardly and timid, so what is the point of their being educated?"[51] Contemporary British opinion of the Bengali *baboos* (middle-class Bengali men) also ran along a similar vein.[52] Her criticism of Bengali *baboos*, however, was due to the fact that they treated Bengali women harshly and did not do enough to improve the condition of the women. She reasoned why Bengali women remained passive observers, as she wrote, "We [women] have been subjugated for a long time and consequently have lost the courage and strength of free life."[53] Krishnobhabini took the Bengali patriarchy to task for being indifferent to the interests of Bengali women and thereby of India.

She believed that Indians had been self-absorbed in their own happiness, like animals, and they indulged in not considering what was best for the country and how to achieve it. She noted that, "Instead of discussing our past glories, we should think of the present and future.... How we can improve the present situation, and what will benefit the future, should be our constant focus."[54] She maintained that all civilized and wealthy countries went through constant changes, and the only way India could solve all her problems was to bring changes in society to improve life for all. She advocated education as an important tool to bring necessary changes and improvement. In this regard, she was a precursor of the early nationalists, whom Seth called "moderate nationalists," who believed English education could be a major benefit to Indians. This view was quite popular in a circle of educated Indians. In his speech to the Congress Party in 1902, S. N. Banerjee stated: "The three great boons which we have received from the British Government are High Education, the gift of a Free Press and local Self-Government.... But High Education is the most prized, the most deeply cherished of them all."[55]

Krishnobhabini's nationalism was based on her comparison of Indians with the English. In that comparison, she perceived that in spite of past achievements, Indians gradually lost their edge and became backward, which caused them to lose their freedom. Krishnobhabini put forward to her readers that freedom is the central issue in the concept of nationalism. She believed that people have to consider themselves worthy of receiving freedom and capable of sustaining that freedom, and especially that they have the strength and courage to receive freedom. She asked her readers to search for ways to become successful and to free themselves from those who dominated them, reminding them to analyze those attributes that have contributed to the domination. She felt that false pride and superstitious, harmful traditional values stood in the way of acquiring the qualities necessary in gaining freedom.

The concept of nationalism in Krishnobhabini Das's writings contained many of the same elements that can be found in Aloysius's article. Krishnobhabini embraced social and philosophical values based on the Vedic era (of ancient India) to nurture the spirit of nationalism, values central to Aloysuis's characterization of Indian nationalist thought. At the same time, she valued some Western concepts of modernity, including Western education. While respecting the values of Western education, she blamed educated elite Bengali/Indian men for being self-absorbed and not trying to reform the system to benefit both women and men. Her brand of nationalism was contrary to McClintock's definition of nationalism, in which women represented conservative principles of continuity. Krishnobhabini rejected conservative traditional values. She became a progressive agent of national modernity.

To Krishnobhabini, travel to England became an educational experience for bringing sociopolitical changes. She believed, with other early male nationalists, that this education would help them to gain independence, become free from ignorance and traditionalism, and gain access to the benefits of modernism. This concept of nationalism, however, clashed with the reality of colonialism.[56] On one hand, there was a respect toward the Western country and its culture; and on the other hand, a desire to project her own cultural values to a higher standard also was present. The contradictory elements have been recognized in Krishnobhabini's travel narrative, *Englande Bangamohila*. In this respect, Krishnobhabini represented the "modern Indian woman," what Mrinalini Sinha claimed "as the unique signifier of Indianness and of the national culture's absolute difference from the West."[57] In a colonized country, nationalism is not a typical replica of Western nationalism. These countries construct their own model of nationalism, as we see in the case of Krishnobhabini. By promoting moderate nationalism, which is to some extent a Western concept, Krishnobhabini symbolized modern Indian woman, and at the same time, by placing a very high value on her Hindu/Indian culture, she became a signifier of Indianness and emphasized the cultural difference between Hindu/India and Britain.

The cornerstone of her nationalism was based on her belief that the weakness of Indian men, especially Bengali men, was responsible for India's subjugation. To prove her point, she repeatedly emphasized the ways Bengali/Indian men deprived women of education and kept them subservient. Thus her narrative provides information not only about middle-class Bengali women's role and status in late-nineteenth- and early-twentieth-century colonial Bengal, but also the mindset of middle-class Bengali men.

KRISHNOBHABINI AND FEMINISM

Her nationalist consciousness also included a vision of feminism. Like many of her contemporaries, Krishnobhabini Das condemned the injustice done to women and tried to remedy the situation but did not ask for gender equality.[58] She emphasized, instead, increased sociopolitical activism for women and education as necessary tools for women. However, the British government banned *Englande Bangamohila* in India. Bharati Ray claimed that Krishnobhabini's feminist beliefs led to the prohibition of this book. Historian Chitra Deb, however, argued that Krishnobhabini's support of nationalism led to the banning of this book.

Indians traveling or educated in England were readily able to understand the importance of education in national life. They all accepted the notion of education as the vehicle for modernization. In their view, England, through superior education, came to be recognized as a civilized nation and came to rule in India. Like these Indians, Krishnobhabini also saw the value of education for India's recognition as a civilized nation. But she maintained that for gains to be made, women must have opportunities for education. She wrote about the status of middle-class English women in order to reach middle-class Bengali women and men. In this respect, she was not very different from contemporary Bengali women. All nineteenth-century Bengali women who left us their writings recorded their desire to learn. Their desire to be educated prompted Tanika Sarkar to write, "The longing for systematic learning was not a desire implanted by male reformers, missionaries and colonialists."[59]

Krishnobhabini wrote in her *Englande Bangamohila* that there were definite opportunities for education for women in England. She was surprised to find out that almost every neighborhood had two or three schools and colleges for girls. She informed her readers that English women attended London, Oxford, Cambridge, and other universities, where they took courses with men, studied under the same professors, passed the same tests, and received the same degrees.[60] Here, indirectly or unconsciously, she was contrasting English women's education with Bengali/Indian women's lack of or limited education. Only a handful of Bengali girls from very progressive families received an education. The vast majority became child brides, like Krishnobhabini, and did not receive any education. Observing that a few women excelled in tests that only a few men dared to take, she maintained women to be as bright as men. In her writings about women's education, she noted that she had heard that well-educated middle-class women in North America became judges and lawyers and gave decisions in legal matters. She claimed that the educated English women, some of whom were engaged in medicine and teaching, did not advance as much as American women. But she believed that English women were making rapid advances in education and they would soon surpass American women in the public sphere.[61]

Krishnobhabini was highly impressed by the willingness of English parents, especially fathers, to spend as much money for their daughters' educations as for their sons', a phenomenon that did not exist in the Indian landscape. She wrote: "When I see that girls are going to school like the boys and young women are going to college like young men, I am so happy that I am unable to express it. Here women start their education from the age of six or seven and continue their schooling until twenty to twenty-five. . . . Not only the daughters of the wealthy," she added, "but also the daughters of the middle-class continue to get lessons in academic subjects as well as music and needle works until they are eighteen or nineteen. Until the girls are well-versed in those subjects, parents spend money for their education without hesitation because they believe it is their duty so they are happy to do it."[62] According to her, daughters of even English lower-class families went to school, so that daughters of almost all families, except the poorest and the lowest-class families, could read, write, and play music and were able to sew and run households. Education opened up opportunities for women, and it helped to produce many female authors, intellectuals, and scientists. She commented that in the 1880s, British women authors wrote the best novels. She had no hesitation to claim that like English women, Indian women possessed the mental strength and courage to do so. But because of illiteracy and subjugation, they could not fully express those qualities.[63]

If women were not respected by their own society, the English nation would not have earned the respect of the rest of the world. She went on to write that only the uncivilized and aborigines would not know how to show respect and take pride in the faithfulness of wives. She felt that England was a country of moral women. In her judgment, many Indian women equated not seeing any man's face or not interacting with other men to intense devotion to their husbands. Krishnobhabini insisted that English women, who constantly interacted with men but still remained committed to their religion and intensely devoted to their husbands, were stronger mentally and spiritually than other women. It is interesting to note that Krishnobhabini's observation of English women in England is completely different from her comments about British women in India, whom she described as "lazy, extravagant and luxury loving."[64]

Krishnobhabini also discussed the treatment of English women by English men. She wrote that to protect the sanctity of their lives, there were strict laws against men who might have committed crimes against women. She believed that by maintaining women's honor, men were protecting in a sense the freedom of women. In her thinking, Indian men were afraid to give freedom to Indian women, judging them to be mentally feeble and incapable of handling freedom. She compared the status of Indian women with children. Unless Indian women were guided toward freedom, Indian women would never learn to rule themselves or travel independently. Krishnobhabini wrote: "Instead of being afraid, society should provide Indian women with good education. If after giving proper education to Indian women, they were given freedom, then one would see that Hindu women were not inferior to British women in any respect."[65]

In England, Krishnobhabini wrote, women always knew how to maintain their honor. They publicly spoke to men and engaged in sports, and from childhood they learned many things about the world. As a result, they did not consider men as gods. Indian wives had been known for their intensely servile devotion to their husbands. Hindu ladies would willingly give up their lives in the funeral pyres of their husbands. The world of English wives was free. They received education, they traveled to various countries, and they listened to and participated in discussions of politics, administration, and other serious topics with their fathers, brothers, and friends. From those discussions, English women developed intellectually and acquired a keen sense of separating right from wrong.[66]

Krishnobhabini captured in her writings the lives of several notable English women. She wrote about Mary Carpenter, Florence Nightingale, Lady Baker, and others. She emphasized that in spite of being single throughout her life, Carpenter used her education to bring many improvements, such as prison reform, to English society and to organize many women's committees. To help Indian students in England, Carpenter established a committee, which existed while Krishnobhabini was in London. She wrote about Carpenter's hard work to promote women's education in India. She told her readers that Florence Nightingale showed her bravery and feminine virtue by helping wounded soldiers during the Crimean War.[67] Krishnobhabini emphasized in her writing that in spite of being married, many of these famous women worked outside the home. She claimed that knowing these ladies who did so much good for the world, with self-help and self-strength, made her very happy. She found that in India, married women seldom volunteered to help the country. In England, even single women and widows found ways to make themselves useful for the needs of the country.[68]

Krishnobhabini wrote that some English women became helpmates to their husbands in their work in adverse conditions. She cited the examples of Lady Baker and Lady Brassey. About Baker, Krishnobhabini wrote that she gladly accompanied her husband to live in African deserts, where men were afraid to go, and in those inaccessible and dreadful lands she traveled extensively to discover new lakes and new rivers. Brassey, who traveled for almost a year and a half on an ocean voyage for research purposes, wrote of her travel experiences and achievements. Krishnobhabini maintained that in reading Brassey's life story, one would find great joy and an inspiration to do good deeds.[69]

Krishnobhabini's narration captures a vision of feminism that grew from a comparative analysis of British women's place in their own society. To advance their own agenda of feminism, British women assigned Indian women relatively inferior status.[70] Thus they had also adopted a comparative approach. Krishnobhabini rejected such an imperial outlook. She held a strong view that the mental capacities of Bengali/Indian women were equal to those of British women. She further maintained that lack of education and Indian men's refusal to open doors of opportunity to women were the root causes of Indian women's inferior and degrading position in society. Krishnobhabini appealed to Bengali women to take up the struggle of freedom for all Indian women. She wrote to these women, "If you ever get the taste of freedom, then you would not like to return to the prison. Come sisters! Break your cages or convince your brothers to cut the shackles, which chain the Bengali women. Come and see how independent life brought happiness to Germany and France where women never shed tears of humility. Notice how men do not ignore women," she continued, "thinking they are useless; they do not keep women in cages of domesticity and treat them like animals. Wherever I go in Europe, I find women are equal to men, but it is totally different in India. Unfortunately, in India women are always oppressed."[71] Again, Krishnobhabini's comparison of Bengali women's lives with caged birds is not new; other Bengali women of that time period also had made this comparison.[72]

Krishnobhabini's poems and her *Englande Bangamohila* provide us with information about the lives of middle- and upper-class Bengali women in late-nineteenth- and early-twentieth-century colonial Bengal. She emphasized the mindset of Bengali *baboos,* who oppressed Bengali women. Thus her life and her writings connected her with the rest of society and made her a representative of her times. Her writings, especially her travel narrative, became an archive. She was courageous enough to break the shackles and come out of the cage. She became a self-taught person and believed that only education would free women. She showed respect for English culture, but at the same time she wanted to cast her own cultural values to a higher standard. In this respect, she became a part of Burton's "history-in-the-making" by becoming a precursor of Sinha's "modern Indian woman" who was a "unique signifier of Indianness and of the national culture's absolute difference from the West."[73]

NOTES

I acknowledge the kind permission of Johns Hopkins University Press to publish this modified version of the essay that appeared earlier in the *Journal of Women's History* (vol. 20, no. 1, Spring 2008). I also thank the editors of the *Journal of Women's History* for their comments and suggestions.

1. *Englande Bangamohila* (A Bengali Lady in England), "written by a Bengali Lady" (Calcutta: Sri Satya Prokash Sarbadhikari, 1885). Krishnobhabini Das published this travel narrative while she was in England with her husband. The front page contains four lines of a Bengali poem, which roughly translates: "Blow the trumpet loudly / Everyone is free in this world / Everyone is proud of this freedom / Only India is asleep!" This verse is taken from Hemendra Lal Roy, a nationalist Bengali poet. *Englande Bangamohila*, reprinted with introduction and notes by Simonti Sen (Calcutta: Stree, 1996). For this essay I have used the 1996 reprint edition. All translations from Bengali texts are my own. To translate accurately I have consistently used the terms "England" and "English" instead of "Britain" and "British."

2. Among these scholars, most noted are Aparna Basu and Bharati Ray, *Women's Struggle: A History of All India Women's Conference, 1927–1997* (Delhi: Manohar Publications, 1990); Meredith Borthwick, *The Changing Role of Women in Bengal, 1849–1905* (Princeton, N.J.: Princeton University Press, 1984); Bharati Ray, ed., *From the Seams of History: Essays on Indian Women* (New Delhi: Oxford University Press, 1995); Tanika Sarkar, *The Words to Win: The Making of Amar Jiban, a Modern Autobiography* (New Delhi: Kali for Women, 1999); Tanika Sarkar, *Hindu Wife, Hindu Nation: Community, Religion, and Cultural Nationalism* (Bloomington: Indiana University Press, 2001); Suruchi Thapar-Bjorkert, *Women in the Indian National Movement: Unseen Faces and Unheard Voices, 1930–42* (New Delhi: Sage, 2006); Antoinette Burton, *At the Heart of the Empire: Indians and the Colonial Encounter in Late-Victorian Britain* (Berkeley: University of California Press, 1998); Geraldine Forbes, *Women in Modern India* (Cambridge: Cambridge University Press, 1998); Barbara Ramusack, "Catalysts or Helpers? British Feminists, Indian Women's Rights and Indian Independence," in Gail Minault, ed., *The Extended Family: Women and Political Participation in India and Pakistan* (Columbia, Mo.: South Asia Books, 1981); and Mrinalini Sinha, "Gender in the Critiques of Colonialism and Nationalism: Locating the 'Indian Woman,'" in Joan Scott, ed., *Feminism and History* (New York: Oxford University Press, 1996).

3. Sutapa Bhatterjee, comp. and ed., *Bengali Meyer Bhabanamulak Gadya: Unish Satak* (An Anthology of Women's Writings in Bengali in the Nineteenth Century) (New Delhi: Sahitya Akademi, 1999); Aruna Chattopadhya, ed., *Krisnobhabini Daser Nirbachita Prabandha* (Collected Essays of Krisnobhabini Das) (Calcutta: Dey's, 2004).

4. Padma Angol, *The Emergence of Feminism in Western India* (London: Ashgate, 2006), Meera Kosambi, *Pandita Ramabai, Through Her Own Words: Selected Work* (India: Oxford University Press, 2000); Rosalind Tarabai Sindhe, *A Comparison between Women and Men*, trans. Rosalind O'Hanlon (New Delhi: Oxford University Press, 1994); Tanika Sarkar, *Words to Win*; Tanika Sarkar, *Hindu Wife*; Tanika Sarkar, "A Book of Her Own, A Life of Her Own: Autobiography of a Nineteenth-Century Woman," *History Workshop Journal* 36 (1993): 35–65; Suruchi Thapar-Bjorkert, *Women in the Indian National Move-*

ment; Mytheli Sreenivas, "Emotion, Identity, and the Female Subject: Tamil Women's Magazines in Colonial India," *Journal of Women's History* 14, no. 4 (Winter 2003): 59–82; Mytheli Sreenivas, *Wives, Widows, and Concubines: The Conjugal Family Ideal in Colonial India* (Bloomington: Indiana University Press, 2008).

    5. Antoinette Burton, *Dwelling in the Archive: Women Writing House, Home, and History in Late Colonial India* (New York: Oxford University Press, 2003), 26.

    6. Quoted in Nwando Achebe, "Getting to the Source: Nwando Achebe—Daughter, Wife and Guest—A Researcher at the Crossroads," *Journal of Women's History* 14, no. 3 (Autumn 2002): 15.

    7. Meera Kosambi's concept as expressed in "The Home as Social Universe: Women's Personal Narratives in Nineteenth-Century Maharashtra," in Glushkova and Feldhaus, eds., *House and Home in Maharashtra*, is easily applicable in Krishnobhabini's case.

    8. Chitra Deb, *Antopurer Atmokatha* (Chronicles from Home) (Calcutta: Ananda, 1984; Abhijit Sen and Abhijit Bhattacharjya, *Sekele Katha: Shatak Suchanai Mayeder Smriti-Katha* (Memories and Sketches by Women in Early-Twentieth-century Bengal) (Calcutta: Naya Udyog, 1997).

    9. Saroj Kumari Gupta was born in 1875 in Bhagalpur, Bihar. Her father was a subjudge. Her brother, an editor of *Tribune* and other Bengali periodicals, was a well-known writer. At the age of fifteen, she married a lawyer who helped her to be properly educated. Her first book was published in 1895.

    10. Saroj Kumari Devi, "Krishnobhabini Das," *Bharati* (December–January 1923), reprinted in Sen and Bhattacharjya, *Sekele Katha*, 169–77; Chattopadhya, *Krisnobhabini Daser Nirbachita Prabandha*.

    11. Antoinette Burton, *At the Heart of the Empire*; Burton, *Dwelling in the Archives*; Inderpal Grewal, *Home, Harem: Nation, Gender, Empire and the Culture of Travel* (Durham, N.C.: Duke University Press, 1996).

    12. Sen and Bhattacharya, *Sekele Katha*, 226.

    13. Sarkar, *Hindu Wife*, 18–19.

    14. Sarkar, *Words to Win*, 29.

    15. Sen and Bhattacharjya, *Sekele Katha*, 173–74.

    16. Ishwar Chandra Vidyasagar (1820–1891), a Brahmin, was a writer and social reformer of Bengal. He was appointed as the head pundit of Fort Williams College in 1850. He promoted female education in 1851 when he was appointed to manage Bethune School for Girls. Observing the miserable lives of widowed girls, Vidyasagar introduced widow remarriage and tried to abolish Bengali polygamy. He was also known for his philanthropy.

    17. Chattopadhya, *Krisnobhabini Daser Nirbachita Prabandha*, 7–8.

    18. Sen and Bhattacharjya, *Sekele Katha*, 171.

    19. Tanika Sarkar, *Hindu Wife*, 48.

    20. Cited by Saroj Kumari Debi from *Jibaner Drishyamala*, 172.

    21. *Englande Bangamohila*, 126.

    22. Sen and Bhattacharjya, *Sekele Katha*, 174.

    23. Simonti Sen, Introduction to *Englande Bangamohila* (Calcutta: Stree, 1996 reprint), 30.

    24. Chattopadhya, *Krisnobhabini Daser Nirbachita Prabandha*, 160.

25. "Striloker Kaj O Kajer Mahatya" (Women's Work and the Glory of Work), *Bharati and Balak Patrika*, 1298 (August–September, 1891), 224.

26. See note 3.

27. Bharati Ray, *Early Feminists and Colonial India: Sarala Devi Chaudhurani and Rokeya Sakhawat Hossain* (New Delhi: Oxford University Press, 2002), 134.

28. Cited in ibid., 134.

29. Ernst Gellner, *Nations and Nationalism* (Oxford: Blackwell, 1983).

30. Anne McClintock, "Family Feuds: Gender, Nationalism and the Family," *Feminist View* 44 (1993): 67.

31. Peter Jackson and Jan Penrose, eds., *Construction of Race, Place, and Nation* (Minneapolis: University of Minnesota Press, 1993).

32. G. Aloysius, *Nationalism without a Nation in India* (Oxford: New Delhi, 1997), 134–35.

33. Sanjay Seth, "Rewriting Histories of Nationalism: The Politics of Modern Nationalism in India, 1870–1905," *American Historical Review* 104 (February 1999): 95–116.

34. R. Palme Dutt, *India Today* (London: 1940), 288–89, cited in Sanjay Seth, "Rewriting Histories of Nationalism," 97.

35. M. N. Roy, *India in Transition*, 168, 174, cited in Sanjay Seth, "Rewriting Histories of Nationalism," 98.

36. Mrinalini Sinha, *Gender and Nation* (Washington, D.C.: American Historical Association, 2006), 12.

37. Nira Yuval-Davis and Floya Anthias, *Women-Nation-State* (London: Macmillan, 1989).

38. Breda Gray and Louise Ryan, "The Politics of Irish Identities and the Interconnections between Feminism, Nationalism and Colonialism," in Ruth Roach Pierson and Nupur Chadhuri, eds., *Nation, Empire, Colony: Historicizing Gender and Race* (Bloomington: Indiana University Press, 1998). For further discussion on race, gender, and nation, see Nupur Chaudhuri's "Issues of Race, Gender, and Nation in *English Women's Domestic Magazine* and *the Queen*, 1850–1900," in David Finkelstein and Douglas M. Peers, eds., *Negotiating India in the Nineteenth-Century Media* (London: Macmillan, 2000), 51–62.

39. McClintock, "Family Feuds," 66.

40. Burton, *Burdens of History*; and Chaudhuri, "Issues of Race," 51–62.

41. Burton, *Dwelling in the Archives*; Inderpal Grewal, *Home and Harem*.

42. *Englande Bangamohila*, 7–8.

43. Ibid., 2.

44. Ibid., 14. Krishnobhabini often used Bengali women and men interchangeably as Indian women and men. However, in reality, the situations of women were different in different regions. See Angol, *The Emergence of Feminism*.

45. Grewal, *Home, Harem*, 169.

46. Ibid., 129.

47. Ibid., 150.

48. Ibid.

49. Ibid., 150–51.

50. Ibid., 150–51.

51. Ibid., 152.

52. The British used the term *Bengali baboos* to describe middle-class Western-educated Bengali men. Often the British used this term in a negative sense.

53. *Englande Bangamohila*, 152.

54. Ibid., 153.

55. 1902 Presidential Address, in A. Molin Zaidi, ed., *Congress Presidential Addresses*, 5 vols. (New Delhi: Indian Institute of Applied Research, 1985–1989), 2:118.

56. Sinha, *Gender and Nation*, 9.

57. Ibid.

58. Deb, *Atmokatha*, 139–40; Ray, *Early Feminists*, 77.

59. Sarkar, *Hindu Wife*, 48.

60. English women could attend universities, but Cambridge University, for example, did not award formal degrees to women until 1948.

61. *Englande Bangamohila*, 74–75.

62. Ibid., 73.

63. Ibid., 80.

64. Ibid., 74.

65. Ibid., 80.

66. Ibid., 79–82.

67. Ibid., 81.

68. Ibid.

69. Ibid., 82.

70. See Nupur Chaudhuri, "The Indian Other: Reactions of Two Anglo-Indian Women Travel Writers, Eliza Fay and A.U." in Tamara L. Hunt and Micheline R. Lessard, eds., *Women and the Colonial Gaze* (London: Palgrave, 2002), 125–34.

71. Ibid., 82.

72. See Kalyani Dutta, *Pinjare Bashia* (Sitting in the Cage) (Calcutta: Stree, 1996), preface; and Sarkar, *Words to Win*, 14.

73. Burton, *Dwelling in the Archive*; Sinha, *Gender and Nation*, 9.

10. UNCOVERING WOMEN AND GENDER IN QAJAR ARCHIVES OF IRAN

Mansoureh Ettehadieh (Nezam Mafi), Elham Malekzadeh, Maryam Ameli-Rezaei, and Janet Afary

This collaborative essay, the work of scholars living in the United States and Iran, offers several new venues for research on women in the Qajar era (1789–1925). In the individually written sections, each scholar uses a different historical source to provide glimpses into gender and sexual constructs of this period. Mansoureh Ettehadieh (Nezam Mafi) examines a court register from the turn of the twentieth century and argues that these registers reveal a legal dichotomy for women between their economic and marital rights. Elham Malekzadeh looks at philanthropic activities to show a change in patterns of charitable donations from the late Qajar to the early Pahlavi eras (1890s–1930s). Maryam Ameli-Rezaei uncovers private letters by wives and daughters of Qajar rulers. And Janet Afary looks at memoirs of a European medical doctor who served as obstetrician/gynecologist in the Qajar court, in order to explore the institution of marriage and sexual practices in the mid-nineteenth century.

* * *

Traditional historical sources of nineteenth- and early-twentieth-century Iran rarely mention women in great detail. From such sources, scholars obtain only a dim view of the lives of a few well-known women in connection with the lives of their menfolk. However, Mansoureh Ettehadieh (Nezam Mafi) shows that with the development of the field of Iranian women's studies, and the new perspective it has thrown upon other aspects of women's lives, feminist scholars have turned their attention to previously neglected sources such as legal records, private letters, contracts, endowments, wills, and official complaints, all of which have yielded new information that enriches our knowledge about women from different walks of life.[1]

WOMEN AND LEGAL CONTRACTS

The register of Sheikh Fazlallah Nuri (d. 1909), a prominent religious figure executed during the Constitutional Revolution of 1906–11 because of his active opposition to the new democratic movement, is one such unique source.² Nuri had a notary office (*mahzar*) where he registered all contracts undertaken in the area under his jurisdiction. Between 1886 and 1889, nearly 1,400 contracts were signed in his office, a majority of which concerned Tehran, then a small city of about 214,000 inhabitants.³ Some of the contracts pertain to other parts of the country, particularly the town of Nur in the province of Mazandaran, which was Sheikh Fazlallah's hometown. The focus of this section is on contracts made by women and registered in Nuri's office.

It is generally assumed that the law considered women immature and childlike in conducting their own legal affairs in the late nineteenth century. Indeed, some people did believe that women were less intelligent than men in such matters. Women were either denied education altogether or received only a rudimentary knowledge of reading, lest they write love letters. They also remained under the tutelage of a male relative—a father, brother, husband, or even father-in-law or brother-in-law—in the absence of their husband. However, the view that the law treated women as children and always placed them under the guardianship and protection of men is not entirely accurate. Rather, the registers of this period demonstrate that women enjoyed much freedom of action in commercial activities. The commercial contracts in the register of Nuri demonstrate that there were no legal impediments to women entering this arena. They could sell, buy, or rent property; they could dispose of their wealth; and they could lend or borrow money. Some women acted through a representative, while others acted on their own. In the case of marriage, divorce, inheritance, and child care, however, women's legal rights were far inferior to men's or nonexistent.⁴ In the following paragraphs, we shall discuss both the freedom women enjoyed in commercial activities and the lack of such freedom in issues concerning their personal lives, particularly marriage, divorce, and care of children. In addition, we shall examine some miscellaneous contracts that are also recorded in Sheikh Fazlallah's register. These contracts shed light on some of the customs of the period.

According to these contracts, it was possible for women to buy, sell, or rent homes and other types of property. Some transactions entailed substantial property and land. For example, Foruq al-Dowleh, one of the daughters of Naser al-Din Shah (r. 1848–96), the most prominent ruler of the Qajar era, and Foruq's husband, Zahir al-Dowleh, made a transaction with the wealthy merchant Amin al-Zarb for the sale of 20,000 *zar* (a unit of length equal to

104 centimeters) of land that included buildings, a water channel, a pool, and trees. Having purchased this property, Foruq al-Dowleh conducted its administration in person through her representative. In fact, she took care of all her husband's business, as evidenced in her correspondence with her representative.[5]

Women could also rent properties. Khanum Kuchak, the widow of Noruz Ali Beyk, rented a room and a storeroom for four and a half months for 7.5 *tomans*. At times special conditions were attached to the rent. In one example, a woman rented a shop to a vendor of forage (*allafi*), the nephew of her late husband, and included all the tools of the shop, on condition that the nephew employ the woman's son and provide him with midday meals. Women also lent or borrowed money. Mirza Ali borrowed 37.8 *tomans* from a woman known as Hajiyeh Masoumeh for a year.

Although it was forbidden to charge interest openly, particularly in a transaction in a religious court, the practice seems to have been common.[6] To circumvent this restriction, the sum recorded in the contract was always a bit more than the actual amount lent. For instance, in one contract a woman lent 37.8 *tomans* for a year, when in reality she probably lent 37 *tomans* and was to receive .8 as interest at the end of the year. In another example, a man borrowed 40.8 *tomans* from Mulla Fatemeh for six months. The .8 of a *toman* was probably interest, calculated on the 40 *tomans* that was borrowed.

In contrast to their relative freedom to engage in commercial activities, women enjoyed much less independence in their personal lives. Marriage was treated as a contract and was registered in religious courts. The wife kept the contract, which usually included various financial and legal conditions. Family members often arranged the marriage, and in most cases the two families had similar social status or were from the same district or province.[7] The case of Morad, a steward who married the daughter of a carriage driver, provides one example. Another example is the daughter of secretary Mirza Abol Qasem, who married the daughter of Habiballah, secretary of the arsenal. A third is Ali Akbar, the haberdasher who married the daughter of Sadeq, the ink maker.

A man was required to pay a sum known as a *mehr* (marriage portion) to his wife, in cash or property. A portion of the *mehr*, known as a *shirbaha*, was usually paid at the time of marriage. The remainder of the *mehr* could be paid at any time during the marriage or upon death of the husband or dissolution of the marriage. Requesting one's *mehr* during marriage usually signaled a huge conflict between husband and wife, and so most women received their *mehr* upon the death of a husband or at the time of divorce. The wife's family provided the *jahiziyeh* (dowry) at the time of marriage. The dowry included household goods, bedding, kitchen utensils, furniture, and so on and belonged to the wife. If she was divorced, she could take her *jahiziyeh* back with her. The families usually fixed the amount of a man's *mehr* and a woman's *jahiziyeh* before the wedding and after much bargaining. The amount of the *mehr* provided prestige for the new bride and was a future safeguard for her. Yet men rarely paid their wives the entire *mehr* in cases of divorce. In the thirty marriage contracts registered in one booklet, the amount paid to the bride was 21 to 28 percent of the total *mehr* owed. Sometimes the price of a volume of the Quran, which by custom the husband donated to the bride at the time of marriage, was also deducted from the cash payment. In addition to the *mehr*, a husband had to pay his wife *nafaqeh* (maintenance) for the duration of their marriage. If for any reason the husband failed to pay *nafaqeh*, the wife could make a formal complaint. Mashadi Ali Gholam and his pregnant wife had a row because he did not provide her with the required *nafaqeh*. He beat her, and she lost the child. He subsequently claimed she had killed the baby to spite him. However, a police inquiry revealed that he actually wanted to divorce her and was looking for an excuse.[8]

The size of a *mehr* depended on the wealth and social status of the husband. When the medical doctor Seyed Mohammad Ali married the daughter of a government official, he agreed to pay a *mehr* of 1,000 *tomans*. At the time of marriage he paid 100 *tomans* as *shirbaha*, from which he deducted a variety of items: the price of a slave[9] at 7.5 *tomans*; the price of 100 *mesqal* (a unit of weight equal to 5 grams) of silk; and 25 *tomans* for the cost of a Quran. He paid the remainder in cash. Their marriage contract also contained the rare condition that if the husband took a second wife within five years, his first wife had the right to seek a divorce.

Men enjoyed a number of privileges over women in the event of a divorce. A husband could divorce his wife at will and without giving cause. The reasons for divorces were not always cited in this register.[10] If a woman sought a divorce, she forfeited the amount of the *mehr* owed her. Robabaeh, for example, gave up 500 *tomans* of her *mehr* in order to obtain a divorce. If a husband divorced his wife, and no prenuptial agreement existed, he had to pay the rest of the *mehr* plus an additional sum for the next three months. These three months were known as the *'idda* period, during which time the woman could not remarry and her husband could take her back if he wished to do so. The *'idda* period gave men the option to return to the marriage. It also established the paternity of any child that might have been conceived before the divorce. Most women insisted on receiving their *'idda* payment. The daughter of Nayeb Karim, for instance, forfeited her *mehr* but received 3 *tomans* as *'idda* when she obtained a divorce.[11]

As already noted, men also enjoyed the particular privilege of revoking a divorce after it had been completed, with or without the wife's consent. To prevent a man from exercising this right, many marriage contracts stipulated that if a husband decided to take his wife back, he had to pay her a certain sum, sometimes the amount of *mehr* still owed her. Still, a man's right to divorce remained his prerogative. He could divorce and take back the same woman three times. Thereafter he could no longer take back his wife unless she married another man, divorced him, and agreed to remarry the first husband. This short-term husband was known as a *mohallel*. Usually the *mohallel* was a low-level cleric who performed this service for a handsome price. It was assumed that the *mohallel* would divorce the woman soon after the marriage, so the first husband could remarry her. In a number of contracts, certain conditions were added in case the *mohallel* refused to divorce the woman. This Quranic provision was aimed at dissuading a husband from using the threat of divorce too many times.[12]

Married men had the right to take additional wives, either a formal *'aqdi* wife or a *sigheh* (temporary wife).[13] In both cases, the first wife had no right to object. In the event of a divorce, the care of children was given to the wife until the age of two for a boy and seven for a girl, although the father was expected to provide for them. Afterward, the man took the children and brought them to his own home. A *sigheh* wife did not inherit from her husband, but the children from the relationship did inherit, so long as they were recognized by the father. The *'aqdi* wife inherited one-eighth of movable assets (furniture and jewelry, for example, but not land), and a daughter inherited half that of her brother. When a man died, his father and mother had a share of his inheritance, which could leave his widow destitute.

According to the register, many family quarrels between the children of different wives arose over inheritance. In such cases, the religious court or the police settled the dispute. For example, in the case of a quarrel between the sons of the late Mirza Aqa Ebrahim, their father's first wife, and their father's second wife, Roqiyeh, and her son, Roqiyeh claimed that the jewels and clothes in question were her *jahiziyeh*. Eventually, the matter was settled by the additional payment of 15 *tomans* and a kilo and a half (one-half *man*) of *nabat* (crystallized sugar).[14] This settlement was reached on the condition that if within fifty years' time any wrongdoing was proven, the sum of 10 *tomans* would be paid to the complainant. Roqiyeh was also asked to pay the sum of 45 *tomans* for her husband's corpse to be transported to Karbala to be buried near a shrine.[15]

Besides such contracts, the registers of Nuri contain a variety of other types of documents, such as endowments, wills, and the settlements of various disputes involving both women and men. They shed light on many customs of the times, some of which no longer exist. For example, there is a contract between a man and a wet nurse to breast-feed his child for two years for 36 *tomans* a year, plus four new dresses worth 4 *tomans* each and two used ones at 2 *tomans* apiece.

* * *

Other archival sources possess enormous potential for understanding the lives of women during the late nineteenth and early twentieth centuries. Elham Malekzadeh argues that women changed the nature of their philanthropic endowments between the late Qajar and early Pahlavi periods. Using archives that have recorded the charitable contributions of women, she argues that the Constitutional Revolution (1906–11) shifted the philanthropic efforts of women from religious charities aimed at keeping the wealth in the family toward charities with wider societal focus that were also under government control.

WOMEN AND ENDOWMENTS (*VAQF*)

The large number of endowments and charitable deeds in the archives dating back to the sixth century A.H. (eleventh century C.E.) indicates a long tradition of philanthropic activities in Iranian society.[16] Women have engaged widely in this activity out of religious devotion, concern for the needy, or the desire to leave a good name to posterity. Documents concerning endowments made by women during the late Qajar and early Pahlavi era are a rich source for the study of women's religious beliefs, wealth, and social standing.[17]

At the end of the nineteenth century, there was a marked change of emphasis in endowments by Iranians. This change became more pronounced during and after the Constitutional Revolution (1906–11). Iranians were inspired by a wave of nationalistic feelings, a nostalgic love for the homeland, and the need for modern reforms. New ideas about health and education were widely discussed in the press and found an outlet in the endowments of both men and women. Whereas before the revolution endowments were mainly concentrated on founding mosques and religious schools, feeding and giving alms to the poor, and/or providing items such as pots, pans, carpets, and lamps for the mosques, after the Constitutional Revolution endowments shifted toward modern private and public social institutions aimed at providing greater educational and health facilities for the public.

The new messages put forward in the press about the need for reform, the new rights gained by women, and the founding of the parliament gave women the occasion to become socially active. Women argued that these developments had awakened them. They discussed their needs as a social class and, in particular, the need to educate girls and to contribute to social justice. These new ideas influenced the endowments they made, as women began establishing schools to educate girls. These schools even paid attention to destitute girls by providing a number of places for them.

Women also organized societies for charitable deeds.[18] For example, in 1926 a wealthy woman, Najm al-Saltaneh, built and endowed a modern hospital and provided a number of beds for needy patients.[19] This endowment sharply contrasted with that of her mother, who had founded a mosque. This contrast and other such examples provide evidence of changing attitudes toward endowments and women's social responsibilities. Inspired by a new spirit of social equality and civic duty, and a feeling of philanthropy, women directed their charity to health matters and education.[20]

In the past, the aim of people in making endowments had been to keep wealth in the family and to contribute to religious institutions. In fact, in the Qajar period, the administration of many endowments was kept in the family. By contrast, people contributed more to educational and health facilities after the Constitutional Revolution, and in the Pahlavi era they agreed to turn over the administration and management of many of the new endowments to government institutions such as the Lion and Sun (an organization similar to the Red Cross) or the Ministry of Education.[21] During the reign (1925–41) of Reza shah Pahlavi, the first Pahlavi monarch, Zahra Sultan Nezam-Mafi, a female philanthropist, created health and educational facilities. She then turned over the administration of these entities to government institutions.[22] Her philanthropic efforts included endowing a vocational school for deaf children.[23] Another example is her endowment in Shiraz, which provided health care for women.[24]

* * *

In addition to archival documents, several examples of prose (as well as a great deal of poetry) from the pen of Iranian women has survived from the late nineteenth century. Of particular interest from this rich body of historical sources are a number of letters written by women connected to the Qajar court. Maryam Ameli-Rezaei examines the content and style of surviving letters by the mother, daughter, and wives of Naser al-Din Shah (r. 1848–96), the fourth Qajar king. Her analysis opens a window into the everyday concerns of such women. Moreover, she argues that the style and content of these letters provide insights into the origins and early development of women's prose in modern Iran.

WOMEN'S PROSE AND LETTERS

Perhaps the first sample of a woman's prose in Iran is the religious thesis of Ameneh Khatun, the daughter of Molla Mohammad Majlesi, in the seventeenth century C.E.[25] Earlier examples of women's poetry are rare, but a number do exist. However, so far we have not come across prose written by women before the seventeenth century. There are various reasons why. First, women's prose did not attract attention and did not survive because it was considered unimportant. Second, poetry was the main method of expression, and women were more prone to write poetry than prose. Third, having an aptitude for poetry did not require much education. Since the majority of women were illiterate, they could recite poetry but not write prose.

The expansion of the royal harem during the reign of Fath Ali Shah (r. 1772–1834), the second Qajar monarch, gave a boost to the education of women.[26] Consequently, a number of Qurans copied in beautiful calligraphy by women have survived from his reign. Original prose writing, however, began later, during the reign of Naser al-Din Shah, and included travel diaries, religious theses, and letters.

The letters from this period include the correspondence of Mahd-e Uliya (the mother of Naser al-Din Shah), letters of Foruq al-Dowleh (one of the Naser al-Din Shah's daughters), and several letters by the shah's wives, especially his favorites, Anis al-Dowleh, Amin Aqdas, and Nadim al-Dowleh. The correspondence of Mahd-e Uliya discusses the endowments of property, orders and letters to her son, and other people at court.[27] The letters of Foruq al-Dowleh, which cover the years 1884–86, are addressed to her personal agent. As contact with a man was not permitted, Foruq al-Dowleh had to correspond through an agent. These letters concern the administration of her property and her personal problems.[28] The shah's wives wrote him letters when he was away traveling at different times.[29]

By studying and analyzing the contents of these letters, scholars can trace the cares, troubles, and other everyday concerns of these women at court. For instance, these letters reveal that Mahd-e Uliya used her influence at court to intercede with the shah in order to help solve some of the problems of people close to her or her relatives. In another example, Negar Khanum, daughter of the late crown prince Abbas Mirza, made a request to receive the salary paid to her deceased husband Sarem al-Dowleh, son of 'Emad al-Dowleh. Another request involved help needed by Nasrallah Mirza Vali, son of Mohammad 'Ali Mirza, in a financial dispute with his brother. A fourth request was to intercede on behalf of the builder Qurban Ali, who was unjustly accused of theft. A final example was a request for the continuation of the salary payments of Taj al-Moluk to her granddaughter.

Other letters reveal everyday concerns and feelings. Mahd-e Uliya sent her son not only fruits and vegetables from her garden, but also pretty girls who served as his concubines. Her letters to her son are full of terms of endearment, expressions of love, prayers for his health, and good tidings. However, the letters of Mahd-e Uliay, sent to courtiers such as Ayn al-Molk or Mo'tamed al-Molk, and especially to her son-in-law and premier Mirza Taqi Khan Amir Kabir (1848–1952, whom she disliked and ultimately sent to the gallows), are quite arrogant in tone and full of contempt. In these letters she complains excessively about her son's lack of attention to her, and other private matters that she would never report to the shah. Letters by the shah's wives repeat many terms of endearment, express their longing for him, and describe the conditions of the harem during his absence. They also ask him for gifts.

Foruq al-Dowleh's letters to her agent are different. They are letters of a princess to a subordinate. To be confined to a sheltered life did not mean a women was totally isolated; she could conduct her own affairs herself or hire an intermediary, especially if she belonged to the royal house. However, she was covered in these meetings as was deemed proper, and not even her face could be seen. The tone of these letters is imperious and strong. They concern the administration of her property, the calculation of the budget of the household, the overseeing of the duties of the gardeners and servants, the payment of debts, and the sale or purchase of property. All of these activities were the responsibility of the agent Hajji Khan, who acted under her supervision. Foruq al-Dowleh requested that Hajji Khan send regular reports to her. She severely reprimanded him when she found fault in his actions. The letters reveal that she was mindful of her position and her good name. For example, if she heard of any misdemeanors, such as converting a part of the garden into a coffeehouse, drinking by servants and gardeners, or using the revenue of the garden as a guarantee of Hajji Khan's debts, she objected severely and thus safeguarded her wealth and her garden.

The prose in all these letters is simple and colloquial. For example, the verb comes before the other parts of the sentence, as in spoken language. Many spelling mistakes suggest that these women were not well educated and were unaware of proper etiquette of writing. Prayers, such as "May I be your sacrifice," abound in the letters and are often repeated.

The letters, particularly those of the shah's wives, are full of descriptive sentences, some of which are so evocative that they conjure images in the reader's mind as in storytelling. In one letter to the shah, Anis al-Dowleh wrote:

> Maryam Khanum came from Tehran to Tabriz to be with her husband, and according to her she came to see me in the northern garden. That same night she fainted, and while she was unconscious she had a bad colic. She fainted

three times. I thought Maryam had died. I cried and beat myself so much that I didn't feel well at all. Throughout this ordeal Maryam's children were also crying. One child was crying because he had no milk. Another said his mother had died and he no longer had a mother.[30]

Nadim al-Slataneh's letter to the shah provides another example:

> On Sunday the 5th of Rabi'al-Avval, after morning prayer I went to Nadimabad and sat there; the colorful flowers had bloomed water lilies, carnations, tulips—I just sat and looked at them. Shokuh al-Saltaneh was also sitting in the poolhouse. She panted badly because of the heat. I saw Yamin al-Dolweh's mother with a cloth over her head; her eyes were sunken as she came out of the room feeling weak. She didn't have the strength to speak. She said: "Nadim al-Saltaneh, what are you doing? Are you gardening again?" I said: "Mashadi, what has happened to you?" She said: "I don't know. I didn't sleep last night until morning. I don't know what is the use of my remaining in this house. I am like a mad person." I advised her not to be sad: "God willing, the shah's kindness will not diminish and your sadness will disappear."[31]

These passages suggest that Qajar aristocratic women described their personal feelings in a manner akin to the writing of a memoir. They described the conditions of society and their internal and personal feelings as women. They wrote without censorship and with great candor. For these reasons, their letters are an appropriate source for the study of the attitudes and inner feelings of the women at the court of Naser al-Din Shah.

* * *

Finally, depictions of Iranian women by foreigners are a valuable source for greater insight into women's history in this period. Janet Afary uses the memoirs of Jakob Polak, an Austrian Jew and physician for Shah Naser al-Din, to examine marriage practices of the time. In spite of the biases contained in Polak's work, Afary demonstrates that such sources contain a wealth of information for historians of women, family, and sexuality in the late Qajar period.[32]

A GLIMPSE INTO SEXUAL PRACTICES

Iran lags far behind Egypt and Turkey in the accessibility of records and registers and in research on the institution of family and sexuality. Yet a close look at harem memoirs and various studies on harem life, especially accounts by European physicians at the court, can shed much light on this issue. Despite their Orientalist prejudices, European travelers' accounts, including memoirs by several women who were keen observers of gender relations, such as Mary Sheil, Carla Serena, M. J. Dieulafoy, Gertrude Bell, and Ella

Constance Sykes, can help draw the outlines of such relations in the court of Nasir al-Din Shah, especially when we combine these sources with religious and legal manuals and, when available, police records.[33]

The memoirs of Dr. Jakob Polak (1818–91), the personal physician of Naser al-Din Shah Qajar, provide us with the most detailed account of urban Iranian sexual practices in the mid-nineteenth century. Polak was in Iran from 1851 to 1860. He served as obstetrician/gynecologist to many women, both inside and outside the harem. He seems to have been genuinely fond of Iranians and intellectually curious about their culture and way of life. He journeyed through the country in the company of the shah, wrote a number of medical treatises about illnesses in Iran, and trained a new generation of Iranian physicians.

Polak was a great admirer of early universal marriage and felt it benefited Iranian women. He judged it to be "a simple fact that when a girl reaches a certain age, she must marry and other matters related to wealth and social class are of less concern. In addition, the ease of divorce does not turn marriage into as difficult a task as it was in Europe. We can understand why there are no bachelors and spinsters, which in civilized countries are in abundance."[34] In his view, early marriage prevented a host of physical ailments that contemporary European society attributed to the womb. Early marriage held the "positive result that hysteria, epilepsy, amenorrhea [absence of menses], dysmenorrhea, and masturbation among virgins almost never happens, only here and there among widows and those strongly guarded, and those neglected by their husbands."[35] Despite Polak's archaic assessments, others confirmed his view on one issue: mothers and elder females did not seem to teach daughters about sex, except for a rudimentary lecture on the importance of defloration on the wedding night. Most girls were too young at the time of their weddings to know much about the process and assumed the wedding feast was about finding new relatives and receiving new gifts of clothes, dolls, jewelry, and perhaps a home of one's own.

Polak also contradicted himself with regard to the benefits of early marriage for girls. Early marriage, coupled with malnutrition, had many harsh consequences for women's bodies. Women aged prematurely and seem to have reached menopause anywhere from the relatively young age of thirty-two to thirty-five.[36] Multiple pregnancies and childbirths, followed by a host of potential gynecological complications, often made sex difficult after a few years.[37]

High infant mortality rates also had an impact on family size. On average, the fertility rate for an urban nineteenth-century Iranian woman was between six and eight children. Polak and Dr. Ernest Cloquet, Naser al-Din Shah's French physician, believed that in Tehran and other urban areas, from half to nearly two-thirds of children died by the age of three, often from seasonal cholera outbreaks linked to contaminated water and food, as well as from famine.[38] There were other reasons for women's multiple pregnancies. Children were seen as "nails" that permanently secured a woman's marriage. As in many other cultures, families assumed that a woman's womb determined the sex of a child. A wife's not giving birth to sons was a valid reason for her husband to take a second wife. Women were thus eager to have many children, preferably boys.

The question of virginity added to the sexual tensions of marriage. A girl's supposed lack of virginity on her wedding night was a "permanent taint" that dishonored her and her entire family.[39] Despite ample advice attributed to the Prophet and religious luminaries such as Imam Ghazali (d. 1111) and Majlesi (d. 1698), who recommended foreplay in order that men arouse women's desire before coitus, many men were ignorant of these practices. On the wedding night, the groom was under immense pressure to prove his virility, while the wife was terrified that for some reason she would not be found a virgin. A cultural emphasis on nuptial defloration often ruined the possibility of amorous intimacy. In such cases, the wedding night could set off a long series of traumas in marital relations.[40]

Freud may have had a point when he emphasized the distressing consequences of a girl's first sexual encounter. In a patriarchal order that places paramount value on a woman's virginity, the girl knows that "her loss of virginity brings a diminution of sexual value."[41] A young woman feels great rage at the man who deflowers her, a feeling that sometimes permanently affects her erotic life. For this reason, Freud thought, "second marriages so often turn out better than first."[42]

Additional anxieties particular to the Middle Eastern culture might arise on the wedding night. Often a midwife was stationed at the door of the wedding chamber to await the auspicious moment and gleefully present the bloodstained sheets to the relatives, proving both the groom's virility and the bride's chastity.[43] A groom's avowal that the young bride was not a virgin would cause great turmoil. Polak reported that "when a girl marries, she must be a virgin with the hymen intact [*dochtar-e bakere*]; if she is without it, it is her fault.[44] Often in these cases a woman could be cast out after the first night on a simple statement from her husband. A cruel and unjust practice, often used with evil intent and with the goal of extorting money, was to call the wife defiled."[45]

Resourceful families knew how to deal with these contingencies, however. Before the wedding, they took the girl to a midwife who testified to her virginity. For a girl who had lost her virginity before marriage, one option was to marry her briefly to a low-level cleric (in return for a handsome payment) and then arrange a second marriage with a person of higher status. Another was to arrange the girl's marriage to an inexperienced youth, oblivious to the markers of virginity. A third common solution was hymen reconstruction, to "stitch her [hymen] with the help of one of several Iranian surgeons who are experts in such matters."[46]

Likewise, there were solutions to illegitimate pregnancies. As part of its recognition of sexual pleasure, Islam has always tolerated contraceptives to a certain degree.[47] In the medieval era, contraceptives in the form of vaginal suppositories and tampons were known to some. Jurists often approved contraceptives and ruled that a husband's permission was preferable, but not absolutely necessary. Both herbs and opium (which was inserted in the vagina) were routinely used for this purpose, with the unfortunate result that women sometimes became addicted to opium or developed gynecological complications.[48] On the whole, coitus interruptus remained the chief method of contraception. All schools of Islamic jurists sanctioned it, provided the formal wife gave her consent.[49]

Polak admired the skill of Iranian midwives in delivering babies and performing other minor surgeries on women, but he particularly singled out their skills in performing abortions:

> If an unmarried woman, a widow, or a divorced woman gives birth, her death would be assured. This situation is unheard of however. Illegitimate children (*haramzade*) are never found among the Shi'is, and the word exists solely as an insult. All pregnancies outside of marriage end in abortion, in which the placenta is punctured. The midwives perform this operation with skill and experience; at least in Tehran they are well-known and frequently visited. After all, these things were somewhat publicly known and no barriers were placed in the way. Only particularly unlucky creatures attempted to help themselves. Some use large numbers of leeches, some slice veins on their feet, some induce vomiting with Sulfas Cupri, or ingest the sprout of a date pit; failing all of these methods, the stomach is massaged and kicked. Many are killed by these crude practices.[50]

Illegitimate births among unmarried girls were probably uncommon, since many wed before menarche. But such incidents did occur among married, divorced, or widowed women.[51] Contrary to Polak's observation, reports from the late nineteenth and early twentieth centuries note that "illegitimate children were abandoned on the benches of mosques or in front of shrines."[52]

Polak claimed never to have performed an abortion, but he did not incriminate midwives who did: "How can we blame these women for appealing to a kinder specialist?"[53] In the Ottoman Empire, elite women apparently used abortion as a method of birth control with their husbands' consent.[54] In Iran, by contrast, 'aqdi (formal) wives seldom used abortion as birth control, because infant mortality rates were so high.[55] The story of Princess Taj al-Saltaneh, daughter of Naser al-Din Shah, suggests that some married women did undergo secret abortions. She chose one after learning her husband had contracted venereal disease and hearing that a favorite niece had died in childbirth. Taj had a botched abortion that left her nerves frail for many years, suggesting a different reality than what Polak describes.[56]

CONCLUSION

Our study of Qajar archives and records of European physicians of the period provide a new view on urban middle- and upper-class women's agency within the confines of their cloistered lives. The legal contracts registered at the notary office of Sheikh Fazlallah Nuri provide a glimpse into the conditions of urban women's lives and the legal dichotomy regarding women in Muslim law. On the one hand, with regard to personal relations, especially marriage and divorce, the law treated women as minors, placing them under the tutelage of their menfolk. On the other hand, women were free to engage in all sorts of commercial and economic transactions, and they took full advantage of these rights. Records of endowments at the turn of the twentieth century also suggest women's active participation in philanthropic affairs and a gradual shift in types of institutions they sponsored in the early years of the twentieth century. Although older types of endowments aimed at mosques and religious institutions did not altogether disappear, better-educated, more political, and more socially aware women were shifting their philanthropic efforts toward health and educational charities, especially women's schools and orphanages.

The prose of elite women also furnishes a window into the closed harem world. From the mid-nineteenth century, prose was gradually replacing poetry as a means of expression, and in the Qajar court we come across a greater number of prose essays written by women. In fact, women's simplified prose was part of the process that led to the overall simplification of Persian prose style. However, just as the cycles of women's lives in the Qajar era differed from those of men, so did women's prose. As opposed to the prose of men, much of which belonged to the public sector, women's prose belonged to the inner and personal sector.

Finally, through the writings of Polak and other European physicians of the period, we see that despite enormous pressures on middle- and upper-class urban women to conform, girls and wives did not always succumb.

There were no "Great Refusals" in this period, no large-scale public forms of resistance, but in James Scott's apt characterization, numerous smaller and more readily available "weapons of the weak" were deployed in daily life.[57] Young women resisted their parents' choice of suitors and attempted to exercise some influence over the marriage process. Aided by resourceful midwives, family members, and love brokers, women also underwent secret hymen repair. For many centuries, the Muslim world seemed to tolerate contraception more than did Christian Europe. In Iran, female contraceptives were widely available to women, but not without dangerous consequences. If these took the form of opiates, health complications would often result. Abortion also seems to have been relatively common. It was sought by married, divorced, and widowed women, perhaps among them those who were victims of cases of incest and rape. The availability of contraception and abortion may help explain why cases of honor killing are extremely rare in the documents of the period. Honor killings became more prevalent later on, as girls were married at an older age and the veil was shed. This change gave young women greater visibility. Neighbors and acquaintances were now able to monitor more closely the actions of young unveiled women on the streets and to pass moral judgment on their behavior.

NOTES

Thanks to Brian Maxson, Mike Green, and Mir Yarfitz for their editorial assistance.

1. For a similar discussion of legal sources in the Ottoman Empire, see Judith E. Tucker, *In the House of the Law: Gender and Islamic Law in Ottoman Syria and Palestine* (Berkeley: University of California Press, 1998), 1.

2. Nuri was a conservative religious leader who tried to undermine the Constitutional Revolution. In 1909, when nationalist forces defeated the king Mohammad Ali Shah and forced him to abdicate, they also tried Nuri in a revolutionary court and subsequently hanged him with permission from ranking constitutionalist clerics in Najaf (Iraq). Other registers from this period have not yet been published. Nuri's register appears in Mansoureh Ettehadieh (Nezam Mafi) and Said Ruhi, eds., *Dar Mahzar-e Sheikh Fazlallah Nuri, Asnad-e Hoquqi-ye Ahd-e Naseri* (In the Law Court of Sheikh Fazlallah Nuri, Legal Documents of the Naseri Era) (Tehran: Nashr-e Tarikh-e Iran, 1385S/2006).

3. The first census of the population of Tehran was undertaken in 1286 A.H./1869 C.E., when the population of the city was about 147,256. This number gradually increased. In 1317/1899, a new census was taken and the population had risen to 244,400, for an average increase of about 3,133 people a year. See Sirus Sadvandian and Mansoureh Ettehadieh (Nezam Mafi), eds., *Amar-e dar al-Khalafeh-ye Tehran, Asnadi az Tarikh-e Ejtema'i-ye Tehran dar Asr-e Qajar* (Census of the Population of Tehran: Documents about the Social History of Tehran during the Qajar Era) (Tehran: Nashr-e Tarikh-e Iran, 1368S/1989).

4. For a parallel discussion of these issues in Sunni Malaki laws of North Africa, see

Mounira M. Charrad, *States and Women's Rights: The Making of Postcolonial Tunisia, Algeria, and Morocco* (Berkeley: University of California Press, 2001).

5. Foruq al-Dowleh's correspondence with her representative is published in Iraj Afshar, ed., *Nameh-haye Foruq al-Dowleh Mashhur be Malekeh-ye Iran* (Letters of Foruq al-Dowleh, Known as the Queen of Iran) (Tehran: Nashr-e Farzan, 1383S/2004). These letters give interesting details about the way she conducted her transactions and oversaw her property and that of her husband, but her letters also suggest she had minimal formal education.

6. There were also professional moneylenders who did not register their transactions and thus could fix an interest rate at will. It is most likely that a promise of payment was exchanged between the parties. A number of exchanges between two relatives exist. One person was the director of the customs in Kashan, and the other was his relative in Tehran, who looked after his affairs. One letter mentions Eliyahou, a Jewish man who did business with them and charged interest. Mansoureh Ettehadieh, ed., *Moraselat-e Tehran, Nameh-haye Mobasher-e Hossein Khan Mobaser al-Saltaneh, az Tehran be Kashan, 1304–1309HQ* (Tehran Correspondence: Letters by the Agent of Mirza Hosein Khan Mobaser al-Saltaneh from Tehran to Kashan) (Tehran: Ketab-e Siyamak, 1384S/2005).

7. The police also recorded marriage ceremonies as part of their cataloging of major events of the capital. From a calculation made of these records, 44 percent of the marriages were between members of the same family. "Zan dar Jame'eh-ye Qajar" (Women in Qajar Society), in *Inja Tehran Ast* (This Is Tehran) (Tehran: Nashr-e Tarikh-e Iran, 1377/1998), 267.

8. Ibid., 369–70.

9. Slavery and the sale of slaves continued in Iran in the early years of the twentieth century. Despite the fact that the African slave trade was declared illegal, slaves were smuggled in for some time. When it proved difficult to find African slaves, local Baluchis were substituted. For more information see Thomas M. Ricks, "Slaves and Slave Traders in the Persian Gulf, Eighteenth and Nineteenth Centuries: An Assessment," in William Gervase Clarence-Smith, ed., *The Economics of the Indian Ocean Slave Trade in the Nineteenth Century* (London: Frank Cass, 1989), 60–70; and Ricks, "Slaves and Slave Trading in Shi'i Iran, AD 1500–1900," in Maghan Keita, ed., *Conceptualizing/Re-Conceptualizing Africa: The Construction of African Historical Identity* (Leiden: Brill, 2002), 77–88.

10. Police reports detail some of the arguments that led to divorce. Often the man simply looked for an excuse to divorce his wife. One prevalent cause of quarreling and wife beating was a wife leaving the house without the permission of her husband. Such beatings also sometimes led to suicide attempts. There are a number of cases when women took opium to commit suicide; many were discovered and saved, probably because houses were overcrowded (sixteen people on average to one house). "Zan dar Jame'eh-ye Qajar," *Inja Tehran Ast*, 249–86.

11. *Dar Mahzar-e Sheikh Fazallah*, document 366, 205.

12. *Dar Mahzar-e Sheikh Fazlallah*, document 7778, 396.

13. For a more detailed discussion of temporary marriage, see the classic work by Shahla Haeri, *Law of Desire: Temporary Marriage in Shi'i Iran* (Syracuse, N.Y.: Syracuse University Press, 1989).

14. Giving *nabat* or crystallized sugar was a common custom to settle quarrels. It was also offered as a wedding gift after contracts were signed to sweeten the transaction.

15. For all Shi'ite who were relatively wealthy, the ideal was to be buried near the tomb of the Prophet's grandson and the revered third Imam, Hossein, in Karbala, Iraq. In such cases someone would usually accompany the corpse to Karbala in a ceremonial manner.

16. Hasan Tajbakhsh, *Tarikh-e Bimarestan-haye Iran az Aghaz ta Asr-e Hazer* (History of Hospitals in Iran from Beginning to the Present) (Tehran: Pajuheshgah-e Ulum-e Ensani, 1379S/2000), 11.

17. For the most detailed social history of charity and philanthropy in the Middle East, see Mine Ener, *Managing Egypt's Poor and the Politics of Benevolence, 1800–1952* (Princeton, N.J.: Princeton University Press, 2003).

18. Janet Afary, *Enqelab-e Mashruteh-ye Iran* (The Iranian Constitutional Revolution, 1906–11), trans. Reza Rezai (Tehran: Nahsr-e Bistun, 1379/2000), 239–43. For the English edition, see Janet Afary, *The Iranian Constitutional Revolution* (New York: Columbia University Press, 1996).

19. Reza'i Omid, 1378/1999, "Bimarestan-e Najmiyeh" (Najmiyeh Hospital), *Majelleh-e Vaqf, Miras-e Javidan* 7, no. 4 (Endowments and Charitable Organization of Islamic Republic of Iran): 281.

20. Rusta'i Mohsen, *Tarikh-e Teb va Tebabat dar Iran az Ahd-e Qajar ta Payan-e Asr-e Reza Shah* (History of Medicine and Medical Practice in Iran from the Qajar Period to the end of Reza Shah's Reign) (Tehran: The National Library and Archives of Islamic Republic of Iran, 1382S/2003), 296, 524–28. See also Ahmadi, *Nezhat-e Vaqf va Gostaresh-e omur-e Darmani dar Tarikh-e Mo'aser ba Takiyeh bar Asnad-e Vaqfi-ye Tehran* (Endowment and the Development of Methods of Remedy in Contemporary Documents Based on Endowment Documents of Tehran) (Tehran: Bonyad-e Pajuhesh va Gostareshe Vaqf, 1387S/2008): 30–35.

21. Ibid. Religious minorities, such as Jews, Christians, and Zoroastrians, had their own endowments whose purpose was solely philanthropic.

22. Abbas Sharaei Ardakani, *Miras-e mandegar va Majmu'eh-ye Asnad Vaqfi-ye Jam'iyat-e Helal Ahmar-e Iran* (Everlasting Heritage Collection of Documents of Endowments and Gifts to the Iranian Red Crescent) (Tehran: n.p., 1381S/2003).

23. Elham Malekzadeh, "Eqdamat-e Kheyriyeh va Moqufat Zahra Soltan Nezam Mafi" (Charitable Deeds and Endowments of Zahra Soltan Nezam Mafi) *Vaqf, Mirath-e Javidan magazin* 13 (1381S/2001): 49.

24. Merritt Hawks, *Afsaneh va Vaqe'iyat,* trans. Mohammad Hossein Nazari Nejad Islamic Research Foundation Astan Qods-e Razavi Mashhad (1371S/1992), 225. For a discussion of social work in the Pahlavi era, see Sattareh Farman Farmaian and Dona Munker, *Daughter of Persia: A Woman's Journey from Her Father's Harem through the Islamic Revolution* (New York: Anchor, 1993).

25. Ruhangiz Kerachi, *Andisheh Garan-e Zan dar She'r-e Mashruteh* (Women Thinkers in the Poems of the Constitutional Revolution) (Tehran: Tehran al-Zahra University Press, 1374S/1995).

26. For a discussion of elite women in this period, see Abbas Amanat, ed., *Crowning Anguish: Memoirs of a Persian Princess from the Harem to Modernity, 1884–1914* (Wash-

ington, D.C.: Mage, 1993); and Lois Beck and Guity Nashat, eds., *Women in Iran: From 1800 to the Islamic Republic* (Urbana: University of Illinois Press, 2004).

27. Abdolhossein Nava'i, *Mahd-e Uliya be Ravayat-e Asnad* (Mahd-e Uliya, mother of Naser al-Din Shah, According to Her Documents) (1385S/2006, Tehran: Asatir Press, 1382S/2004).

28. Iraj Afshar, *Namehha-ye Foruq al-Dowleh* (Letters of Foruq al-Dowleh) (Tehran: Farzan Press, 2004).

29. Esma'il Rezvani, *Ruznameh-ye Khaterat-e Naser al-Din Shah* (The Diaries of Naser al-Din Shah) *Markaz-e Asnad va Ketab Khaneh-ye Melli* (Tehran: n.p., 1378S/1999).

30. Ibid., 359.

31. Nava'i, *Mahd-e Uliya*, 104.

32. For a more detailed discussion of Polak and his insight into Iran's sexual relations, see Afary, *Sexual Politics in Modern Iran* (Cambridge: Cambridge University Press, 2009). For translations of Polak from German to English I am grateful to Brynn Lyerly and Ashley Passmore.

33. Mary Sheil, wife of the British ambassador to Iran, traveled to that country in the 1850s. See her *Glimpses of Life and Manners in Persia* (New York: Arno Press, [1856] 1973); Carla Serena, writer and traveler, was in Iran in 1877–78. See her *Safarnameh-ye Madam Karla Serena* (1877–78), Ali Asghar Saidi, trans. (Tehran: Zavvar Press, [1883] 1983); M. J. Dieulafoy was an artist and the wife of Marcel Dieulafoy, archeologist and engineer. They traveled to Iran in 1881 and 1882. See her *Safarnameh-ye Dieulafoy dar Zaman-e Qajar,* Farahvashi, trans. (Tehran: Khayyam Press, [1887] 1983). Gertrude Bell traveled to Iran in 1892 when her uncle, Sir Frank Lascelles, was appointed British minister in Tehran; Ella Constance Sykes was a sister of Major Percy Sykes, a British officer in Iran. See her *Persia and Its People* (London: Elibron Classics, [1910] 2005). As Nima Naghibi has argued, these sources ought to be used with caution. See her *Rethinking Global Sisterhood: Western Feminism and Iran* (Minneapolis: University of Minnesota Press, 2007). However, in the absence of other sources, they remain essential.

34. Jakob Eduard Polak, *Persien, das Land und seine Bewohner: Ethnographische Schilderungen*, vol. 1 (Hildesheim and New York: Georg Olms Verlag, [1865] 1976), 205.

35. Ibid., 1:207.

36. Ibid., 1:195. See also Sykes, *Persia and Its People,* 218.

37. Hasan Javadi, Manijeh Marashi, and Simin Shekarloo, eds., *Ta'dib al-Nesvan va Ma'ayeb al-Rejal* (Chicago: Historical Studies of Iranian Women, [1895] 1992), 192–200.

38. Polak, *Persien*, 1:195 and 217. See also Sheil, *Glimpses,* 149.

39. Paul Vieille, "Iranian Women in Family Alliance and Sexual Politics," 451–72, in Lois Beck and Nikki R. Keddie, eds., *Women in the Muslim World* (Cambridge, Mass.: Harvard University Press, 1978), 455.

40. Ja'far Shahri, *Tarikh-e Ejtema'i-ye Tehran dar Qran-e Sizdahom*, 6 vols. (Tehran: Rasa, 1990), 1:259. Historian Ja'far Shahri is an indispensable but problematic source. His multivolume study of Tehran at the turn of the twentieth century is replete with prejudicial sentiments and should be used with caution.

41. Sigmund Freud, "The Taboo of Virginity: Contributions to the Psychology of Love III," in *The Standard Edition of the Complete Psychological Works of Sigmund Freud*, vol.

11: *Five Lectures on Psycho-Analysis, Leonardo da Vinci and Other Works,* trans. James Strachey (London: The Hogarth Press, [1910] 1957), 202.

42. Ibid., 202.

43. Morteza Ravandi, *Tarikh-e ejtema'i-ye Iran,* vol. 6 (Tehran: Amirkabir Press, 1984), 250.

44. Deuteronomy, chapter 22.

45. Polak, *Persien,* 1:213. See also Deuteronomy, chapters 13–23.

46. Ibid., 213.

47. B. F. Musallam, *Sex and Society in Islam: Birth Control before the Nineteenth Century* (New York: Cambridge University Press, 1983), 13.

48. Shahri, *Tarikh-e,* 1:269.

49. Musallam, *Sex and Society,* 38.

50. Polak, *Persien,* 1:219. Clot Bay, founder of the schools of medicine and midwifery in Ottoman Egypt, was more critical of Egyptian midwives' ability to deliver babies safely, but he also admired their ability to provide "quick and effective abortions." Mervat F. Hatem, "The Professionalization of Health and the Control of Women's Bodies as Modern Governmentalities in Nineteenth-Century Egypt," in Madeline C. Zilfi, ed., *Women in the Ottoman Empire: Middle Eastern Women in the Early Modern Era* (Leiden: Brill, 1997), 70.

51. Carla Serena writes about the rape of a young widow and the birth of her illegitimate child. The woman's brother killed the baby, but a cleric spared the mother. See *Safarnameh-ye,* 298–99.

52. Shahri, *Tarikh-e,* 1:469.

53. Polak, *Persien,* 1:219. For a discussion of abortion in nineteenth-century Egypt, see Mervat F. Hatem, "The Professionalization of Health and the Control of Women's Bodies as Modern Governmentalities in Nineteenth-Century Egypt," in Zilfi, *Women in the Ottoman Empire,* 66–80.

54. For a different practice in the Ottoman harem, see Leslie P. Peirce, *Imperial Harem: Women and Sovereignty in the Ottoman Empire* (New York: Oxford University Press, 1993), 43.

55. Polak, *Persien,* 1:218.

56. Taj al-Saltana, *Crowning Anguish: Memoirs of a Persian Princess from the Harem to Modernity, 1884–1914,* Abbas Amanat, ed. (Washington D.C.: Mage, 1993), 300–301. See also Amanat, "The Changing World of Taj al-Saltanah," in Taj al-Saltanah, *Crowning Anguish,* 60.

57. James C. Scott, *Weapons of the Weak: Everyday Forms of Peasant Resistance* (New Haven, Conn.: Yale University Press, 1985).

PART 3

CREATING WOMEN'S HISTORY ARCHIVES

11. REVEALING NEW NARRATIVES OF WOMEN IN LAS VEGAS

Joanne L. Goodwin

Research on the subject of women remains a creative and ambitious task decades after the founding of the field of women's history. That is particularly the case when the researcher seeks to answer questions about the experiences of those outside society's mainstream culture. During the period 1950 to 1980, Las Vegas definitely fit American's perception of outsider. Popular ideas about the city include a mob-dominated past, perpetual reinvention of its attractions, and a fantasy land for adults. Oddly, none of these ideas tell us much about the people who lived in the city and whose labor sustained the industry that attracts millions of tourists a year. In fact, the most popular images of women as showgirls and hookers bear little resemblance to the lives of the women who lived there. Yet the absence of alternative sources that would complicate these dominant images serves to perpetuate that master narrative. Consider the differences in the following stories from what we think we know about women in Las Vegas.

Imagine the world of gambling in 1937, when Claudine Williams, not yet sixteen years of age, took her first job in a club. She grew up in Louisiana near the Texas border, where oil fields provided jobs during the Great Depression. She started working in restaurants at the age of twelve to help her mother support the family. When a new club opened a few years later, she convinced the manager that she could deal cards and that she was eighteen. That club provided Williams with on-the-job training as she learned every job and every game. Two years later she moved to Houston, and by the beginning of World War II she opened her own small club. In 1963 she moved to Las Vegas with her husband and son to participate in the transformation of the gambling oasis. Claudine Williams and her husband, Shelby, ran the casino as a partnership. She knew, if needed, she could step into any game and deal the hand. They built their signature property, the Holiday Casino, across the street from Caesars Palace. In 1983 she sold it to Harrah's Entertainment. Until her death in 2009, she remained one of only a few women to own and operate a major casino.[1]

In another part of Louisiana, Lucille Bryant had two work opportunities available to African Americans: chopping cotton or cleaning white women's houses. She earned $5 a week at most. Married at sixteen and the mother of six children, Bryant worked most of her life. Members of her extended family started to move to Las Vegas in 1941; then she followed her husband to the area in 1953 "to get work for myself." She got a job as a housekeeper at the Algiers Hotel on her first morning in Las Vegas. It paid $8 a day. Years later, she recounted her thoughts and feelings on that day. "I got on my knees right there in the Algiers Hotel and I gave God thanks. Eight dollars a day and working in the shade. You know, not backbreaking in the sun. Eight dollars a day—*all* this money. I wrote back and I said, 'Everybody come on out here. White folks gone crazy. They're giving us $8 a day for making a bed and cleaning a bathroom.'" Bryant stayed in Las Vegas and continued to work in housekeeping until her retirement. She became a committed union member and was active in several community groups, including the Parent-Teachers Association, the Cub Scouts, and her church.[2]

The lives of Williams and Bryant, like those of others preserved in the Las Vegas Women Oral History Project, offer new and valuable perspectives on women's choices and challenges during the postwar years. Both women moved away from their homes, in this case from Louisiana to Las Vegas. They came from humble backgrounds and received modest education. Each needed to earn a living, and Las Vegas proved financially fruitful. Their lives also diverged widely. They occupied opposite ends of the employment pyramid: one a member of an elite group of owners, and the other a member of the city's most powerful union. Race distinguished their experiences and opportunities, as it did in the United States as a whole for most of the twentieth century. Gender roles shaped their lives but did not define them. Both women married and raised a family, yet they challenged mid-twentieth-century gender expectations by maintaining an active public life through employment and community activities.[3]

Learning about the women who lived in Las Vegas expands our understanding of U.S. women since 1945. At a most basic level, their stories take us beyond the simple image constructed by casino public relations offices in the 1950s, images that portrayed the city solely as a place with fast women and taboo-breaking behavior. Casino publicists, entertainment directors, and city business interests produced images of starlets and chorines standing by swimming pools, dancing in chorus lines, or otherwise enjoying the entertainment available in Las Vegas. An offshoot of Betty Grable's wartime "sweater girl," this female image became linked in tourists' minds with the city itself. By the 1970s, several showroom spectacles included nudity and the imagery of the statuesque "showgirl" emerged with her suggestion of sexual availability. In an era of increasing tensions between conventional morals and newfound expressions of sexuality, the showgirl image came to overwhelm and obscure the experiences of women as workers and community builders. Going beyond local history, the narratives fill out the story of women's experiences with survival, migration, work, and agency.[4]

The process of reclaiming women's involvement in U.S. culture and history has intrigued me for several decades. As a student finishing my undergraduate studies in the early 1970s, I pestered my art history faculty to tell us about the women artists who remained invisible in books and lectures. Cultural anthropology offered me greater opportunities to study the well-understood and integrated involvement of women in the production of cultural arts of tribal people. After graduation, my interests in gender, art, and culture led me to Los Angeles and the L.A. Woman's Building, a center of feminist art on the West Coast. That cultural institution's archive needed organization, which I provided between 1977 and 1978 while expanding its visual archive of events and exhibits. All of this work led me to understand the crucial relationship between documentation and the writing of history. Both experiences gave me insight into the systems of power that define some cultural actors as marginal and others as central to a cultural mission. In other words, it became clear to me that the process of creating archives was neither natural nor objective. These experiences prepared me for the archival enterprises I would undertake much later in Las Vegas.

Historians of women and social historians first challenged these systems of power in the 1960s and 1970s by raising issues such as who was left out of the historical record, the value of nonconventional materials for research, and the significance of preserving diverse voices and experiences. The necessary actions to include other voices, to make those lives visible, and to create access to previously silenced lives and voices continue to be essential in a diverse society. Postmodern critiques of archives have exposed the hierarchies of power embedded in traditional archives. They have, for example, challenged assumptions of archival neutrality and raised critical questions about what gets archived and, consequently, what and whose history is preserved. Antoinette Burton advanced the critique of archives with her collection of "archive stories," which as a whole challenged the claim to objectivity in archives, both in the composition of the collections and in their maintenance. Burton and others called for historians to assess more critically their archival sources, as well as to recognize alternative sources of evidence.[5]

This essay describes two "archival" projects in which I participated with the goal of achieving a fuller understanding of working women's lives in Las Vegas during the second half of the twentieth century. It begins with a discussion about the necessary process of building an archives and oral history project on Las Vegas women. An academic understanding of the levels of power embedded in the formation of archives did not change the fact that dynamic power differentials continue to exist and make the process of including non-elites in archives a difficult feat. The chapter continues with a discussion of the themes that emerged from the sources and how they change what we know about American women's lives. Both projects give researchers and the general public the opportunity to answer for themselves how women participated in the life of this fast-growing tourist city and how they adapted to the major social transitions under way in American life. Without these sources, midcentury perspectives of women would remain unknown and untold.

LAS VEGAS: CREATING NEW SOURCES

The term *boomtown* truly describes Las Vegas, a place that grew faster than its residents and elected officials often could manage. Living in such a young city provided the opportunity to meet women who were part of the transition from small town to tourist metropolis. As a new resident of this boomtown, I watched as journalists, intellectuals, scholars, and other commentators rushed to interpret Las Vegas and its growth to the rest of the country. Most often, they promoted well-worn stereotypes of glamour and sin. We know that sex sells, but sex work was not the only type of activity engaged in by women in Las Vegas.

Notwithstanding its unique history, Las Vegas shares characteristics with other industry towns. Rather than manufacturing, the service and tourism industries drove the development and expansion of the area since 1945. Tourism, with its embedded gaming and entertainment sectors, provided a wealth of job opportunities for women and men with a basic education. That industry comprises service jobs that continue to attract workers decades later. The city's expansion coincided with larger national trends, like the postwar migration west, an expanding consumer economy, and the transition in the national economy from manufacturing to service jobs. Observers have not only overlooked Las Vegas's place in these national trends, but have also been particularly ignorant of women's participation in them. Similarly, observers' fascination with the promotional images of women in Las Vegas has blinded them to the variety of activities undertaken by women in the workforce and the community.[6]

Conventional approaches to research on the history of women in Las Vegas proved inadequate in 1992, when I began my search. The strongest historical record existed for early-twentieth-century Nevada, a period before Las Vegas distinguished itself as a gambling destination, an entertainment capital, or a fast-growing metropolis. The existing collections at the state archives and university departments of special collections contained a miscellany of manuscripts with an emphasis on business and political leaders as well as pioneers. The archives of the area had not kept up with acquisitions, despite the efforts of a small number of individuals. This weak base of historical sources led to a corresponding dearth of interpretations of women's lives and a scarcity of publications. Yet when asked, longtime residents stressed that women helped build every part of Las Vegas, from the small town's ranches, businesses, churches, and schools to the wartime industries and the resorts that defined the city as a tourist destination since the 1950s. The evidence that could offer answers to the questions about women's historical experiences in Las Vegas, particularly during its period of most significant growth, remained uncollected in private homes or in the greater privacy of individual memories.

The fragmentary evidence of women's lives in Nevada bothered a formidable leader named Jean Ford. She lived in Las Vegas for several years while she raised her family. Like so many homemakers of the 1950s and 1960s, Jean Ford became active in public life through the League of Women Voters (LWV). She led that organization in Las Vegas and statewide. When she decided to run for the state legislature in the 1970s, she did so with the support of hundreds of politicized women and men who came to learn about the issues of equality through the LWV and Jean Ford. After leaving the legislature, she dedicated herself to building an institutional base of support for the preservation of history about women in the state. The results of her efforts include the formation of the Nevada Women's Archives (NWA) located at both state universities, a community organization dedicated to promoting women's history known as the Nevada Women's History Project, and publications including her own oral history.[7]

In 1992, Jean Ford taught women's studies at the University of Nevada, Reno (UNR). She convinced the director of UNR's Special Collections Department to allow her to identify the holdings that pertained to writing the history of women in the state. She worked with the department to acquire additional materials from individuals and organizations whose collections enhanced the archive. They agreed to call the collection the Nevada Women's Archives. Two years later, she visited the University of Nevada, Las Vegas, to measure the degree of interest in starting a similar archive in the southern part of the state. As the History Department's U.S. women's historian, I was aware of the lack of sources for local history and strongly supported the initiative. We quickly convened a committee of faculty from various relevant disciplines to sort out the process and form an advisory board. As I have described elsewhere,

> We wanted to avoid marginalizing a women's collection. In fact, our goal was quite the opposite—to build into an existing repository additional collections that focused on women's lives. We wanted to counteract the charge that women were not included in Las Vegas history because there was a lack of evidence about their lives or about their contributions. At the same time, we wanted to identify the holdings as a unique collection. In this way, we could avoid the invisibility of women's lives that can occur when sources are lost in the papers of a husband or family. We also wanted to avoid the tendency to collect only from the economic and political elite by designing a deliberate acquisition plan that was conscious of many forms of diversity.[8]

After weeks of discussing the mechanics of building the collection, administrative minutiae, and funding, we received administrative approval to begin.

The work progressed in three directions: assessing the existing collections, acquiring new collections, and processing collections for researchers. The advisory board made it a priority to assess the content of the existing collections. Some had been organized, but most had no finding guides or detailed organization. The manager of that task, Carol Corbett, had archival training. She surveyed each collection's content and discussed its relevance for the study of women with the board. Several faculty members had experience with historical methods that guided our preference to include not only collections of and about women, but also materials that could shed light on gender relations. For example, while twentieth-century women's clubs offered an obvious example of community life, the advertisements displayed in entertainment magazines also provided cultural data on gender and sexuality. We advised Corbett to use these broadly defined criteria. While Corbett assessed the holdings, Ford began the long process of acquiring new collections.

Jean Ford's history in the area and her reputation as a legislator helped immeasurably in gaining credibility for the project. She utilized her circle of influence with the League of Women Voters and other civic groups. Again the advisory board set the priorities and advocated a broad set of criteria that would allow gender analysis at a later date. The acquisition stage revealed subtle attitudes that women held about their own histories. A few donors understood the significance of their work to the larger community history. This was particularly true when acquiring papers of women's clubs and organizations. Some groups had identified their own club historian, a member who had been filing away documentary evidence of the group's activities for years. The records of Las Vegas's women's organizations came out of storage areas on outdoor patios, in garages, and in offices. In a city where attics are rare and basements almost nonexistent, space for organizational papers was difficult to come by. Nevertheless, they kept the papers, which speaks to their pride in carrying forward the history of their institutions. Other donors admitted astonishment that their papers might have value to anyone aside from themselves or their families. Ford proved particularly able to convince these initially reluctant donors of the significance their lives would have in telling the larger story of women's experiences in Las Vegas.

The collection assessment and acquisitions came to fruition with the massive effort to process collections for researchers' use. This all-important step often falls to the bottom of priorities, leaving the archival treasures inaccessible. In our case, the board created solutions that met mutual needs. Students with an interest in women's history or women's studies took independent study or internship credits with me to learn about archival methods. Corbett trained dozens of students to process the collections and to make them accessible for research over the years.

By 2007, the Nevada Women's Archives at the University of Nevada, Las Vegas, contained approximately two hundred collections and a wealth of visual documentation from which to study women's experiences. These included the townswomen and ranch families who helped to start Las Vegas at the beginning of the twentieth century; the professional women who by midcentury worked as teachers, businesswomen, and journalists; and the organizations through which women invested volunteer hours to build the community. These sources will help researchers understand the postwar dynamics of women's lives, their economic contributions, and their civic engagement. Manuscripts, audio interviews, and oral history transcripts shed light on women's involvement in the civil rights and antipoverty movements in Las Vegas. Women's rights can be studied through the papers of individuals who worked for the Equal Rights Amendment; the first shelter for battered women, called SafeNest; and the first agency to assist women who had been raped, Community Action Against Rape. The group of community and university volunteers that came together to form the Nevada Women's Archives at UNLV was like a movement in itself. With ongoing institutional support, the collection will continue to expand and serve the public.

During the years it took to create the Nevada Women's Archives, I read broadly to better understand the context in which Las Vegas women lived between 1945 and 1980. The newspapers provided an essential source for local affairs, politics, and personalities. Yet the news circumscribed information of women's lives into women's club news (through the 1960s), crises (murders, arrests, and other headlines), or social news. The commercial visual resources of the era, such as public relations files, advertising, playbills, and entertainment magazines, reinforced the master narrative of the wild vacation town and the exotic women who performed there. The photo archives donated by local families and organizations provided a glimpse of alternative narratives suggesting families, farms, small businesses, trade, workers, and civic groups. Yet the agency of the women in those pictures proved difficult to interpret. The conventional sources proved unable to answer the new questions posed about women. As a result, another project, the Las Vegas Women Oral History Project, began to unfold.

Oral histories provide a vital component of Las Vegas's historical record. The city's youth, as well as business leaders' preoccupation with future developments, has produced relatively few collections for research. Those that existed provided little personal insight or observations on women's lives. Memory and personal reflection, however, are as vulnerable to relativity and reinterpretation as other sources, such as newspapers, diaries, letters, or the omissions of the federal census. Yet considering the flaws of traditional sources, oral histories seemed comparable in their advantages and limits. Furthermore, the oral histories offered information unavailable elsewhere. Using the same sense of critical observation applied to all sources, the researcher must balance the information drawn from the narratives with the understanding that they are constructed entities.[9]

The idea to collect oral histories from women who had built the city, both figuratively and literally, came from three different sources. From my viewpoint, the histories of wage earners, women of color, and women in gaming remained poorly represented in the Nevada Women's Archives. Despite our well-laid plans regarding diversity, a few areas—civic life, professionals, and education—became overrepresented in the acquired collections. A second source of interest came from a small group of graduate students who wanted to learn oral history methods in order to conduct their research for their master's theses. Third, community members from the NWA advisory board repeatedly suggested that the histories of groundbreaking women be collected.

The original design of the oral history project focused on collecting the stories of women in the gaming and entertainment industries. People flooded us with the names of elite women to interview, as they assumed we wanted only those with the greatest wealth and stature. However, we organized the project to include not only the owners and wives of owners, but also the beverage servers, dancers, housekeepers, and dealers who worked in gaming. The occupational segregation of the period allowed us to capture the ethnic, racial, and economic diversity of women workers.

We divided the project into the four areas of work that corresponded to the layout of the hotel casinos. *The back of the house* comprised service workers in food preparation and housekeeping; *the floor* covered dealers and beverage servers; *the showroom* included dancers, entertainers, and showgirls; and *the management* encompassed owners, managers, and directors. Each interviewer used a set of core interview questions that included work as well as social and familial experiences. We added questions about their early history to get a better sense of who they were and how they became a part of the city. The core set of questions could be expanded by each interviewer, allowing flexibility in the interviews. Overall, the interviews sought to better understand the course of women's work lives. "By asking our subjects why they came to the city, how they combined work and family, what opportunities they saw for women, and how employment changed over time with the shift in ownership from families, individuals, or small groups to corporations, the oral history project began to reconstruct the narratives of women's lives."[10]

Initially, few of the working women we encountered understood why their lives might be worth recording. They expressed either modesty or astonishment that people from the university would want to know what they did at work. They assumed that the stories that had the most value were those of close encounters with celebrities rather than the actions they took to build their lives and community. A small handful understood the significance of their stories and their place in the historical record. After talking with the narrators and explaining the project and its goals, their self-consciousness subsided. As we took the time to collect their stories, they relaxed and the pride they took in their work became evident.

Within a few years, the original group had completed their work and moved on to other endeavors, but the project continued. Having just begun to record midcentury narratives, I expanded the project. Adding two more series, on pioneers and on community builders, gave the project a wider scope with which to examine women's choices and transitions. This turned out to enrich the collection in unexpected ways, through revealing truly heroic actions by early pioneering women as well as groundbreaking work to build much-needed social services.

REVEALING NEW NARRATIVES

The Las Vegas Women Oral History Project comprised a total of thirty-five finished oral histories in 2007, with another dozen in various stages of the process. Four major themes emerged from this body of work, themes that intersected with most of the narrators' accounts. Women migrated from other states to Las Vegas. They migrated to take advantage of job opportunities. They balanced employment with marriage. Last, they engaged in the process of community building. In discovering the themes, it became clear that not only did these histories describe the experiences of women's lives in Las Vegas, but the narratives revealed patterns of women's lives within the United States in the decades between 1945 and 1980. The path of one woman, Florence Schilling McClure, demonstrates the confluence of these themes in our narrators' lives.

Florence Schilling grew up in Illinois but left home after a few years of secretarial school to assist in the war effort. At first she worked at the Willow Run Army Airbase near Ypsilanti, Michigan, and then she moved to Miami, Florida, where she worked for the Provost Marshall in the Security and Intelligence Division. She met and married her husband, James McClure, in Florida. Over the next few years, they moved frequently with Jim's military assignments and began their family. After her husband retired, they settled in California, and Florence returned to the workforce. McClure used her executive secretarial skills at the International Hotel in Los Angeles. Her boss, Burton Cohen, found her indispensable and invited Florence to join him on his new assignment—to open the Frontier Hotel and Casino in Las Vegas in 1966. She and Jim agreed to make the move. McClure worked for Cohen in the executive offices of the Frontier Hotel and Casino and later at the Desert Inn Hotel and Casino before she decided to quit and return to school to complete her undergraduate degree.

McClure had a long-standing interest in current events; however, she confessed to being inexperienced in the ways of government and politics. She decided to change that by joining the League of Women Voters in 1967, a choice that had a defining influence on her life. Jean Ford (mentioned previously in the creation of the NWA) mentored McClure and encouraged her to hold offices in the local and state chapters of the LWV. When Ford joined the state legislature, she solicited McClure to lead the statewide organization during the turbulent years of the Equal Rights Amendment campaign. McClure used the LWV training to learn as much as she could about citizens' influence on government. She had no interest in holding office herself but used her knowledge to change Nevada's laws and Las Vegas's practices concerning rape. She worked with others to form Community Action Against Rape (currently called the Rape Crisis Center), which offered counseling and an emergency hotline. McClure housed the first offices in her living room, went to court to support those who had been raped, worked with hospitals to create a procedure that assisted raped women, and led the charge to change Nevada's laws. Legislators called her "Hurricane Florence" because of the gale-force strength of her convictions and her unrelenting actions to change the way the state treated women.[11]

McClure, like others in the study, came to Las Vegas from another part of the United States. She married, raised two children, and valued her family life. Nevertheless, she had a long history of wage earning during her years as a single woman as well as during her married life. After her children were raised, McClure found another avenue for her energies as she became a true community builder, learning from one of the classic organizations of the period, the League of Women Voters. She went beyond the norm and formed one of the important community resources in Las Vegas, the Rape Crisis Center. Not all of our narrators achieved such prominence in their contributions, but their stories demonstrate the impact of these four themes.

Migration

Between 1940 and 1980, the population of Las Vegas doubled five times.[12] Most of the residents came from other U.S. states. We know that many gamblers migrated to the city when law enforcement "back home" cracked down; nevertheless, the numbers indicate that plenty of other people moved during the postwar years. Two-parent families, single mothers with children, couples, and single women moved to Las Vegas. The sample from the oral history project reflects the same pattern. Most of the narrators came from the South, the upper Midwest, and western states. Like Claudine Williams and Lucille Bryant, whose stories opened this chapter, dancers, entertainers, and hotel workers deliberately moved to Las Vegas to find work. Florence McClure had no intention of living in Las Vegas until a job opportunity brought her to the city. That story was repeated constantly in a city where the native-born son or daughter was rare.

Economic Mobility

Economic growth and increased discretionary income defined the 1950s and 1960s for many Americans. The positive economic climate contributed to the growth of the Las Vegas tourism industry with its wealth of jobs. Many of those jobs paid tips, and the high demand for workers provided greater opportunity than the narrators found elsewhere. They came from families that ranged from poor to middle-class in origin. Some never finished high school, while others had some postsecondary education at a university or a professional school. As a group, they remarked on the opportunities to earn a comfortable living without an advanced education and despite job discrimination during many of those years.[13]

Blending Work and Family

Historians initially described the postwar era as one in which the ideals of domesticity limited women to the home, where they cared for their families. Subsequent revisions of that thesis placed greater emphasis on women as agents of change in publications that documented women's efforts in labor unions, social movements, and politics.[14] The Las Vegas oral histories convey a third pattern. Rather than choose between being a homemaker or an activist, many women blended work with family life. Several spent most of their lives in the workforce, and a few continued to work into their seventies and eighties. Women with children made child-care arrangements or broke up periods of employment around child rearing. Others chose to stay childless. They spoke of supportive spouses or of eventual divorces. Those who left the workforce after having children took their voluntary work very seriously, as if it was a career. While we cannot assume this theme represents all working women in the postwar period, we do know that a statistical analysis of the census showed that a higher percentage of women in all marital categories worked in Las Vegas than in the nation as a whole during the years 1940 to 1980.[15]

Community Engagement

While rarely a hotbed of political activity, Las Vegas offered numerous opportunities for women of all backgrounds to improve their communities. Our narrators engaged in activities of the Parent-Teacher Association, church groups, and political parties that they perceived would improve their lives and those of their families. Women also identified with larger social issues, such as rights for racial-ethnic communities, hotel workers, or women. Sarann Preddy and Alice Key participated in civil rights activities since the 1940s regardless of where they lived. Hatty Canty and Rachel Coleman saw the power that the culinary union had to improve workers' lives. Frances Montes completed her own education and then worked to create opportunities for all Latinos/as. Renee Diamond and Harriet Trudell joined the antipoverty effort to reduce poverty and reform welfare. Dorothy Eisenberg and Florence McClure worked through the League of Women Voters to improve numerous policies affecting Nevadans.[16]

Popular culture has eclipsed women's participation in the development of Las Vegas with its focus on "sin city" and the dazzling spectacle of the showgirl. The archival projects described herein reveal alternative life stories of women who created their lives within postwar America. Their stories help explain women's choices and challenges, whether as workers or as volunteers in civic organizations. Together, they describe a highly mobile population. They allow us to understand that despite the limited range of job opportunities as a result of job segmentation by race and sex, women were in the workforce in numbers larger than the national average. They describe individuals who were part of families and, for some, part of a larger community. They felt the influence of mainstream gender perceptions, but they did not fall victim to them. The narratives of Las Vegas women not only change how we view the lives of women in Las Vegas, but they demonstrate how individual women from across the United States adjusted to the changes in American society from the end of World War II to the era of Ronald Reagan. Creating archives of their experiences provides alternative perspectives on women's lives and on gender roles.

NOTES

The author would like to thank the editors of this volume, whose comments helped to clarify my thoughts and write a better chapter.

1. *Claudine Williams: A Life in Gaming,* an oral history conducted with and edited by Joanne L. Goodwin (Las Vegas: Women's Research Institute of Nevada, 2007). The interviews took place on November 20, 1997, and on November 9, 2005.

2. Claytee White, "'Eight Dollars a Day and Working in the Shade': An Oral History of African American Migrant Women in the Las Vegas Gaming Industry," in Quintard Taylor and Shirley Ann Wilson Moore, eds., *African American Women Confront the West: 1600-2000* (Norman: University of Oklahoma Press, 2003), 276-92. The original interviews took place on December 13, 1995, and March 1, 1996.

3. The Las Vegas Women Oral History Project began in 1995 in the History Department at the University of Nevada, Las Vegas. A comprehensive account of its origins may be found in Joanne L. Goodwin, "From the Ground Up: Building Archival Sources for the History of Women in Las Vegas," *Nevada Historical Society Quarterly* 49, no. 4 (Winter 2006): 263-76. The first fifteen interviews on gaming and entertainment were completed by 2001. In the spring of that year, a large reception was held to recognize the women and their contributions to Las Vegas. The recording of the oral histories ranged in length from two hours to fifteen hours and took place within different time periods. Although project members tried to conduct the interviews within a matter of months, in some cases it would be years before all the recording sessions were completed.

4. No synthesis of women's history in Las Vegas exists yet. The best reference work for finding publications on women throughout the state is Jean Ford, Betty J. Glass, and

Martha B. Gould, *Women in Nevada History: An Annotated Bibliography of Published Sources* (n.p.: Nevada Women's History Project, 2000). Anita Ernst Watson, *Into Their Own: Nevada Women Emerging into Public Life* (Reno: Nevada Humanities Committee, 2000), includes some coverage of individual women and organizations in southern Nevada during the first half of the twentieth century. A small group of articles cover women of note, such as Helen J. Stewart, whose land formed the original town site, and specific events, such as the development of women's clubs. Biographies of notable women can be found in M. A. Duval, ed., *Skirts That Swept the Desert Floor: One Hundred Biographical Profiles of Nevada Women in History,* Vol. 1 (Las Vegas, Nev.: Stephens Press, 2006); and Carole Bellmyre, ed., *Distinguished Women in Southern Nevada* (Las Vegas, Nev.: Distinguished, 1995–2000). A slimmer body of scholarship exists for the post-1945 years. Notable additions to the history of women include Annelise Orleck, *Storming Caesars Palace: How Black Mothers Fought Their Own War on Poverty* (Boston: Beacon Press, 2005); Earnest N. Bracey, "Ruby Duncan, Operation Life, and Welfare Rights in Nevada," *Nevada Historical Society Quarterly* 44, no. 2 (2001): 133–46; and Claytee White, "'Eight Dollars a Day.'"

5. Antoinette Burton, ed., *Archive Stories: Facts, Fictions, and the Writing of History* (Durham, N.C.: Duke University Press, 2005). Also see the introduction in Antoinette Burton, *Dwelling in the Archive: Women Writing House, Home, and History in Late Colonial India* (New York: Oxford University Press, 2003).

6. On the history of Las Vegas and its rapid development in the twentieth century, see Eugene P. Moehring, *Resort City in the Sunbelt: Las Vegas, 1930–2000* (Reno: University of Nevada Press, 2000); Hal K. Rothman and Mike Davis, *The Grit beneath the Glitter: Tales from the Real Las Vegas* (Berkeley: University of California Press, 2002); and John M. Findlay, *People of Chance: Gambling in American Society from Jamestown to Las Vegas* (New York: Oxford University Press, 1986). On the development of race and ethnic communities, see Jerry L. Simich and Thomas C. Wright, eds., *The Peoples of Las Vegas: One City, Many Faces* (Reno: University of Nevada Press, 2005).

7. Shortly before her death, Ford completed her oral history. See *Jean Ford: A Nevada Woman Leads the Way,* from oral history interviews conducted and edited by Victoria Ford (Reno: Oral History Program, University of Nevada, 1998). Two books on sources were published through her work with the Nevada Women's History Project. See *Nevada Women's History: A Guide to Archives and Manuscripts in Nevada Repositories,* comp. Jean Ford (Reno: Special Collections Department, University Library, University of Nevada, Reno, 1998); and published posthumously, Jean Ford, Betty J. Glass, and Martha B. Gould, eds. *Women in Nevada History: An Annotated Bibliography Of Published Sources* (Reno: Nevada Women's History Project, 2000). Information about the activities of the Nevada Women's History Project may be accessed online at http://www.unr.edu/wrc/nwhp.

8. Joanne L. Goodwin, "From the Ground Up," 267.

9. For the challenges associated with oral histories as historical sources, see Michael Frisch, *A Shared Authority: Essays on the Craft and Meaning of Oral and Public History* (Albany, N.Y.: State University of New York Press, 1990); Jaclyn Jeffrey and Glenace Edwall, eds., *Memory and History: Essays on Remembering and Interpreting Human Experience* (Lanham, Md.: University Press of America, 1992); and Donald Ritchie, *Doing Oral History* (New York: Twayne, 1995). An expansive bibliography exists on the special

issues of collecting oral histories of women. For example, see Selma Leydesdorff and Luisa Passerini, eds., *Gender and Memory* (New York: Oxford University Press, 1996); Joanna Bornat and Hanna Diamond, "Women's History and Oral History: Developments and Debates," *Women's History Review* 16, no. 1 (2007): 19–39; and Sherna Berger Gluck and Daphne Patai, *Women's Words: The Feminist Practice of Oral History* (New York: Routledge, 1991).

10. Goodwin, "From the Ground Up," 273.

11. Florence McClure, "An Interview with Florence Alberta Schilling McClure," an oral history conducted by Joanne L. Goodwin, January 24, 1996, and February 6, 1996 (transcript), Las Vegas Women Oral History Project, 2006, Special Collections, Lied Library, University of Nevada, Las Vegas.

12. The population grew from 10,389 in 1950 to 350,511 by the 1980 census. The metropolitan area of Las Vegas grew with the development of several sections outside the city proper during this period. I used the Las Vegas township figures to capture most accurately the growth of the area. These numbers do not capture the contingent cities of Henderson and North Las Vegas, however. *Seventeenth Census of the United States, 1950*, Census of Population, Volume 1, Number of Inhabitants, Table 6. Population of Counties by Minor Civil Divisions: 1930–1950; *Twentieth Census of the United States, 1980*, Census of Population, volume 1: Characteristics of the Population, Chap. A Number of Inhabitants, Table 4. Population of County Subdivisions: 1960 to 1980.

13. Gender segregation in employment continued in Las Vegas until 1991. In terms of race, the Moulin Rouge Agreement of 1960 attempted to open up public accommodations and employment, specifically in strip hotel-casinos. In 1981 a consent decree further attempted to open all jobs to African Americans. In 1991 a similar consent decree opened employment to all women and Hispanics. See Moehring, *Resort City*.

14. On postwar domestic containment, see Elaine Tyler May, *Homeward Bound: American Families in the Cold War Era* (New York: Basic Books, 1988). For several revisionist approaches, see Joanne Meyerowitz, ed., *Not June Cleaver: Women and Gender in Postwar America, 1945–1960* (Philadelphia: Temple University Press, 1994).

15. A survey of employment patterns for women in all marital categories can be found in Joanne L. Goodwin, "'She Works Hard for Her Money': A Reassessment of Las Vegas Women Workers, 1940–1980," in Rothman and Davis, *The Grit beneath the Glitter*, 243–59.

16. For example, see Florence McClure, "An Interview with Florence Alberta Schilling McClure," an oral history conducted by Joanne L. Goodwin, January 24, 1996, and February 6, 1996 (transcript), Las Vegas Women Oral History Project, 2006, Special Collections, Lied Library, University of Nevada, Las Vegas. Similar oral histories exist for all the women named in this group.

12. CREATING AN ARCHIVE OF WORKING WOMEN'S ORAL HISTORIES IN BEIRA, MOZAMBIQUE

Kathleen Sheldon

The inclusion of women and gender in African studies has been flourishing in recent decades, but before the 1970s there was little published research on African women's history. Information on women in Africa was more often found in anthropological and ethnographic studies, a focus that continues to be evident in the preponderance of research on African women in development rather than history per se. Existing published materials, reflecting the interests of Africanist anthropologists, documented ethnographic stories with little or no historical context. The absence of a historiography on African women's history meant that there were no ongoing debates on issues and research. Scholars during that era sometimes felt they were working in a vacuum, trying to develop a broader framework as they simultaneously pursued their own specific research.

Scholars were motivated, as with women's history in other world areas, by the international feminist movement, and from the beginning there was a political component to much of the research and writing in African women's history. African women's history also paralleled the expansion of African history following World War II, as scholars inside and outside of Africa began to focus on historical transformations on the African continent. Initially, historians concentrated on showing that women were present and active despite their omission from much historical writing about Africa, and the new wave of research in the 1970s and early 1980s highlighted women and economic change and women as political or community activists.[1] By the mid-1980s, the history of African women was emerging as a vibrant and steadily expanding area of research, and studies of family and sexuality also began to appear.[2] Only in the 1990s did a substantial number of monographs on specific topics begin to be published.

Throughout those decades, historians were hampered by a paucity of published and archival materials related to women in Africa. Researchers developed a variety of methods to retrieve historical information, including using historical linguistics and geography, analyzing folktales and women's songs, and looking at material aspects of women's lives, such as textiles, pottery, and tattoos, among other innovative approaches.[3] But the most common technique was to use some form of oral testimony or oral history. While this approach is used in African history more generally, it has proven particularly central to reclaiming women's lives. Historians have turned to women's life histories and oral testimony to fill lacunae in published sources, methods that have proved to be especially valuable in collecting information about ordinary women's lives in the recent past.[4]

Claire Robertson wrote about her experience collecting life histories of Ga women in Ghana, some of which were incorporated into her book.[5] She also published an article that dealt with such methodological issues as maintaining the informant's privacy, sharing the researcher's own comparable information so that it is not so intensely an exploitative situation, the good and bad aspects of hiring an interpreter from the local area, problems of language and translation more generally, choosing women to interview, balancing the process by asking questions and eliciting more free-form stories, and payment for those who were interviewed. She also addressed the issue of the gender of the researcher and the interviewees. She found that the housing arrangements in central Accra, where women usually lived in compounds with female relations rather than with their husbands, favored interviews. In contrast, interviews conducted with women in suburban housing often found a co-resident husband intervening, either forbidding the continuation of the interview or sitting in and overriding any comments his wife made with his own opinions.[6]

Christine Obbo provided some interesting anecdotes in her discussion of research in a variety of East African communities. On the one hand, men assumed they knew about women's history while women did not have that knowledge. On the other hand, women would often allow men who interrupted to have their say, and then continue with their own stories by stating, "As I was saying...." Obbo suggests that researchers need to create a space in their interviews and conversations so that women can talk, especially when they need to recover from male intrusions.[7]

Francesca Declich's discussion of Tanzania and Somalia revealed how oral histories vary between men and women. She demonstrated how women and men had distinct histories to tell because their experiences were different, and when stories were retold, male and female audiences heard and remembered the information differently. This disparity became a key issue in the historical development of ethnicity and identity, as women from matrilineal backgrounds focused on female ancestors as founders of their group, which later gained an ethnic cohesion centered on the female progenitors. Male narrators completely elided that important source of identity. The broader understanding of their history was impaired because researchers often wrote down the male versions, entirely omitting the female interpretation of historical experiences.[8] Other researchers investigated modern elite women, as with Nakanyike Musisi, who discussed the process of collecting information for a biography of the last Bugandan queen mother, who had died in 1957. Because the biography "demonstrates the intimate relationship between royal women's sexuality, power, and state machinery," she found she had to be flexible in approaching those who had knowledge about the queen, on occasion presenting herself as more religious in order to gain access.[9]

Researchers have used oral information to good effect in African women's history, finding information that was not in archival or other written sources and bringing women's perspective to the study of social change. The words that researchers collect and save become documents of women's history, sometimes expanding on published work and archival sources, and sometimes filling a gap in extant information, providing source material about women's lives that is not available anywhere else.

RESEARCH IN BEIRA, MOZAMBIQUE, IN THE 1980S

When I first went to Mozambique in 1982, I knew that I wanted to engage in research on women's history, but I did not know exactly how I would focus my inquiries. In addition to the effort involved in pursuing a new area of research about Mozambican women's history, I arrived in the early months of what became a devastating internal war that lasted until a peace accord was signed in 1992. Mozambique had won its independence from Portugal in 1975 after a bitter liberation struggle led by the Mozambique Liberation Front, commonly called Frelimo (for Frente de Libertação de Moçambique), which became the ruling party. I had been intrigued by their progressive approach to women and wanted to witness the changes introduced to support women's liberation. Most of the documented materials I had read were pamphlets and nonscholarly articles reporting on Frelimo's socialist approach to reform. Those sources discussed the role of women in the liberation movement, where they generally were only marginally involved in combat but did important work in support activities.[10] The official perspective was found in the widely reprinted speech by Frelimo leader and Mozambique's first president, Samora Machel, "The Liberation of Women Is a Fundamental Necessity for the Revolution"; the title is suggestive of why I wanted to see for myself what changes were occurring in Mozambique.[11] Following independence, Frelimo adopted a new constitution that guaranteed equal rights for women, passed legislation that gave women maternity leave, and introduced reforms that improved access to education for girls and boys.

I had some prior preparation, as I had been involved in one of the first graduate seminars on African women's history at UCLA and I had pursued archival research in Mozambican history in Portugal, Mozambique's former colonial ruler. I had hoped to study Swahili communities in northern Mozambique, but my plans were thrown awry just a month before I was about to leave for Mozambique with my husband and fifteen-month-old daughter. My husband, a pediatrician who had a contract with the Mozambican Ministry of Health, was informed that we would be stationed in Beira, the country's second-largest city and a backwater Indian Ocean port in central Mozambique, quite distant from any Swahili areas.

We were not prepared for the difficulties of simply living in Beira. Beira was extremely isolated from Maputo. Intercity phone service was nonexistent, mail was very slow and unreliable, and computer-based communications and cell phones were in the distant future. Markets and shops sported empty shelves and signs stating, "We don't have salt, meat, bread," indicating the lack of staple foods. In this chapter I discuss how I developed a research project using the sources I found after arriving in Mozambique. Despite ongoing difficulties and obstacles related to extreme poverty and burgeoning war conditions, I was able to complete the research for my dissertation, which analyzed the improvements in conditions for working women following the 1975 socialist victory.[12]

My approach to finding women's history was very broad. With no published or archival sources as a beginning point, all I knew was that women lived in Beira and must have a history, though it had not yet been written. Once we arrived in Mozambique, I introduced myself to as many scholars as possible, especially during the first weeks while we were in Maputo, the capital city and home to the only university at that time. Over the course of two years residence in Beira, I found some documentary materials and I gained some insights when I attended local women's meetings, but my primary sources were oral histories that I collected from working women, women who were invisible in the standard archives. I developed a comparative study that analyzed the history of nurses, garment workers, and cashew factory workers under Portuguese colonialism and followed the varied experiences of each group of women as the new socialist government implemented changes that brought improvements to their lives.

LOCAL ARCHIVES AND OTHER DOCUMENT SOURCES

I began with a conventional approach, looking for documents that would allow me to formulate a research plan. As a perquisite of my husband's work at the local hospital, I obtained official support from Dr. Rui Bastos, the hospital director. His idea to do a history of the hospital gave me a specific way to introduce myself, and he provided a pass called a *guia*. With the *guia* I went to the City Council, where the basement archives housed a repository of municipal history. Although the shelves bulged with manila file folders pertaining to land and property ownership, there was no easy access to information concerning women, and I was not able to use that resource.

I visited the Municipal Library, a modern building near downtown Beira with no card catalog and no obvious organization. I started at one end of the shelves, and over the course of a few weeks I was able to glance at every book owned by the library. While I found a few historical tidbits, there was nothing about women's history. Balbina dos Santos, Rui Bastos's wife and a historian herself, had a short-term job at the library sorting uncatalogued books and papers and determining what should be stored in the national archive in more permanent and secure conditions. She invited me to join her and have a look for myself before the items were sent to Maputo. I spent several days on the second floor of the library, reading various publications and making notes about Beira's history, though again I found next to nothing on women.

I only had slightly better results from looking at local newspapers and magazines. At *Diário de Moçambique*, I began reading issues from the 1940s; for that entire decade, I came across only one photograph of an African, a man arrested for theft. I went to the local bureau of *Notícias de Moçambique*, where again the stories from the colonial era were limited to neighborhood sporting events and white colonial social affairs, with Africans appearing in print only in the police blotter column. An exception was the weekly magazine *Tempo*, which ran a series on Mozambique's history that included information about women in colonial Lourenço Marques (renamed Maputo after independence).[13] Isabel Casimiro, who was pursuing her own research on women in Mozambique simultaneously with me, wrote her master's thesis on newspapers' women's pages during the late colonial period, but I found nothing useful regarding women in Beira.[14]

In Maputo some months later, I went to the Historical Archive of Mozambique, again using my Ministry of Health *guia* to facilitate access. I read reports from the chartered Mozambique Company, which had been the government of Sofala province for several decades in the early twentieth century.[15] I examined numerous official bulletins and reports that gave me more insight into colonial ideas about racially segregating health care, the role of women in that system, and other pertinent topics, though specific information on women was scarce.

Given the absence of material in the formal archives and published sources, I made an effort to develop documentary material. I learned that the provincial labor ministry in Beira was in the process of conducting a survey of workers, and after several visits I was given a handwritten set of numbers that outlined the gender division of labor in basic employment sectors such as industry, agriculture, and government, crucial material that was not available elsewhere at that time. The information in the unpublished report showed more than 24,000 men working in industry, but only 1,380 women holding factory-based jobs.[16] In a city of over 250,000 residents, those numbers reflected the restricted openings for women in the waged sector of the economy.

I found further written sources at the factories where I interviewed working women. At the Belita garment factory, the office staff showed me annual reports, and while I was copying out the reports by hand (there was no working photocopier in the entire city), the director of the factory stopped to talk to me about women's work.[17] He then brought me a report that he thought would be of interest. It was an account of a very intriguing incident in 1979. At independence only five women worked at Belita, none of them at sewing machines, though the process of hiring women had accelerated rapidly after that. During the late 1970s, women in the garment factory were still a new phenomenon, and there were several cases where women were perceived as malingering, claiming they were not well and could not perform their regular work. Rather than simply fire those who were not working as expected, the factory leadership organized a series of meetings and discussions that included representatives from the women's organization (OMM, for Organização da Mulher Moçambicana) and from the Ministry of Health. They set up a protocol for confirming that women who were hired were physically able to do the work. It was a fascinating internal memo that illustrated how the new socialist management was dealing with women workers through involving workers in the decision making.[18]

At the cashew processing factory I was told that the company files from the colonial days had been destroyed, though I was able to copy (again, by hand) a two-page document concerning the nationalization of the factory. And while I was in the cashew management offices, I spotted some work assignment sheets posted on a bulletin board, so I noted which sectors were headed by women. Each of these fleeting and obscure sources added incrementally to my understanding of women's workplace roles and history.

Probably the most unusual discovery was in some trash that was blown onto our apartment balcony. As I picked it up to throw it away, I realized that it included a few pages from a month-old *Diário de Moçambique* containing an extensive centerfold story about workers at the local sugar mill, and it had interviews with women workers.[19] With no easy way to find back issues of the paper, and no microfilm or digital collection of that publication, I doubt that I would have found that article through another avenue. Conventional written sources and archives brought me inadequate information about the history of women in Beira, so I turned to other methods to find their history.

ATTENDING POLITICAL MEETINGS

I gained some important insight into women and politics by attending a provincial meeting of the women's organization held in preparation for the OMM Extra-ordinary Conference planned for the following year. The meeting began with the oral presentation of papers that addressed the topics of divorce, family relations, women's work, prostitution, adultery, promiscuity, and traditional practices including initiation rites, polygamy (when a man may marry more than one wife), bridewealth (an exchange of goods that confirms a marriage), and premature marriage (involving young girls).[20]

The small group I was assigned to debated the policy on initiation rites. One woman gave a graphic description of the process of tattooing, in which small cuts were made in a design on a girl's belly, chest, or shoulders and then rubbed with lotions and ashes to ensure that the cuts were raised and dark. The designs were considered a beautification practice, as well as an erotic adornment that helped attract men. Several people spoke about the common practice of massaging and pulling on the labia to elongate them, a custom prevalent in many parts of Mozambique. The rites were less likely to be pursued in the cities, and many fewer girls went through the procedures than in earlier decades.

More than one delegate voiced the opinion that uninitiated women and women with no tattoos were not properly prepared for adult sexual activity. Some women commented that a girl who had not been initiated would have trouble finding a husband, or the husband might not like his uninitiated wife and would go to other women. Several delegates became nostalgic for the old days, when mothers had control over their daughters; "Daughters were afraid in those days," as one commented. Others complained that urban children did not have proper respect for adults, that they always played and never studied, and implied that continuing the initiation rites would give parents more control. It was clear that the much-quoted revolutionary slogans calling for an end to the rites had been too simplistic and indicated a cultural distance between the government and ordinary Mozambicans. The local paper published a four-part series on the topic, but there was little scholarly work on initiation rites until after my research trip had ended, so I was ill-prepared to ask the right questions or to understand the context of people's comments.[21] As Margaret Strobel pointed out, in a situation where there are few documented sources, it can be difficult to even know what to ask about a particular topic, a problem that dogged me throughout my years in Beira.[22] As I observed activities and participated in discussions at political meetings and workplaces, I was able to develop better questions and approaches that I incorporated into my research.

My group also discussed premature marriage, which was a concern because often girls' education was disrupted when they married at a very young age. One man spoke up to say that he believed that girls provoked men to have sex with them, implying that the girls had to marry early as a result of their own actions. That comment was refuted by Balbina dos Santos and other women, who reminded the group that we still lived in a patriarchal society that placed women in certain categories and gave them few options. And they discussed polygyny (sometimes called polygamy), the practice where a man could marry more than one wife. A marked gender division of perception emerged, as the men thought polygyny was decreasing while the women felt it was increasing, though women believed that second marriages were often secret and were not given the same formal recognition as when polygyny had been accepted.

The closing plenary session included reading aloud all the small-group reports, followed by more discussion and clarification. Each group performed some songs or made another presentation. One group enacted a skit about initiation rites, which I found especially revealing. The play contrasted a modern family, who sent their daughter to school and had a scientific talk about menstruation and ovulation, with a family who took their daughter out of school so that she could undergo the rites. When the modern girl came looking for her friend to see why she was missing school, the traditional father said, "Oh-oh, here comes OMM!" The performance concluded as the second girl decided to end the process of the rite before it was completed and returned to school with her friend.

It was not until years later that I more fully realized the value of some of the traditional practices. At the time of the OMM meeting I agreed with the Frelimo analysis that initiation rites trained women to be subservient to men and that they were obscurantist and detrimental to developing modern women. Later I came to understand the rites as a profoundly woman-centered experience, with a positive focus on female sexuality. Unlike the better-known rites in other parts of Africa that sometimes included cutting women's genitals, the Mozambican rites involved a group of girls of similar ages stroking and enlarging their own labia. And the reality was that people wanted to continue the rituals and they were not going to stop performing rites that were an integral part of their identity just because the government wished it.[23]

The meeting agenda, though long and at times tedious, represented what I thought was an admirable democratic practice, with issues debated by attendees rather than covered up, ignored, or subject to top-down pronouncements. By observing the meeting of the women's organization, I was able to gain a much deeper understanding of political changes taking place.[24] It was less than a decade after independence, and Frelimo and OMM were still groping their way toward a new political process and new ideas about women's role in Mozambican society. I collected printed materials that explained the official point of view, and I was privileged to witness ongoing debates about women's place in a socialist society.

TALKING WITH NURSES

Faced with a meager range of documentary and archival material, I began to develop a program to interview women in sectors where higher numbers of women were employed. Many others have since written about the importance of oral testimony in recovering African women's histories, but before I went to Mozambique, very few such sources had been published. By focusing on three groups of working women, I was able to gain insight into the changes women had experienced.

Because of connections I had through my husband and the Ministry of Health, my first interviews were with nurses and midwives. I had little preparation for these interviews, as there was so little published information about nurses. A friend mailed one new publication to me while I was in Beira, but that research had an anthropological focus that investigated how modern nursing conflicted with traditional ideas about women's place in society and local ideas about health and illness.[25] I was interested in the nurses as workers. My approach was to inquire about their motivations for coming to live in Beira, their educational backgrounds, the day-to-day routines of their work, their experiences under the colonial medical system, the changes they had seen since independence, and how they managed their lives as wives and mothers while continuing to work full-time. The topic of urban working women in Africa had been little studied, with the first publication that focused on women and work in Africa appearing after I was in Beira. Although a colleague did send a copy of that book to me, most of the contributions did not analyze women in factories or the politics of women's work and therefore did not directly address the issues I was investigating.[26]

I spent part of one morning with Lucinda dos Santos, a midwife who had worked in the health service at the colonial railroad. She was the daughter of an African woman and a Portuguese soldier who insisted that the family speak Portuguese. She told about the indignity of the segregated system of that time, commenting, "When a white woman came in, I could not give that white woman an injection. The bed—there was a sheet where a white woman would sleep when she had the injection. When a black woman came in, wasn't it so, when a black woman slept there we had to take off that sheet for another, because we could not mix them." After independence she was promoted to the position of head nurse at the railroad, a place she described as being "the center of racism" in the colonial era. When I asked how conditions had changed following independence, Lucinda cited the new opportunities she had for continuing education, saying, "Now we always study, we are always learning."[27]

One morning I went to the Munhava neighborhood, where I interviewed Gilda Amony, a midwife at the maternity center.[28] Gilda was the daughter of African Protestant ministers from Inhambane. Her father was acknowledged as a religious leader, and her mother had also trained at Chibute, a well-known mission center. Gilda told me that her mother had also preached when her father was away visiting outlying districts. But her mother did not read Portuguese, so she would read the service in Landim, a language common in southern Mozambique and also known as Shangaan. As Gilda commented, "It was only Portuguese that she did not know. In her language, our language, she knew how to read and write." The Portuguese did not consider a person to be literate unless they could read Portuguese, so Gilda's mother was not recognized as an educated woman by the colonial authorities despite her abilities. Gilda also described the coursework she had undertaken in the colonial obstetrical nursing program in the 1950s. She had been transferred frequently, working as a nurse-midwife in a dozen different maternity centers across southern Mozambique before settling in Beira.

I interviewed ten female nurses and midwives, as well as two older male nurses. It was a small cohort but constituted all the older nurses who had trained under the colonial system who were then working in Beira. Each of the stories I heard added to my understanding of women's activities in colonial Mozambique. Though most Mozambican girls had little or no access to formal education, the nurses as a group had enjoyed unusual opportunities. By approaching them as women working for a wage, I was able to make significant comparisons between the nurses and the two groups of factory women.

TALKING WITH CASHEW WORKERS

Members of the local OMM leadership helped arrange interviews with women at Caju, the cashew factory. Cashew exports had made up a major part of the Mozambican economy, amounting to one-third of all foreign-exchange income during the best years in the colonial era, so Caju was a key workplace to investigate. It was also a sector that historically had hired women and was the industrial sector with the highest proportion of female workers. There were officially about 550 workers at Beira's Caju, and 250 of those were women. Though there were difficulties in getting the interviews organized, I was able to talk to twenty-six female and two male cashew workers.

I met cashew worker Raquel Fernando at the OMM office. Raquel was the daughter of a man who had worked in the mines in South Africa and a mother who had been a peasant farmer in Inhambane. She had married at seventeen, and her parents had paid bridewealth of a bull, some fish, one sack of rice and one of cornmeal, a five-liter can of cooking oil, and a few other items. Women often recalled such detail, in part because the value of the goods that were exchanged reflected their own status. But her husband had not paid his taxes to the colonial government, and he left Mozambique to find work in a neighboring country in order to avoid the Portuguese authorities. When Raquel did not hear from him, she decided to move to Beira to find work. In 1967 there were very few options for a nineteen-year-old woman with only two years of formal schooling, but she managed to find a job doing domestic work for a Portuguese woman in Beira.

When the cashew factory opened in 1973, she heard that it was hiring women. She walked to the outlying neighborhood where the factory was located and was one of the first to be hired. She told me about the separation of male and female work, including starkly unequal systems of payment for women and men. She was glad to talk about improvements since independence, as she had completed two more years of elementary schooling at the factory. She was also active in OMM, which she described as responsible for a newly implemented maternity leave and the day-care center at the factory.[29]

When I went out to the cashew factory itself, there were very few people around because the factory was closed. The war had interrupted the transport of cashews, which were mostly from trees owned and tended by individual farming families. With no cashews, there was no work at the factory in sorting and packaging nuts, though a few women continued to come by the site, where they had planted a small plot of sweet potatoes. The factory was managed by the government, a reflection of the historic importance cashews had held. The government plan was to keep some workers on payroll, in the expectation that cashews would return and workers would be recalled.

Each individual cashew nut grows at the base of a fruit that is used for an alcoholic beverage that many women brewed in their own homes. The nuts arrived at the factory inside a tough outer casing, which was removed after the nuts were heated in an oven. Removing that casing released a corrosive liquid that burned the skin of anyone handling it, reflecting the plant's botanical relation to poison ivy. All of the women I spoke with commented on the discomfort of dealing with that stage of the processing with bare hands and no protective gear.

I interviewed cashew workers Luisa Monteiro and Cristina Fanduco. They both spoke Portuguese, but, as was common, it was their second or third language. The cashew workers were often nervous about talking to me and intimidated by the presence of the tape recorder, and as a consequence they were much briefer in response to my questions than other women I interviewed. Both Luisa and Cristina recalled the difficulties of their work during the colonial period, when the daily pay was twenty-five *escudos* (the Portuguese currency used in colonial times, it was replaced by the *metical*), but they were credited for having worked a day only if they filled a twelve-liter tin with properly cleaned cashews. If the tin was not satisfactorily filled, it was carried over to the next day and the women were not credited as having worked that day. If they were successful in filling a tin every day, they would be paid 700 *escudos* at the end of a month, a rate that was rarely achieved. They remembered exactly how the wages had risen after independence, so that by the time of our interview they were receiving 3,500 *meticais* a month (just under $90).[30]

Some cashew workers shared very personal stories about their lives. One woman related how she had been married at age sixteen. Her husband often beat her, until one night he beat her for several hours and she lost consciousness. She then realized that she had to leave, and she returned to her father's house. But her family did not have the funds to repay the *lobolo* (bridewealth), and when her husband kept bothering them for the money, saying, "I want my money from the bridewealth of the marriage," she traveled to Beira to find work. She earned the necessary money, which she sent to her father so that he could repay her husband and officially end that marriage.[31] The need to repay bridewealth in order to dissolve unhappy marriages was a common motivation for women to seek waged work, and was a factor in the work histories of several of the cashew workers.

I was learning how their experiences as cashew workers were shared. In contrast to the nurses, many of the cashew women had married young and unhappily, and their desire to escape from the desperate poverty of rural villages and forlorn home lives was their incentive for moving into the city and going to work at the cashew factory. Most had had bridewealth exchanged when they married. Bridewealth was usually a sum of money along with household goods and food given by the groom-to-be to the bride's family. Historically it had consisted of cattle or hoes, which were directly related to family-based production.[32]

Frelimo intended to end the practice, which was officially regarded as being oppressive to women. The cashew workers' experience corroborated that policy, as they had to earn the money through factory labor in order to repay the *lobolo* and formally end their marriages. But it was not simply a repressive custom that could be ended by government decree, as the Frelimo analysis implied. During informal conversations while I waited for my transportation back to town, the cashew workers told me that "the government wants to end *lobolo,* but they won't be able to." They explained that a legal paper did not give value to a relationship or bring families together—that only the *lobolo* exchange could accomplish those goals. They had similar views about polygyny, the still-common practice of men marrying more than one wife. Frelimo saw polygyny as oppressive to women, but the cashew workers told me that men will have two or more wives, and it was not likely to end because of new government policies. In a legal situation that disallowed previously existing polygyny, junior wives might have fewer protections under the law and thus be more vulnerable to abandonment and ill-treatment than in a society that accepted polygyny.

TALKING WITH GARMENT WORKERS

During the provincial women's meeting, I had approached a woman who worked at the Belita garment factory, and with her support I arranged to do interviews there. I wanted to include Belita because, like the cashew factory, it had a high proportion of women workers. At the time I began visiting the site, there were 320 workers, and 103, or about one-third, were women. The factory was much brighter and cleaner than the cashew factory, with sewing machines clattering away on the upper floors. The ground floor held the main offices, the warehouse, and a small shop with some demonstration clothing. The warehouse was empty, though garment worker Ana Maria dos Santos told me that it used to be filled with material imported from Hong Kong, Japan, the United States, and all over. By 1982 they were relying on the more limited selection of cloth from a local textile factory. The third floor was the main work area and included the cutting and pattern departments. The center section of the floor was filled with sewing machines organized into groups of twelve, men and women all working together, some hemming white sheets, others sewing red skirts or military caps when I visited.

The working conditions were considered to be unusually good. They had a monthlong vacation and sixty days' maternity leave, and near the end of a pregnancy a woman could move to less strenuous work. The workers participated in annual discussions about production goals, though the increasing problems in maintaining electricity and in obtaining cloth made it difficult to meet the production targets. I admired the high level of organization, which seemed to set a notable example of a socialist workplace.

I had a pleasant interview with Rita Bacare, who was exactly my age, had been educated at a mission school, and was married with a five-year-old daughter, a son who was just over one year, and a third baby due in about two months. When I asked about her marriage, she commented that *lobolo* had been exchanged when she married. She laughed a bit about it: "I was *loboloed*, two *contos* five hundred. It is the custom, isn't it? He paid *lobolo* to my parents; my in-laws along with my parents made a traditional ceremony . . . the family made a little food to eat."[33] In apparent contradiction to the exchange of *lobolo*, her parents had been known, in her words, as "conscientious churchgoers, my father was very religious, so the Father of the Murraça mission came to take me to the mission when I was eight." She learned to sew in the mission school and later took a course in Beira, where she earned a certificate in sewing.[34]

Aurora Soares was an older garment worker, over forty when I spoke with her. Her father had been a teacher and then trained as a nurse. When I asked if she had been "*loboloed*," she responded, "No, my father did not accept *lobolo*, it was a civil union [government-recognized marriage] and in the Catholic Church." Though Aurora Soares's attitude seemed more logical than Rita Bacare's, the Bacare family's continued expectation of *lobolo* was a good example of how such cultural practices continued in the face of religious and political disapprobation. Aurora Soares had also learned to sew in a mission school on a manual machine, first encountering electric sewing machines at Belita. She had twelve children living, ranging in age from twenty-five down to four years old. The oldest, who were still at home, watched over the younger ones, helped with the housework, and assisted with the cultivation of rice in her urban *machamba*, or cultivated plot of land. That year she expected to harvest three or four sacks of rice, a yield much reduced from her output in previous years.[35]

Joana Madeira was another garment worker who had been educated to the fourth grade in a mission school and had taken further training in Beira. She told me, referring to a particular training manual, that she "had taken a course in patterns . . . that olive-colored book, I took the olive course." Her father bought a sewing machine for her, and for several years she had a successful small home-based business as a dressmaker. She was one of the first women to come to work at Belita, so I asked her about the incident from 1979 that I had read about in the document, when women were possibly malingering. She avoided speaking of individuals by telling me that "where a lot of women work, there are always problems . . . because no one can understand another person's situation. I can understand my own illness. Another person's, I cannot understand. . . . But now we are fine, there are no more problems."[36]

Ana Maria Cristino told a story of how the new laws under Frelimo supported women. Her first pregnancy had ended in a miscarriage, so when she became pregnant a second time her doctor ordered her to rest in bed beginning in her fourth month. She stayed home and, as she remembered, "At home also I did nothing; I did not pound in the mortar, I did not go to my *machamba*, nothing. Until the ninth month, [when] I had the baby, I had a normal birth."[37] In the poorest nation on earth at that time, she had benefited from paid medical leave for the entire five months that she was away from the factory and was able to return to her former position, an indication of the important legal provisions for women that had been introduced by the socialist government.

With a series of interviews with seven female and one male garment worker, I could see aspects of their shared experiences. Mozambique under colonialism had a very poor record of educating girls, with the result that only 7 percent of Mozambican women could read and write in Portuguese at independence. Yet at Belita I had found a group of women who had been educated during the colonial era in mission schools, where they had learned to sew. Belita's workforce had been almost entirely male until after independence, so the female garment workers had been trained in the colonial era for jobs that did not exist for women until years later, when the provincial labor ministry, along with the women's organization, had devised a plan to hire more women. As with the nurses, jobs that were commonly associated with women in much of the world had been reserved for men in Mozambique. Women's job opportunities had expanded only with the ascension of a socialist government.

CONCLUSION

After arriving in Beira with no organized research plan beyond finding the women, I met people who helped me to gain access to archives and, more importantly for my eventual analysis, to attend political meetings and interview a range of working women. My interviews provided the primary source material for my conclusion that all three sectors of working women gained some form of improvement in their working conditions as a result of new government policies. The nurses were no longer subject to the oppressive racism that had tainted their work under colonialism, and they spoke happily about the expansion of health care to sectors of the Mozambican population that had been previously excluded. The garment workers had found employment in an industry that had been nearly entirely male before new policies deliberately recruited women to work in the garment factories. And the cashew workers benefited from a more equitable wage payment system. All three groups also voiced approval for the social changes related to child care, legal supports for marital rights, and similar issues that I was not able to discuss in this article.

My observations also led me to reformulate my ideas about urban life and women's history. Literature about Africa tended to emphasize a stark division between urban and rural life, with the assumption that rural conditions were simply left behind when people moved to the city.[38] Urbanization may have meant a greater separation from rural life for men, but I was learning that women were continuing their primary rural agricultural work in the city. All around me women were growing maize, rice, and vegetables, and most of the women working in the cashew and garment factories cultivated crops. Placing women at the center when describing Beira's urbanization suggested an entirely different process than what was generally understood about the development of African cities, which was more often associated with industrialization and wage labor.[39]

We were living in the middle of an escalating conflict that meant worry about the availability of food, cuts in the electric supply, frequent problems with contaminated water, and other conditions that were the result of poverty and war. But the women I met all welcomed the opportunity to talk about their families, their work, and their hopes for a future that would mean better lives for themselves and their daughters. Women's history was all around me, though for the most part not in the standard archival repositories. I found it by talking to women whose memories of Portuguese colonial oppression influenced their appreciation for the improvements they were experiencing under a socialist government in a newly independent Mozambique.

NOTES

1. For example, Nina Mba, *Nigerian Women Mobilized: Women's Political Activity in Southern Nigeria, 1900–1965* (Berkeley: Institute of International Studies, University of California, 1982); Claire C. Robertson, *Sharing the Same Bowl: A Socioeconomic History of Women and Class in Accra, Ghana* (Bloomington: Indiana University Press, 1984); and Margaret Strobel, *Muslim Women in Mombasa: 1890–1975* (New Haven, Conn.: Yale

University Press, 1979). Conversations in 2008 with Margaret Strobel were helpful in clarifying how my research experience fit into the field of African women's history.

2. Kristin Mann, *Marrying Well: Marriage, Status, and Social Change among the Educated Elite in Colonial Lagos* (New York, 1985); Luise White, *The Comforts of Home: Prostitution in Colonial Nairobi* (Chicago: Chicago University Press, 1990).

3. I have written about these research methods in greater depth in "Writing about Women: Approaches to a Gendered Perspective in African History," in John Edward Philips, ed., *Writing African History* (Rochester, N.Y.: University of Rochester Press, 2005), 465–89. An important historical linguistics publication is David Lee Schoenbrun, *A Green Place, a Good Place: Agrarian Change, Gender, and Social Identity in the Great Lakes Region to the 15th Century* (Portsmouth, N.H.: Heinemann, 1998); a key geographical history source is Heidi J. Nast, *Concubines and Power: Five Hundred Years in a Northern Nigerian Palace* (Minneapolis: University of Minnesota Press, 2005); on folktales, see Mary C. Bill, "Refusal to Eat and Drink: A Metaphor for 'Safe Sex' in Tsonga Folktales," *African Languages and Cultures* 7, no. 1 (1994): 49–77; and on songs, Leroy Vail and Landeg White, "The Possession of the Dispossessed: Songs as History among Tumbuka Women," in Leroy Vail and Landeg White, eds., *Power and the Praise Poem: Southern African Voices in History* (Charlottesville: University Press of Virginia, 1991), 231–77. Textiles sources include Colleen Kriger, "Textile Production and Gender in the Sokoto Caliphate," *Journal of African History* 34 (1993): 361–401; and Judith A. Byfield, *The Bluest Hands: A Social and Economic History of Women Dyers in Abeokuta (Nigeria), 1890–1940* (Portsmouth, N.H.: Heinemann, 2001); and the research that looks at pottery and tattoos is by Heidi Gengenbach, "Where Women Make History: Pots, Stories, Tattoos, and Other Gendered Accounts of Community and Change in Magude District, Mozambique, c. 1800 to the Present" (PhD dissertation, University of Minnesota, 1999).

4. Susan Geiger, "Women's Life Histories: Method and Content," *Signs* 11, no. 2 (1986): 334–51; Marjorie Mbilinyi, "'I'd Have Been a Man': Politics and the Labor Process in Producing Personal Narratives," in *Interpreting Women's Lives: Feminist Theory and Personal Narratives*, ed. Personal Narratives Group (Bloomington: Indiana University Press, 1989), 204–27; and Sarah Mirza and Margaret Strobel, eds., *Three Swahili Women: Life Histories from Mombasa, Kenya* (Bloomington: Indiana University Press, 1989).

5. Robertson, *Sharing the Same Bowl*.

6. Claire Robertson, "In Pursuit of Life Histories: The Problem of Bias," *Frontiers* 7, no. 2 (1983): 63–69.

7. Christine Obbo, "What Do Women Know? . . . As I Was Saying!" in *Oral Narrative Research with Black Women*, ed. Kim Marie Vaz (Thousand Oaks, Calif.: Sage, 1997), 41–63.

8. Francesca Declich, "'Gendered Narratives,' History, and Identity: Two Centuries along the Juba River among the Zigula and Shanbara," *History in Africa* 22 (1995): 93–122.

9. Nakanyike B. Musisi, "A Personal Journey into Custom, Identity, Power, and Politics: Researching and Writing the Life and Times of Buganda's Queen Mother Irene Drusilla Namaganda (1896–1957)," *History in Africa* 23 (1996): 369–85. See also Nwando Achebe, "Getting to the Source: Nwando Achebe—Daughter, Wife, and Guest—A Researcher at the Crossroads," *Journal of Women's History* 14, no. 3 (Autumn 2002): 9–31; Sondra Hale, "Feminist Method, Process, and Self-Criticism: Interviewing Sudanese Women,"

in Sherna Berger Gluck and Daphne Patai, eds., *Women's Words: The Feminist Practice of Oral History* (New York: Routledge, 1991), 121–36; and Onaiwu W. Ogbomo, "Oral Field Techniques and Women's History: The Case of Owan, Nigeria," *Ufahamu* 22, no. 3 (Fall 1994): 7–25.

10. For instance, "'We Women Have the Right to Fight,'" *Mozambique Revolution* 51 (April–June 1972): 15; Josina Machel, "O papel da mulher na revolução," in *7 de Abril: Dia da Mulher Moçambicana* (Maputo: Frelimo, 1975), 9–13; Michèle Manceaux, *As mulheres de Moçambique* (Lisbon: Editora Arcádia, 1976); and Stephanie Urdang, "Women Workers Making Changes," *Southern Africa* 15, no. 3 (1982): 2–3. For more detail, see Kathleen Sheldon, *Pounders of Grain: A History of Women, Work, and Politics in Mozambique* (Portsmouth, N.H.: Heinemann, 2002), especially chapter 4, "'Today in FRELIMO the Mozambican Woman Has a Voice': The Struggle for Independence and Socialism."

11. Samora Machel, "The Liberation of Women Is a Fundamental Necessity for the Revolution," in his *Mozambique: Sowing the Seeds of Revolution* (London: Committee for Freedom in Mozambique, Angola and Guiné, 1974), 21–36.

12. Kathleen Sheldon, "Working Women in Beira, Mozambique," (PhD dissertation, University of California, Los Angeles, 1988).

13. Hilário Matusse, "Chamanculo: memórias de um bairro," *Tempo* 682 (November 6, 1983): 22–28; and Hilário Matusse, "Mafalala: fronteira entre a cidade e o subúrbio, o passado," *Tempo* 685 (November 27, 1983): 14–19.

14. Isabel Casimiro, "Transformação nas relações homem/mulher em Moçambique 1960–74" (Dissertation de licenciatura, Universidade Eduardo Mondlane, 1986).

15. Companhia de Moçambique, *Annuario do Territorio Manica e Sofala* (Beira: 1908), among others.

16. Typescript of preliminary unpublished census results prepared at my request by staff members of the Direcção Provincial do Trabalho de Sofala, Secção de Recursos Laborais, May 1984.

17. Belita, Ltd., *Relatório anual*, 1978, 1980, 1981, 1982.

18. Belita, Ltd., *Relatório sobre problema de algumas trabalhadoras da Empresa Belita 1979, 20 Out.* (1979). This report was published in Kathleen Sheldon, "A Report on a 'Delicate Problem' Concerning Female Garment Workers in Beira, Mozambique," *Signs* 16, no. 3 (1991): 575–86, and included in Sheldon, *Pounders of Grain*, 193–94.

19. António César, "Mulheres-tractoristas: quebram-se os tabus," *Diário de Moçambique* (December 30 1982): 8–9.

20. Organização da Mulher Moçambicana, Gabinete Central de Preparação da Conferencia Extraordinária, "Temas-base para discussão" (Maputo: typescript, 1983).

21. Albano Naroromele, "Ritos de iniciação: qual é a contradição?" *Domingo* (April 29, 1984). This was the final article of a series of four about initiation rites that Naroromele published in *Domingo* during April 1984. See also Lourenço Jossias, "Ritos de iniciação: aspectos positivos devem ser valorizados," *Notícias* (December 8, 1983). For scholarly analysis, see Signe Arnfred, "Notes on Gender and Modernization: Examples from Mozambique," in Agnete Weis Bentzon, ed., *The Language of Development Studies*, (Copenhagen: New Social Science Monographs, 1990), 71–107.

22. Margaret Strobel, "Doing Oral History as an Outsider," *Frontiers* 2, no. 2 (Summer 1977): 68–72, reprinted in Susan H. Armitage, Patricia Hart, and Karen Weathermon,

eds., *Women's Oral History: The Frontiers Reader* (Lincoln: University of Nebraska Press, 2002).

23. For more detail and analysis, including ethnographic and geographic variations, see Sheldon, *Pounders of Grain,* 1–43, 117–18, and 134–35.

24. A report on the provincial meetings is in "Pelo sucesso da sua conferência, mulher moçambicana saúda partido Frelimo," *Domingo* (December 2, 1984): 1; and Fernando Manuel, "Problemas da mulher: para além das aparências," *Tempo* 694 (January 29, 1984): 14–17. For more on the national meeting, see Signe Arnfred, "Women in Mozambique: Gender Struggle and Politics," *Review of African Political Economy* 41 (1988): 5–16.

25. Ilsa Schuster, "Perspectives in Development: The Problem of Nurses and Nursing in Zambia," in Nici Nelson, ed., *African Women in the Development Process* (London: Frank Cass, 1981), 77–97.

26. Edna G. Bay, ed., *Women and Work in Africa* (Boulder, Colo.: Westview, 1982).

27. Interview by author with Lucinda dos Santos, June 30, 1983. All interviews were conducted in Beira, Mozambique.

28. Interview by author with Gilda Amony, October 6, 1983.

29. Interview by author with Raquel Fernando, July 18, 1983.

30. Interviews by author with Luisa Monteiro, July 21, 1983, and Cristina Fanduco, July 25, 1983.

31. Interview by author with Marta Eliz, July 25, 1983.

32. Adam Kuper, *Wives for Cattle: Bridewealth and Marriage in Southern Africa* (London: Routledge and Kegan Paul, 1982), 10; see also Joaquim Nunes, "Costumes gentílicos: o lobolo," *Moçambique Documentário Trimestral* 8 (October–December 1936): 89–117, regarding the positive role bridewealth played in African communities.

33. The cash component of her bridewealth payment was approximately U.S. $80 in the mid-1970s.

34. Interview by author with Rita Bacare, November 28, 1983; Rita Bacare's interview is included in the appendix to Sheldon, "Working Women in Beira, Mozambique," 307–13.

35. Interview by author with Aurora Soares, November 29, 1983.

36. Interview by author with Joana Madeira, January 26, 1983.

37. Interview by author with Ana Maria Christina, January 26, 1984.

38. For more analysis of urban African women, see Kathleen Sheldon, ed., *Courtyards, Markets, City Streets: Urban Women in Africa* (Boulder, Colo.: Westview, 1996), especially the introduction, which discusses the historiography of women in African cities.

39. I wrote about this aspect of my research in Kathleen Sheldon, "Machambas in the City: Urban Women and Agricultural Work in Mozambique," *Lusotopie* (1999): 121–40; and "Markets and Gardens: Placing Women in the History of Urban Mozambique," *Canadian Journal of African Studies* 37, nos. 2 and 3 (2003): 358–95.

CONTRIBUTORS

JANET AFARY is a professor of Middle East history and women's studies at Purdue University. The author of *Sexual Politics in Modern Iran*, her previous publications include *The Iranian Constitutional Revolution: Grassroots Democracy, Social Democracy, and the Origins of Feminism*; and (with Kevin B. Anderson) *Foucault and the Iranian Revolution: Gender and the Seductions of Islamism*.

MARYAM AMELI-REZAEI was born in 1974 in Tehran and received a PhD in Persian literature from Shahid Beheshty at the University of Tehran in 2007. The subject of her PhD thesis is "The Improvement of the Position of Women in the Prose of the Qajar Era." She has published *Images in the Foroogh Farokh Zad's Poetry*, "Wise Women in Iran's Culture," and "The Development of the Status of Women in Pre-constitution Prose."

NUPUR CHAUDHURI is a professor of history at Texas Southern University (Houston). She is the coeditor of *Western Women and Imperialism: Complicity and Resistance*; *Nation, Empire and Colony: Historicizing Gender and Race*; and *Voices of Women Historians: The Personal, the Political, the Professional*. She has published in *Victorian Studies*, *Journal of Women's History*, and *Women's History Review*.

JULIA CLANCY-SMITH is a professor of history, University of Arizona. She is the author of *Rebel and Saint: Muslim Notables, Populist Protest, Colonial Encounters*; *Mediterraneans: Tunis, North Africa, and the Mediterranean in an Age of Migrations*; and *Exemplary Women and Sacred Journeys: Women and Gender in Judaism, Christianity, and Islam*. She edited *North Africa, Is-

lam, and the Mediterranean and coedited *Domesticating the Empire; Writing French Colonial Histories;* and *The Walls of Algiers.*

MANSOUREH ETTEHADIEH (NEZAM MAFI) is a historian of modern Iran and author of numerous publications on Qajar Iran. She is the director of Nashr-e Tarikh-e Iran, a center for historical research and publication in Tehran.

MALGORZATA FIDELIS is an assistant professor of East European and Polish history at the University of Illinois at Chicago. She received her PhD from Stanford University in 2006. Her research focuses on social and cultural issues, particularly everyday life and the relationship between individuals and state power in communist societies. She is completing a book tentatively titled *Between Tradition and Revolution: Women, Communism, and Industrialization in Postwar Poland*. Her new project concerns consumer and popular cultures in post-1945 East Central Europe.

JOANNE L. GOODWIN is an associate professor of history at the University of Nevada, Las Vegas, and founding director of the ten-year-old Women's Research Institute of Nevada. Her publications include *Gender and the Politics of Welfare Reform; Women in American History, 1585-Present, an Encyclopedia,* as coeditor; and articles in *Gender & History, Journal of Women's History, Signs,* and the *Journal of Social History*. She is writing a manuscript on women in Las Vegas.

KALI NICOLE GROSS, associate professor of history and politics, is director of Africana studies at Drexel University. Her book *Colored Amazons: Crime, Violence, and Black Women in the City of Brotherly Love, 1880–1910* received the John Hope Franklin Center Prize and the Letitia Woods Brown Memorial Book Prize from the Association of Black Women Historians. She is currently working on *A Ghastly Find: Mary Hannah Tabbs and the Case of the Disembodied Torso, Philadelphia 1887.*

DANIEL S. HAWORTH teaches Latin American history at the University of Houston–Clear Lake. His most recent publication, "Civilians and Civil War in Nineteenth-Century Mexico: Mexico City and the War of the Reform, 1858–1861," appears in *Daily Lives of Civilians in Latin America from the Wars of Independence to the Drug Wars*. His current research explores the intersection of family life and public authority in the lives of adolescents in nineteenth-century Mexico.

SHERRY J. KATZ teaches in the Department of History at San Francisco State University. She has published essays on radical women's political activism in the edited volumes *We Have Come to Stay: American Women and Political Parties, 1880–1960*; *One Woman, One Vote: Rediscovering the Woman Suffrage Movement*; and *California Progressivism Revisited*. She is currently completing a book manuscript titled "Dual Commitments: Socialist-Feminism in Progressive Era California."

ELHAM MALEKZADEH teaches history at Azad University while completing the PhD at Al-Zahra University. Her research focuses on women's endowments and philanthropic work from the Qajar period to the present era. She received the Best Researcher Award in 2004/2005/2006. Her publications include *Sargozasht-e Safariyan* and *Omur-e Khayriyyeh dar Doreh-ye Qajar*. With Dr. Navai she has published *Asnad-e Daneshjoyan-e Irani dar Uropa 1313–1307; Tarikh-e Ravabet-e Iran va veniz*; and *Ruznameh-ye Khaterat-e Nasir al-din shah*.

MARY ELIZABETH PERRY is a research associate at the UCLA Center for Medieval and Renaissance Studies and a Fulbright Senior Specialist. She has published five books on early modern Spain, most recently *The Handless Maiden: Moriscos and the Politics of Religion in Early Modern Spain*. She is particularly interested in researching underrepresented people in history, and her books and many articles have appeared in translation in countries such as Austria, Mexico, Spain, and the United Arab Emirates.

KATHLEEN SHELDON is an independent historian with a research affiliation at the UCLA Center for the Study of Women. Her publications include *Pounders of Grain: A History of Women, Work, and Politics in Mozambique* and the *Historical Dictionary of Women in Sub-Saharan Africa*.

LISA SOUSA is an associate professor of history at Occidental College in Los Angeles. She coedited and cotranslated *The Story of Guadalupe*, with James Lockhart and Stafford Poole, and *Mesoamerican Voices*, with Kevin Terraciano and Matthew Restall. She has published articles on subjects such as women and crime, native views of the Spanish conquest, and the Devil in the indigenous imagination. She is currently completing a book manuscript on indigenous culture and gender in colonial Mexico.

ULA Y. TAYLOR is an associate professor in the Department of African American Studies at the University of California, Berkeley. She is the author of *The Veiled Garvey: The Life and Times of Amy Jacques Garvey*. Her essays on Black Nationalism and black feminisms have appeared in a variety of journals and edited collections.

INDEX

abortions, xxii, 110, 168–70
Achebe, Nwando, 136
adolescents in Mexico, xvi, 21
Afary, Janet, xxii
African American women, xvii; in archives, xx, 126–33; and crime, 56–67; and feminism, 128–29; in Las Vegas, 178, 191n13; as migrants, 58, 68n8; multiple narratives of, 130; and the Nation of Islam, 130–32; oral histories of, 126; and sexual propriety, standards of, xvii, 62–63
African studies, 192–93
agricultural activities of indigenous women, 82
Ali, Qurban, 163
Ali, Seyed Mohammad, 159
Aloysius G., 142
alternative archives, xxi, 136, 179–80
Ameli-Rezai, Maryam, xxii
Amony, Gilda, 201
Aniela, Pani, 117, 119
Anna, Pani, 118–19
Anthias, Floya, 143
Antonio, Joseph, 82
Aqdas, Amin, 163
'aqdi wife (formal wife), 160
Archive of New Documents (Warsaw, Poland), 110
archives: African American women in, xx, 126–33; alternative, xxi, 136, 179–80; assessment of historical accuracy, xxii, 132, 180, 182–83; collection building, xxii, 182–83; about Frances Noel and socialist-feminism, 92–100; gaps in, xvii–xiv, 193–94; of Las Vegas, 181; of Polish trade unions, 108, 110; potential sources of information, 39–46; processing of materials, xxii, 183; and production of knowledge, xiii; relocation in post-colonial period, 40; subjective nature of, xiv, 4, 179–80; underrepresentation of women and minorities, xiv; of woman suffrage movement, 96–97. *See also* journals as sources; newspapers as sources
Archive Stories (Burton), xiv, 179
Archivo General de la Nación (Mexico City), 77–78
Archivo Histórico Nacional (Madrid, Spain), 6
Ar'n't I a Woman (White), 125
artisans, indigenous women as, 75–76, 83
assessment of accuracy of archival documents, xxii, 132, 180, 182–90
assumptions, challenges to, 52, 55n40
autobiographical writings, xxi, 165

Bacare, Rita, 205
Baker, Ella, 129
Baker, Lady Florence, 150–51
Banerjee, S. N., 146
Banks, Bessie, 60, 64
Barbera, Annetta, 35, 45
Bastos, Rui, 196
Bell, Gertrude, 165, 173n33

INDEX

Bell, Laura, 58–59, 65–66
Bengali *baboos* (middle-class Bengali men), 146, 155n52
Bengali Lady in England, A (Krishnobhabini Das), xxi, 135–51
Bengali women, xxi, 135–51, 153n16
berberiscas (Muslim women who have converted to Christianity), 5, 9–10
Bernstein, Irving, 92–93
Bharati (Bengali journal), 137
Bharat Stree Mahamandal (Great Circle of Indian Women), 141
biographical dictionaries, 100
Black Power movement, 130–32
Brassey, Lady Anna, 150–51
breast cancer, 101–2
bridewealth, 198, 202–5, 210n33
Bryant, Lucille, 178
Buhle, Mari Jo, 90
Burden of Feminism, The (Burton), 143
burglaries, 49–52
Burton, Antoinette, xiv, 4, 136, 143, 179–80

California Equal Suffrage Association, 96
California Outlook, The (Calif. women's movement publication), 98
California State Federation of Labor, 98
Canty, Hatty, 188
Carmichael, Stokely, 131–32
Carpenter, Mary, 150
cashew factory workers in Mozambique, xviii, 194, 197, 202–4
Casimiro, Isabel, 196
Casolot, Antonio, 26–28
Catholic Church: in communist Poland, 113–14, 117, 119; Inquisition, 4–6; in Mexico, 25; missionary women, 39, 43
censorship of women's voices, 111
census records: and indigenous people, 78; Iranian, 170n3; of Las Vegas, 191n12; and socialist-feminist leaders, 99; of Tunisia, 42
Cesana, Emanuele, 47
charitable endowments by Iranian women, 161–62, 169
Chaudhurani, Saral Devi, 141
Chaudhuri, Nupur, xxi
Cheap Amusements (Peiss), 62
children, raising of, 23, 82–83, 110, 114, 160. See also families balanced with employment

Chizawska, Katie, 65–67
Cincard, Katie, 60
Citizen, The (Los Angeles, Calif., labor publication), 98
City Council of Beira (Mozambique), 196
city directories, 99
civil marriage, 110, 205
civil rights, 183, 188
Clancy-Smith, Julia, xvi–xvii
Cloquet, Ernest, 166
Codex, Florentine, 78–79, 81, 83
Codex Borgia, 87n11
Codex Laud, 87n11
Codex Mendoza, 80–81, 83–84
Codex Vaticanus B, 87n11
Cohen, Burton, 186
Cole, Josephine, 94–96
Coleman, Rachel, 188
collection building, xxii, 182–83
colonialism, 142, 147, 201–3
common-law marriage, 46
communism and women in Poland, 107–21, 123n18
Community Action Against Rape, 187
community builders, women as, 186–88. See also women's clubs or organizations
community feminism, xx, 128, 130
concubinage, 45–46
Congregation of Saint-Joseph de l'Apparition (French missionary order), 39
Constitutional Revolution (Iran), 161
Construction of Race, Place and Nation (Jackson and Penrose), 142
contextualization of documents, xiii, xv, 5
contraband trade, 49–52, 55n39
contraception in Iran, 168, 170
contracts, Iranian, xxi, 157–61
conversion and conversion narratives, 5–7, 131–32
Cook, Henrietta, xvii, 56–67
Cooperative Commonwealth, 89
Corbett, Carol, 182–83
counsular system of justice, 44, 47–48
Cowan, James, 65
Cowley, Catherine, 62–63
crime and criminal records: and African American women, 56–67; and gender roles, 82–83; and indigenous women, 77–78; and social context, 57. See also prison records
criminal justice system in Baltimore, 59, 64

Cristino, Ana Maria, 206
Cueva, Francisco de la, 84
cultural nationalism, 142, 145
Cutler, Annie, 62

Darmska, Josephine, 63
Das, Debendranath, 138–40
Das, Krishnobhabini, xxi, 135–51
Das, Srinath, 138–39
Das, Tilottoma, 138–41
Das, Upendranath, 139
Davis, Natalie Zemon, 50
death certificates, 99
Deb, Chitra, 148
Declich, Francesca, 193–94
Devi, Saroj Kumari, 137
Diamond, Renee, 188
Diário de Moçambique (newspaper in Mozambique), 196, 198
Dieulafoy, M. J., 165, 173n33
Dimitri (the English man), 35
"Discontented Black Feminists" (Terborg-Penn), 125
discrimination in Mozambique, 202
"disembodied" quality of research material, 100
disenfranchisement of women, xvi, 4–5, 16
divorce: in communist Poland, 110; in Iran, 158–60, 166, 171n10; in Mozambique, 203
documentation and writing of history, 179
Dowleh, Anis al-, 163–65
Dowleh, Foruq al-, 157–58, 163–64
Dowleh, Sarem al-, 163
Dowleh, Zahir al-, 157–58
Dowley, Nadim al-, 163
Dual Commitments: Socialist-Feminism in Progressive Era California (Katz), 91–92
DuBois, Ellen, 91, 97, 103n4
Duval-Davis, Nira, 143
Dwelling in the Archive (Burton), 4

Early Feminists of Colonial India (Ray), 141
East Africa, women of, 193
eating and drinking as social and sacred acts, 85
Ebrahim, Mirza Aqa, 160
economic activities: economic mobility, xviii, 187–88; of indigenous women, xviii, 82; revealed in criminal records, 77–78; of women in Iran, xxi–xxii, 157–61, 163–64, 169, 171n5

economic independence of women, 89–90, 103n3
education of women: in India, xxi, 145–50; in Iran, 162–63; in Mozambique, 199, 201
Eisenberg, Dorothy, 188
emancipation of women: in communist Poland, 107; in India, xxi, 146, 148–51; in Mozambique, 194–95; and socialist-feminism, 89–90, 97–98
employment of women: balanced with marriage and families, xviii, 186–88; in communist Poland, 110, 114–20; discrimination against, 191n13; in Mozambique, xviii, 194–95, 200–207
empowerment of women, xvi, 89–90, 112, 128
Engels, Frederick, 109
Englande Bangamohilia (Krishnobhabini Das), xxi, 135–51
entertainment industry, women in, 177–78, 184–85, 189n3
Equal Rights Amendment, 186
equal rights in communist Poland, 109–10
ethnography, 40. *See also* social context
ethnohistory and Latin American history, 87n4
Ettehadieh, Mansoureh, xxi
exploitation and tribute labor, 78, 84

factory workers in Mozambique, xviii, 194, 197, 202–6
families balanced with employment, xviii, 186–88
Fanduco, Cristina, 202
Fargion, Elia, 45
Fatima/Ana, xv–xvi, 3–15
Federal Writers Project, 100
feminism: and African American women, 128–29; and African women's history, 192; community feminism, xx, 128, 130; and nationalism, xxi, 135, 142–51; socialist-feminism, xix, 89–102, 103nn3–4
Fernández, María Petra, xvi, 20–30
Fernando, Raquel, 202
Fertig, Joseph, 64
fertility in Iran, 166–67
Fidelis, Malgorzata, xix, 108
financial standing, evaluation of, 26–28
Fisk University archives, 127
Florentine Codex, 78–79, 81, 83
Ford, Jean, xxii, 181–83, 186

formal texts of indigenous people, 78–84, 87n11
Foster, Caroline, 98
France, official documents, 41–42
Frente de Libertação de Moçambique (Frelimo), 194–95
Friday Morning Club (Los Angeles, Calif.), 98

Gaffney, Joseph, 61
Galván, Joaquín, 28
gaming industry, women in, 177–78, 184–85, 189n3
Garbutt, Mary, 94–95, 99
garment workers in Mozambique, xviii, 194, 197, 204–6, 207
Garvey, Amy Ashwood, xx, 127–30
Garvey, Amy Jacques, xx, 127–30
Garvey, Marcus, 127
gauridan (Hindu wedding arrangement), 138
Ga women of Ghana, 193
Gellner, Ernst, 142
gender: and memory, 118, 123n29, 124nn36–37, 193–94; and nationalism, 142–47
Gender and Nation (Sinha), 142
gender ideology, 77–78, 82–83, 108, 123n18
Ghana, Ga women of, 193
Ghazali, Imam, 167
Gholam, Mashadi Ali, 159
Giddings, Paula, 125
Girlfriend (Polish journal), xix–xx, 108–16
Goodwin, Joanne L., xxii–xxiii
Gordan, Avery, 126
Gordon, Linda, 91
Grant, Joanne, 129
Gray, Breda, 143
Great Circle of Indian Women, 141
Grewal, Inderpal, 137, 143–44
Griffin, Charles, 131
Gross, Jan, 112
Gross, Kali Nicole, xvii
Gupta, Saroj Kumari, 153n9

habilitación de edad (declaration of adulthood), 20, 25–26, 29
harem memoirs, 165
Harlem, N.Y., xx, 129–30
Harris, Cheryl, 126
Haworth, Daniel S., xvi
Hayden, Dolores, 93
Hiberras, Gianmaria, 47–50
Hindu Law, 138–39

Hine, Darlene Clark, 126
Historical Archives of Mozambique, 196
historical context: and African American women, 128–29; and anthropological studies of African women, 192–93; of images, 79–81; and the Inquisition, 6; and Mexican adolescents, 22–30; and Moriscas/Moriscos in Spain, 7; and Philadelphia's criminal justice system, 60–61; and women in communist Eastern Europe, 108; and women in Las Vegas, 184; and women in Tunisia, 40–43
honor killings, 170
hospital records, 46
household make-up, 44–45, 56–57
Huntington Library (San Marino, Calif.), 97
hymen repair, xxii, 168, 170

'*idda* period (three months after divorce), 159
identity. *See* personal identity
ideology of women in communist Poland, xix, 111
illegitimate children, 168, 174n51
illiteracy: in India, 149; in Iran, 163; in Mozambique, 201; in Tunisia, 35, 37, 44, 46, 53n2
images of women's roles, 79–81
immigrants and immigration. *See* migrants and migration
incidental information, xviii, 77–78, 82
Indian women, xxi, 135–51, 153n16
indigenous women of Mesoamerica, xviii, 75–86, 86n2
industrialization and socialist-feminism, 91–92
infanticide, xvii, 56–67
infant mortality, 166–67
inheritance, 29, 159–60
initiation rites in Mozambique, 198–200
Inquisition, 4–6. *See also* Catholic Church
interest on loans, 158, 171n6
interviews. *See* oral histories
Iran, women in, xxi–xxii, 156–70, 171n5, 171n7, 171n10, 174n51
"Issues of Race, Gender and Nation" (Chaudhuri), 143
Italy, official documents of, 40–41

Jackson, Peter, 142
jahiziyeh (dowry), 158–59
Janina, Pani, 118

Jelinek, Estelle, 136
Jennings, Louella, 65
Jeronima, María, 82
Jesuits, 75, 85–86
Jiboner Drishyamala (Krishnobhabini Das), 138
Jones, Jacqueline, 125
journals as sources: in communist Poland, xix–xx, 108; in Mozambique, 196; socialist, 94–96, 104n16; of the women's movement, 98
jurors, impartiality of, 64, 70n53

Kabir, Mirza Taqi Khan Amir, 164
Karim, Nayeb, 159
Karriem, Anna, 131–32
Katz, Sherry J., xviii–xix, 91–92
Key, Alice, 188
Khan, Hajji, 164
Khanum, Maryam, 164–65
Khanum, Negar, 163
Khatun, Ameneh, 163
King, Franklin, 58, 62, 63
Knight, William, 62
Kosambi, Meera, 136
Kotsch, Georgia, 96

labia elongation in Mozambique, 198–200
Labor Clarion (San Francisco, Calif., labor publication), 98
Labor of Love, Labor of Sorrow (Jones), 125
labor unions, 108, 110, 188
land ownership records in Mexico, 78
language: of indigenous women, 76, 87n5; translation of, 46–47, 53n2
Lanota, Anna, 111
Las Vegas (Nev.), women in, xvii, 177–89, 191n13
Las Vegas Women Oral History Project, xxii–xviii, 178, 184–88, 189n3
League of Women Voters, 181–82, 186–88
legal documents: evaluation of testimony, 43–51; Iranian, xxi, 156–61; translation of, 46–47; Tunisian, 43–51, 54n28; women as subject of, 30
legal status: of Bengali/Hindu women, 138–39; and religious affiliation, 46; of slaves, 10; of women in Iran, xxi–xxii, 157–61, 169; of women in Mozambique, 206
Lehr, Harry, 60
Leiva, Antonio, 20–21, 23–24, 27–28
letters, personal, xxii, 101–2, 162–65, 169

letters to the editor, xix–xx, 99, 108–16
"Liberation of Women Is a Fundamental necessity for the Revolution, The" (Machel), 194–95
Lindsey, Estelle Lawton, 100
lobolo (bridewealth), 198, 202–5, 210n33
López, Maria, 10–11
Los Angeles Public Library, 97

Machel, Samora, 194–95
Madiera, Joana, 205–6
magazines as sources. *See* journals as sources
Majlesi, 167
Malcolm X, 130
Malekzadeh, Elham, xxii
María, Agustina, 82
Maria, Pani, 117
María, Petra, 82
market vendors, 75–78
marriage: and African American women, xvii, 62–63; balanced with employment, xviii, 186–88; civil marriages, 110, 205; common-law, 46; to escape parental authority, 21; in India (Bengali/Hindu), 138, 153n16; in Iran, xxii, 158–60, 166, 170, 171n7; in Mexico, 21, 24–25; in Mozambique, 198–99, 202–6, 210n33; polygyny (polygamy), 199, 204. *See also* divorce
Martin, Rachel, 56
Marx, Karl, 109
Matka Polka (ideal of Polish mother and patriot), 123n18
matrilineal cultures, 194
McClintock, Ann, 142, 143, 147
McClure, Florence Schilling, 186–88
McGowan, Georgianna, 59
McGuigan, John, 64
medical facilities endowed by Iranian women, 162
mehr (marriage portion), 158–60
Mellon, Knox, 92–93, 101
memoirs of Iranian women, 165
memory and gender, 118, 123n29, 124nn36–37, 193–94
methodology: and assessing accuracy of archival documents, 132; "disembodied" quality of research material, 100; and multiple, often contradictory documents, xviii, 76, 82; need for emotional detachment, xx, 126–28; of oral history collection, 116–18, 193–94; for research-

ing African American women, 126–29; researching around a subject, 90–91, 99; of researching women in Mozambique, 194–206; and single documents, xv, 5, 15–16, 36. See also "spinning and weaving" methodology

Mexico, women in, xvi, xviii, 20–21, 25–30, 75–86

"Midwife's Speech" (in *Florentine Codex*), 79

Midwife's Tale, A (Ulrich), 44

midwives, xviii, 79, 83, 168, 174n50

migrants and migration: of African American women, 58, 68n8; assumptions about, 55n40; to Las Vegas, xviii, 177–79, 187–88; mobility of populations, 38; in Mozambique, 203; in official documents, 40–43; reasons for emigration, 45; to Tunisia, xvi–xvii, 35–52

Miguel, Juan, 82

Milone, Nicola, 41

Minnis, William, 59

minorities, underrepresentation of in archives, xiv

missionaries, 39, 43

mobility of populations, 38

modernization of India, 142–44

mohallel (short-term husband), 160

Molk, Ayan al-, 164

Molk, Mo'tamed al-, 164

money-lending, 158, 171n6

Monteiro, Luisa, 202

Montes, Frances, 188

Montgomery Bus Boycott and the Women Who Started It, The (Robinson), 125

Morales, Leonor de, 8

Morantz-Sanchez, Regina, 100

Moriscas/Moriscos, 3–4, 7

mothers' pensions, 90, 92, 97–99

Moulin Rouge Agreement (Las Vegas, Nev.), 191n13

Mozambique, women of, xviii, 194–207

Mozambique Liberation Front (Frelimo), 194–95

Muhammad, Elijah, 130–32

Muhammad Speaks (newspaper of Nation of Islam), 130–32

multiple narratives of African American women, 130

multiple wives (polygamy), 159–60, 199, 204

Municipal Library (Beira, Mozambique), 196

Muslims and slaves, 7–15

nabat (crystallized sugar), 160, 172n14

nafaqeh (maintenance allowance), 159

Nahuatl language, 76

Nahua women, xviii, 75–86

names, importance of, 9–10

nationalism: and feminism, xxi, 135, 142–51; and gender, 142–47; Indian, 142–47; Iranian, 161

Nationalism without a Nation in India (Aloysius), 142

Nation of Islam (NOI), 130–32

Nevada, women in, 177–89, 189n3, 191nn12–13

Nevada Women's Archives, 181–85

"New Christians," 6–9, 11

New Compilation (Spanish legal code), 24–25

newspapers as sources: and African American crimes, 66; in communist Poland, 107; in Las Vegas, 184; mainstream press, 96; in Mozambique, 196; of Nation of Islam, 130–32; socialist, xix, 94–96, 104n16; about socialist-feminist leaders, 99; of the women's movement, 98

Nezam-Mafi, Aahra Sultan, 162

Nightingale, Florence, 150–51

Noel, Frances Nacke, 89–90, 92–93, 101–2

Noel, Francis, 93, 101

NOI (Nation of Islam), 130–32

non-European women, 37

non-government documents, 42

Norton, Anne, 7

Notícias de Moçambique (newspaper in Mozambique), 196

Nuri, Sheikh Fazlallah, 157, 170n2

nurses in Mozambique, xviii, 194, 200–201, 207

Obbo, Christine, 193

Ocuila (Mexico), 75, 85–86

official documents: of communist Poland, xix, 108–9, 111; French, 41–42; on immigration, 40–43; and indigenous people, 78; Italian, 40–41; Mexican, 20–30; and reading against the grain, xii, xv, 4–6, 22

"Old Christians," 7–8

Olmedo, Cayetano, 20, 24, 26–30

Olmedo, Clara, 28–30

Omasta, Edward P., 67n2

OMM (Organização de Mulher Moçambicana—women's organization in Mozambique), 197–200, 202 oral histories: of African American women, 126; Las Vegas Women Oral History Project, xxii–xviii, 178, 184–88, 189n3; methodologies, 193–94; of women in Africa, 193; of women in Mozambique, xviii, 194, 200–207; of women in Poland, xix, 108–9, 113–14, 116–20. *See also* memory and gender

Organização de Mulher Moçambicana (OMM—women's organization in Mozambique), 197–200, 202

organizational archives, 126. *See also* women's clubs or organizations; *specific organizations*

organized labor, 92

orphanhood, 23–24, 32n17

Osman, Fred D., 64

Ottoman Turks, 8–9, 41

Painter, Nell Irvin, 91

Pan-Africanism, xx, 127, 129–30

pardon-tales discourse, 50

Park, Alice Locke, 97

patriarchal societies: and Hindu women, 139; Iran, 157–61, 166–68; Mexico, xvi, 20–21, 25–30; Mozambique, 199; and virginity, 166–68; widows in, 29–30

Peiss, Kathy, 62

Penrose, Jan, 142

Perry, Mary Elizabeth, xv–xvi, 125

personal identity, 9–10, 15, 194

personal letters, xxii, 101–2, 162–65, 169

personal mythmaking, 131–32

personal narratives, xxi, 131–32, 165. *See also* conversion and conversion narratives; oral histories; physicians' narratives; travel narratives

Peterson, Annie, 59, 66

Philadelphia, PA, xvii, 56–67

philanthropic endowments by Iranian women, xxii, 161–62, 169

physical environments, xx, 48, 129–30

physicians' narratives, xxii, 165–69

pictorial writing, 79–81

pioneers, women as, 186

poetry of Iranian women, 163

Polak, Jakob, 165–69

Poland, women in, xix–xx, 108–21, 122n6, 122n11

police, coercion by, 60

police records, 171n10. *See also* crime and criminal records

Polish United Workers' Party, xix, 108, 110

politics: challenges to in communist Poland, 113–16; and socialist-feminism, 91–92; women crossing boundaries of, 131; and women in communist Poland, xix–xx, 110, 113–16; and women in India (Bengali), 135, 141–51; and women in Mozambique, 198–200

polygyny (polygamy), 159–60, 199, 204

post-communism backlash against women, 108

Preddy, Sarann, 188

pregnancy, xvii, 62–63, 168, 174n51

premature marriage, 138, 199

preservation of history of women in Nevada, 181–85

press. *See* newspapers as sources

prison records, xvii, 51, 56–57, 68n6. *See also* crime and criminal records

Proceedings (California State Federation of Labor), 98

processing of archival materials, xxii, 183

Progressive Era and socialist-feminism, 92

propaganda, 107, 131

property transactions and Iranian women, 157–58, 163–64, 171n5

prose writings of Iranian women, xxii, 162–65, 169

punishments, 51

Qajar period in Iran, 156–70

racism, 59, 64, 201

Ralston, Judge, 61, 67

Ramabai, Pandita, 137, 140

Ramírez, José Maria, 26, 29

rape of Iranian women, 174n51

Ray, Bharati, 141, 148

reading against the grain, xiii, xv, 4–6, 22

religion and women, 113–14, 161–62, 170n21. *See also* Catholic Church

religious affiliation and legal standing, 46

reproductive role of women, 110

researching around the subject, x, xv, xix, 90–91, 99, 102

riots, 75, 85–86

Robabaeh, 159

robberies, 49–52

Robertson, Claire, 193

Robinson, JoAnn Gibson, 125

romanticizing the past, 116–17, 120, 123n29. *See also* memory and gender

Roqiyeh, 160
Rowe, G. S., 66
Rozalia, Pani, 117
Ryan, Louise, 143

Sabuquillo, Niccola, 35
Sahagún, Fray Bernardino de, 79
Saltaneh, Najm al-, 162
Saltaneh, Taj al-, 169
Santa Anna, Antonio López de, 25
Santos, Ana Maria dos, 204
Santos, Balbina dos, 196, 199
Santos, Lucinda dos, 201
Sarker, Tanika, 148
Scenes from a Life (Krishnobhabini Das), 138
Scott, James C., 12, 170
scrapbooks, 96
Seed, Patricia, 27
self-empowerment, 4–5, 16
Serena, Carla, 165, 173n33
service industry, women in, 180, 185
Seth, Sanjay, 142
Sewell, Tony, 129
sexual propriety, standards of, xvii, 62–63
Shahri, Ja'far, 173n40
Sheil, Mary, 165, 173n33
Sheldon, Kathleen, xviii
shirbaha (portion of *mehr*), 158–59
showgirl image, 179
sigheh (temporary wife), 160
single documents, methodology for understanding, xv, 5, 15–16, 36
Sinha, Mrinalini, 142, 147
Sklar, Kathryn Kish, 125
Slataneh, Nadim al-, 165
slaves and slavery, 7–15, 171n9
SNCC (Student Non-Violent Coordinating Committee), 131–32
Soares, Aurora, 205
social class, 47
social context: and crime in Baltimore, 57; and Tunisian system of justice, 44, 47–48; and women in Iran, 157–61
socialism in Mozambique, 194–206
socialist-feminism, xix, 89–102, 103nn3–4
Socialist Woman/Progressive Woman, The (socialist newspaper), 99
social networks, 77–78, 119–20
social norms, women crossing boundaries of, 131
social welfare and reform: in India, 141–42; in Iran, xxii, 161–62; legislation, 97–98; in Mozambique, 207; in Nevada, 183, 188; and socialist-feminism, 91–92
Somalia, women of, 193
Sorabji, Cornelia, 137
Sousa, Lisa, xviii
Spain, Muslim slaves in, 7–15
Spencer, William, 61
Spillers, Hortense, 63
"spinning and weaving" methodology, xviii, 76, 81
street strolling, xx, 129–30
Strobel, Margaret, 199
Student Non-Violent Coordinating Committee (SNCC), 131–32
suicide in Iran, 171n10
survival strategies of slave women, 13
Sykes, Ella Constance, 165–66, 173n33

Tanzania, women of, 193
Tapia, Mordachai, 48
taqiyya (Muslim tradition of precaution), 4
tattooing in Mozambique, 198–200
Taylor, Ula, xv, xx
Tellini, Giovanna, xvi, 35–52
Tempo (magazine in Mozambique), 196
Terborg-Penn, Rosalyn, 125
textile workers in communist Poland, 117
Thomas, Helen, 64
totalitarian states, 109, 112, 122n6
tourism industry, women in, 180, 187
Towes, John, 125–26
trade or labor unions, 108, 110, 188
traditional sources. *See* official documents
translation, 46–47, 53n2
travel narratives, xxi, 135–36, 140, 143–44, 165–66
tribute payers, indigenous women as, 75–76, 84–85
Trudell, Harriet, 188
Truth, Sojourner, 91
Tunisia, women in, 35–52, 54n28
Turner, Ethel Duppy, 101

Uliya, Mahd-e, 163–64
Ulrich, Laurel Thatcher, 44
undesirable women, xvi, 42–43
unemployment of women in communist Poland, 115, 117
UNIA (Universal Negro Improvement Association), xx, 127, 129–30

unions, labor or trade, 108, 110, 188
Universal Negro Improvement Association (UNIA), xx, 127, 129–30
University of California, Los Angeles, Special Collections Department, 92–93
University of Nevada, Las Vegas, xxii, 182–83, 189n3
University of Nevada, Reno, 181–82
urbanization in Mozambique, 207
urban space, xx, 129–30

Vali, Nasrallah Mirza, 163
values, traditional *versus* modern, 142, 147
Vedic Brahminism, 142, 147
Vidyasagar, Ishwar Chandra, 138, 153n16
virginity of Iranian women, 166–68, 170
virtue, appearance of, xvii, 63–66. *See also* virginity of Iranian women
vulnerability of women, 11–15, 27, 60–61

Wanda, Pani, 117, 119
Welsh, Kate, 56, 66
wet-nurses, 161
When and Where I Enter (Giddings), 125
White, Deborah Gray, 125–26
Whitehead, Ethel, 96, 99
widows in Mexico, xvi, 29–30
Williams, Claudine, 177–78

Woman's Bulletin, The (Calif. women's movement publication), 98
Woman Socialist Union, 95
woman suffrage movement, 95–97
women: comparison of British and Indian, 148–51; ignored in academic literature, 37; underrepresentation of in archives, xiv
Women, Communism and Industrialization in Postwar Poland (Fidelis), 108
Women and American Socialism (Buhle), 90
women's clubs or organizations, 95, 183, 197–200, 202. *See also* League of Women Voters
women's movement, 95–98, 141–42, 183
women's roles, 82–83. *See also* families balanced with employment
Works Progress Administration, 100

Xochitl, Juana, 82

Yellow Ribbon (California Equal Suffrage Association), 96

Zabtiya (Tunisian police force), 41
Zjednoczona Partia Robotnicza (Polish United Workers' Party), 108, 110
Zuavi Sa'id, 41
Zuzanna, Pani, 118–20

The University of Illinois Press
is a founding member of the
Association of American University Presses.

———————————————————

University of Illinois Press
1325 South Oak Street
Champaign, IL 61820-6903
www.press.uillinois.edu